REAGAN, BUSH, GORBACHEV

REAGAN, BUSH, GORBACHEV

Revisiting the End of the Cold War

Norman A. Graebner, Richard Dean Burns, and Joseph M. Siracusa

PRAEGER SECURITY INTERNATIONAL
Westport, Connecticut • London

Library of Congress Cataloging-in-Publication Data

Graebner, Norman A.
Reagan, Bush, Gorbachev : revisiting the end of the Cold War / Norman A. Graebner,
Richard Dean Burns, and Joseph M. Siracusa.
    p.   cm.
  Includes bibliographical references and index.
  ISBN 978–0–313–35241–6 (alk. paper)
    1. United States–Foreign relations—Soviet Union.   2. Soviet Union—Foreign
relations—United States.   3. Cold War.   4. Reagan, Ronald.   5. Bush, George, 1924–
6. Gorbachev, Mikhail Sergeevich, 1931–   7. United States—Foreign
relations—1981–1989—Decision making.   8. United States—Foreign
relations—1989–1993—Decision making.   9. Rhetoric—Political aspects—United
States—History—20th century.   I. Burns, Richard Dean.   II. Siracusa, Joseph M.   III. Title.
  E183.8.S65G73   2008
    347.73047—dc22   2008008983

British Library Cataloguing in Publication Data is available.

Library of Congress Catalog Card Number: 2008008983
ISBN-13: 978–0–313–35241–6

First published in 2008

Praeger Security International, 88 Post Road West, Westport, CT 06881
An imprint of Greenwood Publishing Group, Inc.
www.praeger.com

Printed in the United States of America

The paper used in this book complies with the
Permanent Paper Standard issued by the National
Information Standards Organization (Z39.48–1984).

10 9 8 7 6 5 4 3 2 1

CONTENTS

PREFACE

The end of Moscow-dominated communism, in particular the events between November 9, 1989, when the Berlin Wall came down, and December 25, 1991, when the Soviet Union was abolished, has loomed large in historical research for the past fifteen years and is likely to be the main focus of the historiography of the end of the Cold War for many years to come. Among the reasons that explain the interest aroused by this period, the apparent unpredictability of the events in question ranks high. There is indeed a growing consensus among historians and political scientists alike that the unfolding of these events had hardly been foreseen by contemporaries, including key politicians, policymakers, and strategic analysts[1] who were genuinely taken by surprise both by the rapidity of events as well as the pacific character of the Velvet revolutions of 1989 and their sequel. Equally important, perhaps, we have an obligation to remember and learn, *as agreed upon conclusions,* as to why events played out as they did, particularly as they are likely to shape current public discourse as well as serve as future foreign policy axioms in Washington and Moscow. In this sense, it is absolutely crucial that students of modern history and politics, no less than the political successors of Ronald Reagan and Mikhail Gorbachev, whose own personal gamble of perestroika and glasnost internally triggered the collapse of the Soviet system,[2] develop these conclusions with far more care than has been characteristic in the pre-nuclear past.

What is presented here is a contemporary, realist appraisal of the events leading up to the end of the Cold War, an analysis that employs contemporary observers with their penetrating assessments of the superpowers' policies and rhetoric. In this fashion, the current study, the considered judgment of three generations of diplomatic historians, shows clearly the thinking that was driving policies (where there were coherent policies), assumptions, and events during the last years of the Cold War. Understanding exactly what happened and why in these crucial years is paramount. For the stakes are high, and the endgame matters.

Perceptions of who "won" or "lost" the Cold War will be at least as significant as the "Who lost Vietnam?" debate and the next, "Who lost Iraq?" While neoconservatives, the standard bearers of so-called Cold War triumphalism, claim to be "realists", they do not appear to have grasped either the lessons of the Cold War or for that matter the very fundamentals of the foreign policy realism found in historical experience. The realist philosophy that informs this study has long been grounded on a forthright calculation of the necessities, possibilities, and parameters of foreign policy action related to war and peace since the costs of miscalculation could become exorbitant. The realist critique, which itself was a reaction to the mindless American anticommunism ideology of the early Cold War, posits several important questions before embarking on a war of choice: Are objectives clearly defined, and do they include precise, generally recognized national interests or danger? Do the ambitions and abilities of the enemy of the moment endanger vital national economic or global security interests? Would victory enhance the equilibrium of the region? Is victory assured at a cost commensurate with the interests at stake, and will the costs be sustained by necessary public and government support? Vice President Dick Cheney's observation after 9/11 that "old doctrines of security do not apply" takes on a double irony as America replaced the "war on communism" with "the global war on terror" as the nation's leading organizing principle. The military-industrial-research complex could not believe its good fortune.

For this reason, the concluding chapter—"In Retrospect"—focuses on the basic themes that emerge from the contemporary assessments, especially the policy assumptions and rhetoric, and seeks to relate these themes to more recent, "historical" assessments based upon new documentation. Presidential rhetoric, which we basically define as the public statements and utterances of the president, will come in for special scrutiny—and for two simple reasons: first, that it is language about political events, rather than such events in any other sense, that people experience, and thus political rhetoric constitutes political reality; and, second, that of all the rhetoricians involved in American politics, it is the president himself who is the most influential architect of political reality.[3] The presidency is and remains "the ultimate source of action," in John F. Kennedy's felicitous expression.

Norman A. Graebner
Charlottesville

Richard Dean Burns
Claremont

Joseph M. Siracusa
Melbourne

CHAPTER 1

Introduction: The Carter Years

The excesses of the so-called imperial presidency of Richard M. Nixon had led to widespread public disillusionment with both the White House and Congress. The ghosts of Vietnam and Watergate haunted Nixon's successors Gerald Ford and Jimmy Carter who struggled to reclaim the faith of the nation. Ford's task was an especially difficult one, for while he inherited the foreign policy of his predecessor, when he came to office the economy was facing its worst recession since the Great Depression. Carter's pledge to heal America was also undermined by unforeseen circumstances. For his part, Carter pursued arms control and engaged the Soviet Union on its human rights record, especially in Afghanistan, yet the administration's involvement in the Middle East finally led to its undoing and a severe public backlash.[1]

With Henry Kissinger in charge of the State Department, Ford continued to pursue the foreign policy goals of the Nixon administration. A major breakthrough was in fact reached in the second phase of the SALT II negotiations at a meeting in Vladivostok in November 1974 between Ford and Soviet General Secretary Brezhnev. With a view to striking a compromise between the Soviet advantage in numbers of strategic launchers permitted by the temporary five-year accords and America's three-to-one advantage in multiple nuclear warheads, the two sides agreed to an overall limit of strategic nuclear delivery vehicles, a ban on the construction of new land-based intercontinental ballistic missile launchers, and limits on the deployment of new types of strategic offensive areas.

Even more significantly, as it turned out, Ford also traveled to Helsinki in late summer 1975 to sign, along with the heads of the thirty-five nations of Europe, the so-called Final Act of the Conference on Security and Cooperation in Europe. The high-water mark of détente, the Helsinki Conference declared the current frontiers of Europe "inviolable", thereby endorsing the Soviet Union's post-World War II territorial gains, as well as its hegemony in eastern Europe. In return, Moscow pledged to open its east European empire to a freer flow of people and ideas, reaffirming the ideal of the dignity of the individual. Although neither Moscow nor Washington understood it at the time, the Soviets had opened the door to the winds of change—the end of their European empire.

There was no shortage of critics of détente in the United States; so many, in fact, that Ford quit using the term. To make matters worse, Americans came to believe that Moscow had abandoned the conventional rules of the game through the use of East German and Cuban surrogates in the Angolan Civil War. It seem to indicate a new, more belligerent Soviet approach to the Third World. Cribbed and confined by congressional resolutions barring American involvement of any kind in the conflict, the administration (while "encouraging" South African and other mercenaries) protested that Moscow's presence there was "harmful" to détente. Perhaps more significant was the public revelation of the CIA's assessment of Soviet defense spending in 1976; according to the study, the percentage of the U.S.S.R.'s gross national product absorbed by defense spending had increased from 6–8 percent to 11–13 percent. Media reports that the CIA had "doubled" its estimate of Soviet defense expenditures sent shockwaves through the national intelligence community. That the new figures might have reflected how far less efficient Soviet defense industries were than the CIA formerly believed seemed to escape public attention.

The Democratic National Convention in the summer of 1976 nominated outsider and political moderate Governor James (Jimmy) Earl Carter, Jr., of Georgia to challenge Ford for the presidency. The strategy of outsider versus insider worked well enough. "I have no new dream to set forth today," declared the thirty-ninth president of the United States at his inauguration on January 20, 1977, "but rather urge a fresh faith in the old dream . . . Let us create together a new national spirit of unity and trust." Carter, a deacon in the Southern Baptist Church with a penchant for quoting Old Testament prophets, committed his administration to: enhancing equality of opportunity; preserving the nation's natural beauty; fostering respect for human rights at home and abroad; keeping the nation strong militarily; eliminating nuclear weapons from the face of the Earth; and, before all else, recognizing the nation's limits in being able to solve all problems, much less afford to do everything.

FROM HUMAN RIGHTS TO SALT II

The personnel, style, and emphasis on foreign policy of the Carter administration differed substantially from that of his recent predecessors. The so-called Lone Ranger approach to international affairs, as presumably

The Carter foreign policy team. (L to R): National Security Adviser Zbigniew Brzezinski, President Carter, and Secretary of State Cyrus Vance. *Source:* Jimmy Carter Library.

practiced by Henry Kissinger, was to be replaced by a more open, team player concept espoused by Secretary of State Cyrus Vance, National Security Adviser Zbigniew Brzezinski, and the president's "ideas man" Andrew Young, U.S. ambassador to the United Nations, a former Georgia congressman, and black civil rights activist.

"As president," recalled Carter, "I hoped and believed that the expansion of human rights might be the wave of the future throughout the world, and I wanted the United States to be on the crest of this movement." Soon, cognizant of pursuing such a policy too rigidly, the administration came to define human rights on a number of levels: the right to be free from governmental violation of the integrity of the individual (torture); the right to the fulfillment of such vital needs as food, shelter, health care, and education; and the right to enjoy civil and political liberties. Despite the obvious difficulty of translating general theory into uniform bureaucratic action, and despite charges by western European allies that the administration was naive and formulated "policy from the pulpit," the president's advocacy of human rights went a long way toward enhancing America's reputation as the leading defender in this area.

In other areas (Panama and China), President Carter built on the firmer foundation of the Nixon and Ford policies. He completed renegotiation of an entirely new treaty respecting the Panama Canal Zone. In 1977, two new treaties emerged: the Panama Canal Treaty, extending to America the continued primary responsibility for the operation and defense of the Canal until the end of 1999,[2] and a treaty pledging Panama to maintain the permanent neutrality of the Canal. All in all, the administration managed to retain adequate control of the operation of the vital waterway, reestablish good relations with Panama, and derail the issue of North American colonialism.

With regard to the thorny issues surrounding the formal recognition of the People's Republic of China (PRC) the president, led by his national security adviser, set out to resolve the problems of how best to effect the resumption of diplomatic relations with Beijing without unduly undermining the stability of the Taiwanese regime.[3] On the evening of December 15, 1978, immediately after the November congressional elections, Carter announced that Washington and Beijing had at last agreed to recognize each other and reestablish diplomatic relations. Touted as a long overdue "normalization" of relations, the surprise move redefined U.S. relations with both China and Taiwan. In return for placing relations with Beijing on an official footing, the administration consented to break diplomatic relations with Taiwan, withdraw its remaining 700 troops from that island, and abrogate its 1954 defense treaty with Taipei. Failure to secure a pledge from Beijing not to use force in the ultimate reabsorption of Taiwan into China aroused a growing chorus of mainly conservative critics. Among the most vocal critics of the normalization of relations with China were Ronald Reagan and George H. W. Bush, both of whom already had an eye firmly on the 1980 presidential election.[4]

In the Middle East, Carter mounted a major effort to bring about a comprehensive settlement of the problems left there since the Arab-Israeli War of 1973. The administration's three basic elements to the solution to the Middle East question included a firm commitment to complete peace in the area, the establishment of recognized borders, and a resolution of the Palestinian issue. Much to the dismay of the newly-elected Israeli government (the right-wing Likud Party, headed by Menachem Begin), Carter personally stressed the necessity of resolving the Palestinian question by finding a "homeland" for the Palestinians as opposed to creating a separate Palestinian state carved out of the occupied West Bank and Gaza Strip. He hoped to bring all the concerned parties to Geneva where the U.S.S.R., co-chair of the short-lived Geneva Peace Conference in the Middle East, would preside over "a just and lasting settlement of the Arab Israeli conflict."

Little was accomplished, however, until the spectacular diplomatic initiative of Egyptian president Anwar el-Sadat who on November 19, 1977 electrified the world by traveling to Israel to put his peace proposals before the Israeli Parliament. One month later, Begin reciprocated with a similar unprecedented visit to Egypt, bringing his peace proposals. Replying to Egyptian demands for the withdrawal from territories occupied during the

Egypt's President Anwar Sadat shakes hands with Israel's Prime Minister Menachem Begin at Camp David. *Source:* Jimmy Carter Library.

1967 Middle East War and the establishment of a Palestinian state, Begin offered the demilitarization of the Sinai, the gradual withdrawal of occupied territory, and limited self-rule for Palestinian Arabs on the West Bank and Gaza. By the end of January 1978, Cairo and Jerusalem had become deadlocked. In another dramatic development, Carter met Sadat and Begin from September 5 to 17, 1978, at the presidential mountain retreat, Camp David. The outcome, generally considered the most important foreign policy achievement of the administration, resulted in two major agreements: The Framework for Peace in the Middle East and Framework for the Conclusion of a Peace Treaty between Egypt and Israel. While the so-called Camp David accords resolved Egyptian and Israeli differences, the peace process continued to be bedeviled by problems such as defining of Palestinian autonomy in the West Bank and the accelerated establishment of Israeli settlements there.[5]

In curbing the arms race, one of Carter's central promises during the campaign, the administration was spectacularly unsuccessful. Despite campaign criticism of Republican preoccupation with the Soviet Union in general and arms controls in particular, the Carter administration found itself devoting equal time and energy to the same matters. Carter eventually approached the Soviets with two arms control proposals. The first proposal, which was regarded by some as the most revolutionary arms proposal so far, would require substantial overall weapons *reduction*—thereby lessening the vulnerability of both nations to a nuclear first strike, imposing stringent qualitative limits on weapons improvements, and reducing the threat of the large Soviet intercontinental missiles and the proposed American MX missiles. The Kremlin replied immediately and negatively, since it was basing its weapons policies around the Vladivostok accords. Subsequently, Carter accepted the Ford administration's Vladivostok guidelines, albeit with overall weapons limits about 10 percent below the previously accepted figures, as the basis for negotiating SALT II. For the first time, equal ceilings were placed on both strategic arsenals, ending a previous numerical balance favorable to the U.S.S.R. while preserving American options to proceed with forces, deemed necessary to maintain the balance. The last minute details were ironed out in June 1979 when Carter traveled to Vienna to meet with Soviet leader Leonid Brezhnev and to sign the agreement. They also worked out guidelines for what was to have been SALT III. Brezhnev's admonition, "If we do not succeed, God will not forgive us," struck a particularly responsive chord in the president, who sent the treaty to the Senate for approval on June 22, 1979.

But events were against ratification. The Republicans decided to make a campaign issue of the treaty and the Soviets, inadvertently, decided to assist them. Soviet involvement in the dispute between Somalia and Ethiopia in the Horn of Africa and in the Vietnamese invasion of Cambodia led critics to question the worth of signing a treaty with the Kremlin at that or any other time. The "discovery" of a Soviet brigade in Cuba, consisting of 2,000–3,000 troops, a deployment, incidentally, that had remained in Cuba since the Cuban missile crisis of 1962, was seen as contributing to tensions in the Caribbean and Central America.

Whatever chance the treaty had of acceptance had disappeared altogether with the Soviet military intervention into Afghanistan in December 1979, an invasion that aroused concern for Pakistan and Iran. Carter, who viewed the invasion as a stepping-stone to possible control of the Middle Eastern oil supplies, reacted fiercely to the situation. His January 1980 State of the Union message pledged, "An attempt by any outside force to gain control of the Persian Gulf region will be regarded as an assault on the vital interests of the United States of America, and such an assault will be repelled by any means necessary, including military force." In addition to proclaiming the "Carter Doctrine," the president ordered a partial grain embargo of the U.S.S.R., halted exports, and called for a boycott of the summer Olympic games scheduled to be held in Moscow—the boycott was only partially successful, though the United States stayed home. Because of the Soviet invasion, Carter announced that further Senate consideration of SALT II was to be deferred.

Publicly admitting that he misjudged Soviet intentions, Carter proposed a record high peacetime military budget of $196.4 billion—a 14.6 percent hike over the previous year with a "real" increase, after inflation, of 4.6 percent.

More than half of the budget was earmarked for personnel and preparedness costs, with the remainder for the new MX land missile, cruise missiles to be launched from bombers, more navy ships, improved army tanks, marine equipment positioned in the Indian Ocean theater as part of the newly created Rapid Deployment Joint Task Force, and research on laser guns for space warfare. The Task Force, renamed Intervention Force, made up of army, Marine, navy, and air force units, was designed to project rapid and effective strength to any part of the world where it may be required.

THE IRANIAN HOSTAGE CRISIS

Such a force, however, proved unable to help the administration from its most damaging situation. The Iranian Revolution of January 1979 set in train a series of crises that would be the virtual undoing of the Carter administration. In a late 1977 visit to Teheran, Carter lauded the supreme leader of Iran, Shah Mohammed Reza Pahlevi, a "'progressive" autocrat and ruler of the Peacock Throne, as one who had managed to maintain an oasis of stability in a troubled region. The fact of the matter was that the Shah had been propped up by American support since the CIA-staged coup in 1953 had restored the young monarch to his throne after he had been deposed by Prime Minister Mohammed Mossadegh, who had nationalized West-owned oil fields. Oil-rich and preoccupied with military security, the Shah was allowed unlimited access to American arms. Force-marching his people through changes in decades that in other similar societies would have taken centuries prompted intense domestic resistance, from the Westernized middle class and radical students to right-wing Islamic fundamentalists led by repressed Shi'a mullahs and ayatollahs. Under pressure from human rights advocates in the Carter administration, the Shah reined in the dreaded secret police and allowed unopposed street demonstrations. From that point on the roof fell in on the Peacock Throne, as the Shah fled Teheran in January 1979 taking up refuge, consecutively, in Egypt, Morocco, the Bahamas, Mexico, and then Panama.

Meanwhile, Ayatollah Ruhollah Khomeini, the charismatic leader of the Islamic Revolution who had lived in exile in Paris, returned to Iran and established himself as the revolutionary leader of Islamic fundamentalists, ruthlessly pushing aside Marxists, liberals, and any other opponents. Khomeini made it clear, moreover, that he sought the return of the Shah "to Iran to stand trial in public, for fifty years of crimes against the Persian people." It thus became a matter of great concern when, on October 22, 1979, torn between the prospect of rebuilding normal relations with the new Iran and under drumbeat pressure from the Shah's closest American friends, including former Secretary of State Henry Kissinger and chairman of the Chase Manhattan Bank, host to Iranian assets, David Rockefeller, and based on official Iranian assurances that the American Embassy in Teheran would

President Carter meets the hostages returning from Iran. *Source:* Jimmy Carter Library.

continue to be protected, Carter against his better judgment gave in and admitted the Shah to the United States, ostensibly for cancer treatment.

This was not to be the case. On November 4, a group of Iranian militants consisting of Islamic fundamentalists and anti-American factions united mainly in their opposition to what they perceived as the bourgeois, pro—Western government of Iranian Prime Minister Bazargan, seized the American Embassy and took sixty-five American hostages, demanding that the United States return the deposed Shah. While thirteen hostages were released two weeks later, the plight of the remaining fifty-three hostages dominated the imagination of the national and international public until their release 444 days later. In America it became, without question, *the* media spectacle of the last half of the twentieth century, with daily reminders from CBS's Walter Cronkite and ABC's Ted Koppel on *Nightline* of how long the hostages had been held.[6] Carter moved cautiously, ordering the halt of oil imports from Iran and freezing all Iranian assets in the United States.

In retrospect, it is clear that plans for freeing the hostages obsessed the administration, opening the way for bizarre diplomatic contacts of all kinds with Iran. Although supporting their president for many months, Americans were gradually overwhelmed by a sense of collective impotence, stimulated each day by some new affront to a hostage or a new insult to the flag. Even Carter's decision to call off formal campaigning for the 1980 presidential election until the crisis was solved had little effect. The administration itself was torn apart. Secretary of State Cyrus Vance believed that continued diplomatic negotiations would eventually bring the release of the hostages. National Security Adviser Zbigniew Brzezinski was persuaded it would take the use of force, and while the president vacillated between his two top advisers, the administration drifted for several months. As opinion polls turned against Carter, public impatience ruled the day.

With all rational avenues closed—it was practically impossible to find any one in Iran with whom to deal—the president reached for the military option. On April 24, 1980, Carter ordered into Iran a rescue team of six C-130 transports and eight RH-53D helicopter gunships from the aircraft carrier *Nimitz*, on patrol in the Arabian Sea, to effect the hostages' release. Equipment failure in three of the helicopters had already forced the decision to abort the mission, when two of the remaining aircraft collided on the ground following a refueling operation in a remote desert location in Iran, dubbed "Desert One." Early on the morning of April 25, the president candidly accepted responsibility for the failure of the mission. Secretary of State Vance resigned in protest against Carter's use of force and was replaced by Senator Edward Muskie of Maine.

After much taunting of the administration and the death of the Shah in Cairo in July, Khomeini set down in September the conditions for the hostages' release: the return of the Shah's wealth, cancellation of American claims, unfreezing of Iranian assets in American banks, and a promise not to interfere in Iran's affairs. After 444 days in captivity, the hostages were finally freed on January 20, 1981, Inauguration Day. Their release came after weeks of round-the-clock negotiations between the United States and Algeria, selected by Iran to act as intermediary in exchanges concerning the hostages. The relief to the national psyche was overwhelming, and no more so than to the Georgian during his last hours in White House: "It is impossible for me to put into words how much the hostages had come to mean to me, or how moved I was that morning to know they were coming home." Carter's greatest wish had been achieved; every single hostage had been released alive and well.[7] But it had come with a heavy price for his presidency.

The 1980 election was won by an opponent who raised the alarm about the new Soviet threat, insisted on a military build-up, and condemned the nation's slide in American pride and prestige. Ronald Reagan launched his bid for the presidency, Hedrick Smith noted, with a vision that was truly apocalyptic. America was now entering "one of the most dangerous decades" ever to confront Western civilization, he declared in January 1980.[8] No successful candidate since the early days of the Cold War had railed so loud and so often against the Soviet Union.

CHAPTER 2

Ronald Reagan and the Second Cold War

Ronald Reagan caught the country's post-Afghanistan alarms at full tide, embellished them, and rode them to victory. During his run for the White House, he and his party pilloried the Carter administration for leading the nation into the posture of "weakness, inconsistency, vacillation, and bluff" that enabled the Soviet Union to surpass the United States in military power. "We're already in an arms race," Reagan complained, "but only the Soviets are racing." U.S. power continued to stabilize a divided Europe, but to Republican critics it had failed dangerously to restrain Soviet expansionism in the Middle East, Africa, and Latin America. By rebuilding the country's defenses, Reagan and his supporters hoped to reverse the putative decline of the Carter years. But that reversal demanded far more than augmented military power; it required as well the development of a realistic foreign policy strategy and the successful exorcising of the Vietnam syndrome and the limitations it imposed on the exertion of national will. The latter proved to be far easier addressed than the former.

It was the public's desertion of its earlier isolationism that permitted the extension of American commitments into distant regions where the United States had had no historic interests. The Vietnam War effectively broke that American consensus. To renew that consensus Reagan advised the nation in April 1980, "[W]e must rid ourselves of the 'Vietnam Syndrome'. It has dominated our thinking for too long."[1]

During the campaign Reagan termed Vietnam a "noble war," an unselfish American effort to help a new Asian country defend itself against a "totalitarian neighbor bent on conquest." He assured the American people that the United States had not been defeated in Vietnam; the country had failed because its antiwar elements would not permit it to win. Reagan's

Reagan's Senior Staff in Oval Office: (L to R) Allen, Deaver, Meese, Brady, Baker and Reagan with back to camera. *Source:* Ronald Reagan Library.

Secretary of State designate, Alexander M. Haig, Jr., shared that conviction. The United States could have triumphed, he averred, had it employed its available power against the Communist enemy. "America," he lamented, "is no longer the America it was, . . . [and] this is largely attributable to the mistakes of Vietnam." Reagan's determination to erase the adverse memories of Vietnam won the overwhelming approval of the war's defenders. In transforming Vietnam into a necessary, laudable, and winnable encounter, Reagan embraced the dual proposition that the United States dare not abjure the use of force in Third World crises; neither did it dare lose. Through the reinstitution of its military dominance and commitment to global containment, the United States would at once regain the capability and the will to check Soviet expansionism. It would re-emerge as the defender of the free world.

Reagan entered office in January 1981 with an advisory team committed to the reassertion of the country's global leadership. Under Reagan, the Committee on the Present Danger, of which he was a member, gained the influence that Carter had denied it; fifty-one of its members received positions in the new administration. At the core were such ardent Cold Warriors as a defense analyst from the University of Southern California William R. Van Cleave, Harvard historian Richard Pipes, and former director of the Defense Intelligence Agency General Daniel O. Graham. Other key advisers were: Richard V. Allen, Soviet specialist and Reagan's principal campaign coordinator for foreign policy; Fred C. Ikle, former director of arms control; and Robert W. Tucker, political scientist at Johns Hopkins. "There are differences within the group," Allen acknowledged, "but if we have any area where there's unanimity, it would be for increased defense spending." Pipes, repeating the dire conclusions of the group, warned in *Commentary* that nuclear deterrence was losing its effectiveness because the U.S.S.R. was preparing to fight and win a nuclear war. The Soviet regime, he noted, was "driven by ideology, internal politics and economic exigencies steadily to expand." Tucker observed that the United States, reflecting its loss of power and will, had virtually invited the Soviets to misbehave by refusing to confront them.[2] Van Cleave concluded that the United States suffered from an indefensible decline in readiness, modernization, maintenance, and force levels. "Today," he asserted in an October 1980 *New York Times* interview, "the United States is almost irrelevant."[3]

UNITED STATES' GLOBAL ANTICOMMUNISM EFFORTS

For the Reagan team, U.S. security interests placed a higher priority on anticommunism than on human rights. Many traditional friends of the United States such as South Korea and the Philippines, Allen explained, would never have governments that conformed to American principles.[4] Whether Third World governments had poor human rights records mattered less than their opposition to communism. As early as December, the Reagan transition team placed such career diplomats as Robert E. White on the list of "social reformers" that the new administration should remove as quickly as possible. White had spent a career locking horns with Latin American dictators friendly to the United States. In El Salvador, White had become the embodiment of a policy of encouraging social reform to prevent the political extremes from submerging the country in civil war. Ambassador to Nicaragua Lawrence Pezzullo, also on the blacklist, accused the Reagan team of attempting to appease the right wing in Latin America, whatever its infringement of human rights.[5]

Jeane Kirkpatrick of Georgetown University impressed the Reagan team with a 1979 article in *Commentary*, entitled "Dictatorships and Double Standards." Joined by Ernest W. Lefever, also of Georgetown University, and other Reagan favorites, Kirkpatrick distinguished between Communist totalitarianism and right-wing authoritarianism. The former, they pointed out, trampled on human rights in pursuit of ideological purity; authoritarian regimes did so to counter subversion or external pressure. Totalitarian regimes, they argued, never became democratized, whereas many autocracies did. What Hungary, Czechoslovakia, and Poland demonstrated, this distinction seemed to overlook, was not the absence of reformist potential in Communist societies but the power of Soviet armies to control. Yet such distinctions filled a serious need by rationalizing aid to pro-American dictatorships as well as endless opposition to Communist regimes. Kirkpatrick received a Reagan appointment as ambassador to the United Nations. When Reagan nominated Lefever to become Assistant Secretary of State, in charge of human rights affairs, Lefever accused those who opposed him of favoring a crusade against authoritarian allies while they ignored human rights violations in Communist-controlled Afghanistan, Angola, and eastern Europe. The United States, he asserted, should support friendly governments, whatever their character. Eventually Senate opposition compelled Lefever to withdraw his name from consideration.[6]

Such fears of Soviet power and expansionism dominated the outlook of the new administration. Reagan defined the Soviet danger at a White House news conference in late January 1980:

> From the time of the Russian revolution until the present, Soviet leaders have reiterated their determination that their goal must be the promotion of world revolution and a one world socialist or communist state . . . They have openly and publicly declared that the only morality they recognize is what will further their cause; meaning they reserve unto themselves the right to commit any crime; to lie [and] to cheat in order to obtain that.[7]

Haig shared that somber view of the world. At his confirmation hearings in early January 1981, he reminded members of the Senate Foreign Relations Committee that "the years immediately ahead" would "be unusually dangerous. Evidence of that danger . . . [was] everywhere." The country had no choice but to marshal its resources to shape the future. "Unchecked," he warned, "the growth of Soviet military power must eventually paralyze Western policy altogether."[8] Haig accused the Kremlin of abetting international terrorism. In April he informed the American Society of Newspaper Editors that the United States focused its policies on the U.S.S.R. "simply because Moscow" was "the greatest source of international insecurity today," saying, "Let us be plain about it: Soviet promotion of violence as the instrument of change constitutes the greatest danger to world peace."[9] Haig never supplied evidence to support such charges. From the outset the Reagan policies presumed that Soviet expansionism underlay unwanted developments everywhere. The Republican platform had detected "clear danger signals indicating that the Soviet Union was using Cuban, East German, and now Nicaraguan, as well as its own, military forces to extend its power to Africa, Asia and the Western Hemisphere."

The Central American Threat

In Central America the immediate challenge facing the Reagan administration was Congress' decision, of September 1979, to offer $75 million

President Reagan meets with newly elected President Jose Napoleon Duarte
of El Salvador at the White House. *Source:* Ronald Reagan Library.

in economic aid to Nicaragua's radical Sandinista regime. Actually Congress
had added so many conditions that the Nicaraguan government turned to
Moscow for help; subsequent Soviet-Nicaraguan economic arrangements
produced some $100 million.[10] During 1980, the Sandinistas tightened
their grip on the country and proceeded to strengthen their army as a defense against counterrevolution. The Republican platform acknowledged the
growing power of communism in Central America; it deplored the Marxist takeover of Nicaragua and Marxist attempts to destabilize El Salvador,
Guatemala, and Honduras. "As a result," noted the platform, "a clear and
present danger threatens the energy and raw material lifelines of the Western world."[11] Under the conviction that authoritarian governments were
acceptable allies, the Reagan team condemned Carter's failure to defend
the previous pro-American Nicaraguan government. The dictator Anastasio
Somoza, wrote Kirkpatrick, had established nothing other than an efficient,
urban political regime, and should have received whatever U.S. support
would have kept him in power. In April 1981, Haig announced that he was
stopping all American assistance to Nicaragua, including shipments under
the PL-480 food program.[12]

Reagan decided early to convert tiny El Salvador into a major arena
of Soviet-American confrontation. Washington understood long before

inauguration day that Cuba and other Soviet bloc nations had shipped arms to Salvadoran guerrillas through Nicaragua. By launching a counteroffensive in El Salvador, the administration could not only reassert American responsibility for hemispheric defense but also do so under conditions that would eliminate the danger of a direct U.S. involvement. The Carter administration had hoped that moderate elements in El Salvador would gain power and stop the burgeoning Communist-led insurgency. A reform effort, inaugurated in October 1979, ended almost before it began as the hardliners within the military regrouped and placed Colonel Jose Guillermo Garcia in the office of Minister of Defense. Thereafter demands for reform met bloody repression. The moderate Jose Napoleon Duarte acted as head of state, while the security forces ran the country. Organized "death squads" eliminated enemies of the regime by the thousands. During November and December 1980, the violence and murder reached grotesque levels as government military units acted as if they could do no wrong in the eyes of the incoming Republican U.S. president. Suspected Americans did not escape mistreatment. In a notorious incident, Salvadoran soldiers abducted, raped, tortured, and murdered four American churchwomen and buried them in a shallow grave. Still, Reagan and his advisers rejected the notion that the struggle within El Salvador had its roots in horrid indigenous conditions of widespread poverty, gross inequality (with a few families owning the country), political and judicial corruption, and vigorous repression of dissent.

By the end of 1980 the strength of the insurgency had begun to ebb. On January 10, the Salvadorian rebels responded to the Reagan challenge with an antigovernment offensive. It failed miserably in three days. But for much of Washington the Salvadoran danger had become hemispheric. Reagan resurrected the domino theory to explain the necessity of meeting the Soviet challenge in El Salvador. "What we're doing," he told newsmen, "is try to halt the infiltration into the Americas, by terrorists and by outside interference, and those who aren't just aiming at El Salvador but, I think, are aiming at the whole of Central America and possibly later South America and, I'm sure, eventually North America."[13]

Others in Reagan's Washington took up the Salvadoran cause. A State Department report of February 1981 declared that an external conspiracy was endangering the whole of Central America. Already one government, the report noted, had been the victim of "a well-coordinated, covert effort to bring about the overthrow of [its] established government and to impose in its place a . . . regime with no popular support." Another Central American state had been transformed "into a base for indirect armed aggression" against its neighbors. "In short," the report concluded, Central America had become "a textbook case of indirect aggression" that could destabilize the entire hemisphere.[14] Lawrence Eagleburger, Reagan's Under Secretary of State for Political Affairs, again applied the domino theory to the dangerous trends in Central America. "[I]f the Sandinistas and the Salvadoran guerrillas

(L to R) CIA director William Casey, Secretary of Defense Caspar Weinberger, Reagan, V.P. George Bush, Secretary of State Alexander Haig, Ed
Meese, in the Oval Office. *Source:* Ronald Reagan Library.

are successful in overthrowing the Government in El Salvador," he warned,
"that's the beginning, not the end, of the problem. The Costa Ricans, the
Hondurans and the Guatemalans are certainly going to face the same sort
of threat. I can't even say that the Mexicans wouldn't have a problem."[15]

Secretary of State Haig quickly elevated the Salvadoran challenge to a
symbol of world crisis. He expected the Kremlin, he said, to control its clients
in Cuba, Nicaragua, and El Salvador or take responsibility for their behavior.
Testifying before the House Foreign Affairs Committee in mid-March, Haig
declared that El Salvador was one entry on "a priority target list—a hit list,
if you will, for the ultimate takeover of Central America." Unless the United
States stopped the spread of Soviet-sponsored terrorism, he declared, "[W]e
will find it within our own borders tomorrow."[16] Nicaragua had already
fallen under Soviet domination; El Salvador, Guatemala, and Honduras
were destined to follow.[17] Clearly the administration had overplayed its
hand. In subsequent explanations of the Salvadoran danger, officials were
forced to acknowledge that the political realities of Central America were
more complex than Haig's hit list suggested.

Despite the proclaimed dangers, Reagan's crusade to free Central America
of Soviet influence scarcely contained the elements of a national policy. Many
wondered how poverty-stricken and revolution-prone El Salvador could be

the keystone of hemispheric security. A disillusioned ex-Marine commented in *The New York Times* that the cavalryman's bugle was again assembling Americans "to protect" their "encircled wagon trains of destiny," saying, "Cubans are coming; the Nicaraguans; and Salvadorans (hard to find a more microscopic place, except maybe Monaco and Andorra)."[18] Even for Haig the defense of U.S. interests in Central America required going to the source: Cuba. He pressed the administration for a program to eliminate the Castro regime, but the president's other advisers demurred. If the goals of policy remained elusive, the means for effective U.S. action remained equally so. The administration had no intention of sending American forces into Central America to protect the nation's security. In lieu of direct U.S. military involvement, Reagan, on March 9, issued a "finding" (written statement required by law) that authorized U.S. covert action in Central America through allies and surrogates.

The Middle East, Africa, and Asia

Reagan's new globalism required that the United States confront Soviet expansionism in Africa and the Middle East no less than in Central America. The Soviet invasion of Afghanistan destroyed the illusion that the United States could accept unwanted developments in that strategic region with indifference. The U.S. failure to confront the Soviets in Afghanistan, warned Robert Tucker in *Foreign Affairs*, "has laid bare as never before the vulnerability of the American position in a region of vital interests. . . . [T]he invasion of Afghanistan must signal, even for the most obtuse, that we have entered a very dangerous period."[19] Such fears of Soviet encroachment dictated Reagan's approach to Middle Eastern security. Despite the doubtful premises of the Carter Doctrine for southwest Asia and the Persian Gulf, the Reagan administration accepted it uncritically.

During April 1981, Haig toured the Middle East to seek "a consensus of strategic concerns" among the countries of the region. What he sought above all was agreement that Soviet expansionism comprised the chief threat to the Middle East, a challenge to be met by a series of bilateral arrangements that would strengthen the region against Soviet adventurism.[20] Haig soon discovered that the Arab states regarded the issue of Palestinian autonomy, not Soviet expansionism, the chief danger to regional peace. Egypt made it clear that it had no interest in any anti-Soviet strategy for the Middle East. Washington was more successful in its offer of $3 billion in military aid to Pakistan. Immediately India mounted a counteroffensive to prevent any U.S. effort to convert Pakistan into a frontline defense against Soviet expansion. To Saudi Arabia the administration prepared to deliver an $8.5 billion-dollar defense package, including five advanced Airborne Warning and Control Systems (AWACS). But Israel, backed by much of Congress, bitterly opposed the sale of such equipment to its Arab antagonist. In recognition of

Israel's strategic importance to the Middle East, the president refused to condemn that country for its air strikes against Soviet-equipped missile bases in Syria or its preemptive destruction in 1981 of a nuclear energy installation in Iraq.

Some wondered against what enemy Pakistan, Saudi Arabia, and Israel would defend southwest Asia and the Persian Gulf. The Reagan team could not convert these countries into effective allies against the Soviet Union. If the Arab world dared not confront Israel militarily, it could hardly serve as a defense against Moscow.[21] At any level of expenditure or alliance making, the United States could not garner the means to face Soviet conventional power in the Middle East. Fortunately, Soviet caution and limited interests in the region sustained the apparent solvency of American policy.[22]

In South Africa the administration's support for the Republic of South Africa, against the Soviet-backed, but United Nations-recognized, Southwest Africa People's Organization (SWAPO) in Namibia, comprised another Reagan effort to transform a local revolutionary conflict into a Soviet-American confrontation. In late August 1981, Pretoria, assured of U.S. cooperation, sent its forces into Angola in pursuit of SWAPO forces. Angola itself had long settled down to developing its resources, largely through American multinational corporations, and had improved its relations with the United States. The continued presence of Cuban troops scarcely rendered Angola a danger to Western interests in Africa. After a weeklong engagement in Angola, the South Africans claimed success in eliminating hundreds of SWAPO guerrillas, capturing a Soviet officer and large quantities of Soviet equipment. Black African leaders demanded sanctions against South Africa through a UN resolution, but Washington refused to oppose Pretoria at the United Nations. This decision reversed the United Nation's anti-Soviet alignment created by Afghanistan, again isolating the United States from the main currents of international opinion. The price was high: South Africa controlled only a small percentage of Africa's population and resources.[23]

What prevented the Reagan administration from pressing the Chinese mainland into its anti-Soviet strategy was the Taiwan Relations Act of 1979, which promised continued support for the island against Beijing's known acquisitiveness. Conservative Republicans, moreover, continued to favor the Chinese nationalist cause.[24] In its efforts to avoid the issue of military sales to Formosa, the administration faced Beijing's growing threat to withdraw its ambassador from Washington. Continued application of the Taiwan Relations Act, Beijing warned, would provoke a crisis in the western Pacific. Finally, in mid-August 1982, Washington and Beijing issued a joint communiqué in which the administration agreed to curtail arms sales, especially advanced equipment, to Taiwan. Behind the concern for better relations with Beijing was the danger, articulated forcefully by Admiral Robert L. Long, commander of U.S. forces in the Pacific and Indian Ocean, that the United States had long passed the point where it could defend the periphery of south and southeast Asia alone.[25] Scarcely less threatening to the U.S. position in east Asia was Moscow's determination to end two decades of bitter relations with the Communist Chinese.

MILITARY BUILDUP AND REVISIONIST EXPECTATIONS

Indicating to the Soviets that their days of presumed military dominance were numbered, the new president unveiled the costliest defense program in the nation's peacetime history. Caught in the momentum of expanding fears and strategic concerns, the administration eventually pushed its budget requests far beyond the promises of the campaign. Reagan's military advisers, led by Van Cleave, a long-time critic of the nuclear arms limitation treaties, searched for new levels of defense expenditures without the customary review procedures or the willingness to reconsider agreements once reached. Defense Secretary Caspar W. Weinberger, earlier an advocate of budget cuts, accepted the Pentagon's "wish list," with its assumption that nothing less than an annual 7 percent increase in defense spending above inflation would meet the Soviet threat. The president accepted the figure and included it in his new budget.[26]

Most Americans seemed to agree with the president that the United States could best regain its capacity to shape events and support friends reliably by restoring the country to a position of military predominance. New high technology weapons would reassure allies and enhance U.S. negotiations with the Kremlin, especially in negotiations on nuclear weapons reduction where Washington would deal from a position of greater strength. The Reagan expenditures—$1.6 trillion in 5 years—would be spent to acquire new missile systems, especially the mobile MX. Additionally, they would underwrite the most ambitious naval program in the nation's history, enhance existing air force resources, and create a stronger, more mobile conventional force prepared to strike effectively anywhere in the world.[27] Afghanistan, argued Secretary Weinberger, demonstrated that the United States must plan to fight several conventional wars simultaneously. "We have to be prepared," he said, "to launch counteroffensives in other regions and to exploit the aggressor's weaknesses wherever we might find them. . . . We must be prepared for waging a conventional war that may extend to many parts of the world." It was not clear how the administration could obtain the necessary personnel to man its ships, tactical air wings, and divisions without some form of public service. More immediate was the problem of distinguishing weapons that were necessary, effective, and manageable from those that were merely expensive.[28]

Many businessmen and even Pentagon officials believed that military planning transcended the needs of national security. Convinced that the Pentagon was wasteful, they wondered whether Weinberger would ever force the Pentagon to clean its fiscal house. Congressmen, equally troubled by the perennial price of national defense, found it difficult to argue that certain expenditures were excessive when the experts, with their control of critical information, insisted that they were not. (Moreover, most congressmen benefited from the monies spent in their districts and realized substantial reductions of defense expenditures would result in the loss of jobs at home.) For some critics, at least, there existed a strange lack of concern in Washington for the proper distribution of defense funds. The needed message to the Soviets, it seemed, would emerge from the expenditures themselves.

The "Crusade for Freedom"

No less than many of their predecessors, Reagan and his advisers anticipated far more than the perpetuation of the status quo from the country's costly defense efforts. Some anticipated long-desired changes in Soviet behavior from the higher levels of U.S. preparedness. To speed the Soviet collapse, the Republican team would supplement the buildup of American power with a program to deny the U.S.S.R. the benefits of Western trade, credits, and technology. For Reagan the time had come for the United States to assert its revisionist goals in its dealings with the Kremlin. Any future summit meeting, the president warned, must include a discussion of the "imperialism of the Soviet Union." For Haig, the ultimate American objective remained simple and compelling. "We have a right, indeed a duty," he said, "to insist that the Soviets support a peaceful international order, that they abide by treaties, and that they respect reciprocity."[29]

Such implied warnings to the U.S.S.R. raised revisionist expectations elsewhere in Washington. One high administration official declared that he would no longer accept the Soviet withdrawal from Afghanistan and Angola as a precondition for a more moderate U.S. posture; he would demand nothing less than an extensive reduction in Soviet military spending. Strategists anticipated the time when the United States would achieve nuclear supremacy of such magnitude that it would coerce the Soviet Union into an acceptance of conditions everywhere that conformed to American design. Reagan offered a strong statement of his administration's revisionist goals when he spoke before the British Parliament on June 8, 1982: "Let us now begin a major effort to secure the best—a crusade for freedom that will engage the faith and fortitude of the next generation. For the sake of peace and justice, let us move toward a world in which all people are at last free to determine their own destiny."[30]

Reagan's approach to the U.S.S.R. was, in some measure, a reaffirmation of the earlier concept of massive retaliation, with its underlying assumption that the Soviets could not, in the long run, survive American competition. The conviction that American power would ultimately permit Washington to face down the Kremlin leadership seemed to give the Soviets the dismal choice of enduring confrontation, bankruptcy, or capitulation.

Any national investment in a defense structure of such promise would be expensive indeed. Reagan found the answer to vastly increased military budgets, not in higher taxes, but in supply-side economics. The theory of supply-side economics took form from the Laffer curve, named after its creator, conservative economist Arthur Laffer of the University of Southern California. Laffer argued that severe tax cuts, by stimulating demand and production, would produce more federal revenue than high taxes in a stagnant economy. The economic explosion would increase output and jobs, while the gains in productivity from new equipment would curtail inflation.[31] Laffer offered the country a formula designed to eliminate all its economic woes with the enticing and painless expedient of tax reduction.

With Budget Director David Stockman leading the way, Reagan presented his economic program to a joint session of Congress late in February 1981. In what he called "America's New Beginning," he proposed a slashing budget cut of $41.4 billion, a sweep that would spare only the military and deserving needy. He called for passage of the Kemp-Roth tax cut of 10 percent a year for three years, with steeper tax write-offs for business investment. His program, he assured the nation, would ultimately produce thirteen million new jobs and a balanced budget by 1984. Democrats fought the Reagan tide in vain. During May and June congressional committees approved the president's program; at the end, the House and Senate agreed to a 23 percent income tax cut over three years. Reagan's proposed new military spending, by 1986, would exceed the budget cuts by $1.5 trillion.[32] With good reason the president's victory over his congressional opponents presaged trouble. *The New York Times* anticipated deficits as high as $60 billion for 1982; others predicted deficits as high as $90 billion.[33]

REAGAN'S VIEWS CRITICIZED

So completely did Reagan isolate foreign affairs from his congressional relations that the first eight months of his administration produced no coherent foreign policy debate. Still, the criticism of his single-minded anti-Soviet crusade was unending. Writers and analysts renounced the fears that motivated the administration's rhetorical concentration on American weakness and insecurity. Alexander Cockburn noted in *The Wall Street Journal* edition of March 12, 1981, "The world map apparently being scrutinized by Reagan and Haig must be a rather small affair, dominated by Moscow and covered by immense red arrows proceeding there from." Speaking at Dartmouth College in November, George Kennan termed the Reagan view of Soviet power and expansionism "so extreme, so subjective, so far removed from what any sober scrutiny of external reality would reveal, that it . . . [was] not only ineffective but dangerous as a guide to political action."[34] Certainly the Soviet peoples dreaded mass death and destruction no less than did others. "To cite Russian activity in Afghanistan, Ethiopia, and Angola as credible evidence to the contrary," wrote Robert L. Bard of the University of Connecticut Law School, "is an absurdity of truly monumental proportion."[35]

Nowhere could critics detect the Soviet advances that allegedly threatened world peace and stability. The Soviets had failed to dominate any country that they had not occupied militarily. Only in Afghanistan, a desert country on its border, had the U.S.S.R. committed armed forces to actual combat. That invasion, in no measure, threatened the integrity of Britain, western Europe, Japan, China, or even the oil regions of the Middle East. Nowhere had the Soviets revealed any willingness to risk a military engagement with any Western power. Somehow the administration could not explain how its anti-Soviet posture and arms buildup would eliminate unwanted regional pressures for change.

The Reagan program was designed to establish a satisfactory order throughout the Third World simply by blocking Soviet encroachments. But try as it might, the administration could not make a case for its central thesis—that it could explain any counterrevolutionary turbulence in Central America and elsewhere by attributing it to Moscow. Nowhere could its objective of confronting Soviet expansionism everywhere with superior power eliminate local sources of turmoil. "It won't work, of course," Cockburn concluded, "Discontented peoples around the world will continue to rise against their oppressors, whether in El Salvador or Pakistan or Namibia."[36] In El Salvador the American anticommunist crusade brought neither security to the cities nor peace to the countryside. Unfortunately, the Reagan administration's preoccupation with alleged Soviet exploitation of Third World revolution almost eliminated its capacity to recognize and address the continuing problems that flowed from indigenous sources of instability—poverty, corruption, local oppressions, regional tensions, and looming economic collapse. For many analysts it seemed imperative that the Reagan leadership reassess the nation's Third World challenges to determine with greater precision what dangers it faced and what commitments to regional stability were vital to its security.

European Skeptics

Europeans shared the dismay of many Americans at Washington's intense anti-Soviet outlook. After three decades of declining cohesion, the NATO alliance, by the early 1980s, had reached an acute sense of crisis. In large measure, the later strains within the alliance resulted less from policy differences than from the partnership's impressive catalogue of successes. Not once in over thirty years did NATO face an actual Soviet aggression; yet it was only the fear of such an attack that rationalized the alliance's existence. Long before 1980, many Europeans, enjoying perennial peace with no apparent danger, viewed the trans-Atlantic relationship as simply an expression of U.S. interest. With similar logic, they held the United States responsible for whatever strains existed in that relationship under the assumption that they owed far less to the alliance than the alliance owed to them.

Some European analysts wondered how long NATO could survive the Reagan worldview. Early in June, *The Economist* (London) declared characteristically, "The relationship between Western Europe and North America is in the early stages of what could be a terminal illness. The alliance has been in trouble plenty of times before, but this time is the worst yet." That month President Francois Mitterand of France commented, "What I do feel is that in the West . . . there is no guiding thought." Similarly, French Foreign Minister Claude Cheysson admitted to feelings of despair over the future of the Atlantic Alliance. One senior American official observed in July, "There is no papering over the fact that basic disputes exist on the major issues." And James Reston noted in December that no one could listen to the news "without feeling that something . . . [was] deeply wrong within the Western Alliance."[37] There seemed to be, in 1981, greater diversity of opinion within NATO than at any time since mid-century. Three factors contributed to the growing tensions: the unanswered problems of European defense; the unfortunate state of U.S.-Soviet relations, characterized by the decline of détente; and Europe's awareness of the continuing Soviet-American strategic rivalry across the Third World.[38]

Thirty years of successful containment in Europe had never resolved the perennially divisive military dilemmas inherent in the alliance. Europe's defense structure contributed to the region's unprecedented peace, but the defense formula itself remained in doubt. The heavy reliance on nuclear weapons, as the only effective and affordable deterrent and guarantee of peace, placed Europe completely under the decision-making power of the United States. Washington alone would determine how Europe would be defended during any hostilities. Whereas this allied strategy reduced Europe to the status of a protectorate, the Europeans had no intention of matching the Soviet bloc in conventional forces or becoming a genuine partner of the United States in defending their own territories. Allied strategic planning presumed, moreover, that any East-West conflict would center in Europe, perhaps be fought there exclusively. But it was always understood that a war for Europe could escalate into a long-range nuclear war that would also destroy much of the United States. McGeorge Bundy, speaking in London in September 1979, observed, "[N]o one knows that a major engagement in Europe would escalate to the strategic nuclear level. But the essential point is the opposite; no one can possibly know it would not."[39] It was the latter assumption that underlay the credibility of the American nuclear deterrent as a guarantee of peace. But the supposition that the United States itself was vulnerable to Soviet attack had long created doubts that the United States would risk its cities and population by attacking Soviet targets in retaliation for any Soviet aggression against western Europe. It was, in part, to quiet such doubts that NATO adopted the dual track decision to position U.S. medium range weapons on European soil.

Europeans agreed overwhelmingly that the long-range American nuclear arsenal was adequate for the protection of Europe. For that reason they regarded the Reagan administration's pursuit of military superiority as unnecessary, destabilizing, and dangerous. To Europeans it made considerable difference whether the Reagan rearmament program was the beginning of a new crusade against the U.S.S.R. or an end in itself. Europeans had no reason to believe that additional U.S. military would make the administration's anti-Soviet posture any more effective, intelligent, or reassuring. No country, Peter Jenkins observed in *The Guardian*, could build policy on words and power alone; what mattered in a country's behavior was the quality and precision of the interests that it pursued."[40] What American interests, Europeans wondered, underlay the administration's often-repeated intention to face the Soviets down with superior power everywhere from Central America to the Middle East? At the Rome meeting of NATO foreign ministers in May 1981, Haig secured a formal communiqué in which the European allies recognized the U.S. concern over Soviet expansionism in exchange for a promise that Washington, before the end of the year, would begin negotiations with the Soviets over theater nuclear weapons in Europe.[41]

Europeans found Reagan's decision, of August 1981, to assemble and stockpile neutron bombs disquieting; such weapons, no longer regarded vital, merely increased the prospect that any European war would be nuclear. Equally troubling was the continuing evidence of American unilateralism in reaching decisions that touched European interests directly. European officials complained that President Carter had failed to consult them about his decision to postpone the development of the neutron bomb. Undaunted by that criticism, the Reagan administration made another fundamental neutron bomb decision without seeking any advice in Europe. The *Financial Times* (London) editorialized on August 11, "Consultation or not, this decision taken during the summer recess reinforces the impression that the U.S. is riding roughshod over its allies in . . . the creation of a new nuclear weapon which can only be destined for a European theater of war." Schmidt added, "If the American government had consulted with Bonn and Rome before making the decision, both Governments would have recommended to Reagan that he not make this decision at this time." Columnist Tom Wicker warned, in *The New York Times*, that the neutron decision would encourage the European desire "to dissociate from either side of the Soviet-American competition viewed as moving dangerously toward war, in the probably vain hope that Europe might not become the ultimate battleground."[42]

With the attitude of the rich and powerful, Reagan's Washington remained careless in its relations with its allies, seldom troubling itself with the assets and liabilities that they represented. Sandro Viola of *La Republica* (Rome) reflected the views of many Europeans when he wrote in the autumn of 1981, "Regarding relations between America and Europe, Reagan spoke in the first months of his Government of the need for consultations with European allies. There has been no consultation."[43] Earlier, when the power of the United States assuaged Europe's fears and underwrote its prosperity, the allies willingly accepted a master-servant relationship. With the recovery of their productivity and confidence, they became increasingly unsympathetic toward American Cold War fears and corresponding distractions in other regions of the earth. Facing profound disagreements on numerous critical issues touching the Soviet problem, the United States, less and less, sought or received European support for its global reactions. Such unilateralism assumed that either the U.S. power was too dominant, the Soviet danger too remote, the allies too insignificant or ill-informed, or the interests too negligible to require the cultivation of an effective Western coalition.

Few Europeans expected that Europe, where East and West were armed to the teeth and the lines of demarcation long established, would become an actual battleground. What troubled them was the continuing Cold War in the Third World where, after decades of decolonization, the turf and the stakes were still undetermined. Earlier in the Cold War Europeans accepted their vulnerability to Soviet attack as the price of existing at the center of the East-West confrontation. If Western strategy assumed that the next war would be fought in Europe, Europeans acknowledged their danger, knowing that the major Cold War issues were European and that western Europe would be the primary objective in any war. By the 1970s, however, many Europeans no longer regarded Europe the center of the East-West conflict. It was not, for them, a self-evident truth that western Europe need suffer disaster because of the perennial failure of Washington and Moscow to settle their differences or terminate their everlasting global confrontations in regions and over issues that concerned most Europeans remotely, if at all. Britain, France, West Germany, and Italy had significant numbers of intellectuals and socialists who believed that western Europe could establish and sustain a position of neutrality between the United States and the U.S.S.R. As an effective third force, Europe—according to one French official—would escape the "supersuicide of the superpowers." To protect Europe from a Soviet-American war begun elsewhere, France's Charles de Gaulle repeatedly demanded that Britain and France have some voice in determining U.S. objectives outside Europe. "If there is no agreement among the principal members of the Atlantic Alliance on matters other than Europe," he asked, "how can the Alliance be indefinitely maintained in Europe?"[44]

For good reason, U.S.-Soviet détente topped the priority list of most western Europeans; it remained the essential condition for the region's prosperity, confidence, security, and peace of mind. Unable to govern U.S.-Soviet relations, Europeans lauded every change in policy or attitude that reduced East-West tensions across Europe. Reagan's tough anti-Soviet posture troubled

Europeans because it confirmed either the death of détente or an American disinterest in it.

The "Basic Principles of Relations" agreement signed by President Richard Nixon at the SALT I summit in 1972, initiated by the Kremlin and ignored by American leadership, was Moscow's attempt to formalize the concept of détente. It might have substantially reduced tensions between the superpowers if the pact had been better defined and realistically explained to the American public. While Nixon and Kissinger sought a "linkage" between arms control and resolution of Third World issues, the Kremlin hoped that this pact would provide the basis for superpower cooperation in resolving basic differences and allow quiet negotiation of "minor" problems in Third World regions. Soviet officials considered it "an important political declaration" that they hoped, as Ambassador Anatoly Dobrynin recalled, would be the basis of a "new political process of détente in . . . [their] relations." Moscow hoped the agreement would recognize the Soviet doctrine of peaceful coexistence (or détente) and acknowledge the "principle of equality as a basis for the security of both countries." The failure to develop détente's boundaries and gain public acceptance for it, doomed the idea as American leaders interpreted détente simply to mean that the Soviet Union, China, and Cuba were to maintain a "hands off" policy in the Third World.

However, Europeans saw value in the idea. Chancellor Schmidt, in an interview with *The Economist*, explained why Germany could not dismiss its reliance on détente. "One of the necessities of the alliance as well as for Germans," he said, "is to get along with the eastern power. . . . There is nothing to be gained for the Germans in a cold war, divided as our nation is, divided as our capital of Berlin is."[45] Western Europeans argued that détente was divisible, that any settlement was better than none and should be pursued whatever Soviet behavior elsewhere. "Détente," wrote Rudolf Augstein, editor of *Der Spiegel*, "is not something we can give up for anybody."[46]

Europeans clearly expected less of détente than did Americans. They saw little danger to their security in Soviet policies that troubled the more globally oriented United States. They denied that the Soviets had gained more than the West from détente. For them the years of relaxation had demonstrated the bankruptcy of the Soviet system, and the unreliability of the Soviet Union's eastern European allies. If Europeans did not regard the U.S.S.R. a benign presence, they overwhelmingly rejected U.S. fears that "the Russians were coming." They saw no need of a Western confrontation with the Soviet world. Moreover, they regarded the U.S.S.R. so beset with internal and external problems that it desperately desired improved relations with Europe. Accepting the possibility of a major reduction in East-West tensions, *The Sunday Times* (London) complained in February 1981, "President Reagan celebrates his assumption of the Presidency by a polemic in which he describes the Soviets as cheats and liars. General Haig, entering upon his high office, accused them of terrorism. . . . It all sounds tough, but abuse and bombast are not toughness. They are simply abuse and bombast and they achieve nothing."[47]

Europe and Third World Conflicts

Many European leaders and analysts rejected every facet of the Reagan approach to Third World challenges. They condemned and ridiculed Washington's assumption that Soviet expansionism was the universal source of turmoil. "Americans see danger, revolution and terrorism everywhere," observed Germany's *Der Spiegel*, "and behind it all are the Russians." The Reagan approach to Central America was troubling to western Europeans because it challenged directly their own widely held perceptions of Third World revolution and change. Why, many wondered, would the Reagan administration attempt to convert El Salvador into a major arena of U.S.-Soviet confrontation and then attempt to suppress the Salvadoran civil war with aid, advisers, and military shipments to the notoriously repressive government in San Salvador? True, European writers such as Robert Held of the *Frankfurter Allgemeine Zeitung* (Frankfurt) accepted the administration's case. "The Americans," he wrote, "simply cannot afford to let the land bridge to the South American continent become a hegemonic zone of the Soviet Union." Critics, however, continued to far outnumber supporters of U.S. policies. In its pervading criticism of the U.S. commitment to El Salvador, Rome's *Il Messaggero* warned that it could lead to a repetition of past American mistakes, such as Vietnam. The conservative *De Telegraaf* of Amsterdam added that by sending troops to El Salvador "[Reagan] would lose the right to criticize Moscow's involvement in Afghanistan and Poland."[48]

French President Mitterand, pointedly rejecting the Reagan approach to Central America, made the decision, in January 1982, to sell Nicaragua's Sandinista regime arms, equipment, helicopters, patrol boats, trucks, and rocket launchers worth $17 million. Mitterand not only ignored Reagan's plea to reconsider but also suggested that Washington follow the lead of the Mexican government in negotiating away its conflict with El Salvador.[49] European critics, no less than their American counterparts, regarded the upheavals of Central America regional rather than global, indigenous rather than external. Andre Fontaine, editor of Paris's *Le Monde*, viewed them thus in April 1982. "But," he complained, "President Reagan still sees in any Third World crisis the hand of the Soviet Union. From here that appears ridiculous. You don't need Russians to create situations like Nicaragua and El Salvador." London's *The Sunday Times* added, "The tendency to measure everything that happens in the world by the scale of East-West relationships . . . has done much to increase the sense of disunity and mistrust within the alliance."[50] If Europeans had little interest in Third World conflicts, it was because they could find in them no threat to their peace and security.

The Polish Issue

Europeans challenged Reagan's anti-Soviet crusade in Europe no less than in the Third World. Poland thus emerged as a divisive issue when, on December 13, 1981, Polish General Wojciech Jaruzelski executed a successful military crackdown that extinguished, at least temporarily, the popular union-led Solidarity movement. The Polish government rounded up and arrested union leaders, including Solidarity head Lech Walesa, announced a state of national emergency, and the institution of martial law. European leaders responded with expressions of sympathy and shipments of food, with the relief that the Soviets had not invaded and the conclusion that Solidarity had attempted too much. Washington, however, focused on Soviet iniquities and the need for retribution. When State Department officials arrived in Bonn with a list of punishments to be imposed on the Kremlin, Foreign Minister Hans-Dietrich Genscher refused to discuss them. Undaunted by the looming absence of European cooperation, Reagan, in late December, announced an embargo on all shipments of technology to the Soviet Union, the suspension of Aeroflot flights to the United States, and limitations on Soviet access to U.S. ports. He ordered American firms to stop selling equipment to the Soviets that related to the production and transportation of oil and gas. The president forbade the renewal of exchange agreements in energy, science, and technology.[51] During his visit to Washington early in 1982, Schmidt complained that the Reagan administration had embarked on its program of economic sanctions against the U.S.S.R. without consulting any of its European allies.[52] Washington officials agreed that the sanctions would be effective only if they received allied cooperation.

Europe's rejection of the Reagan sanctions was almost total. European leaders denied the president's presumption that the U.S.S.R. was responsible for the Polish crackdown. West Germany announced that it would avoid sanctions short of an actual Soviet invasion of Poland. For the federal republic, with 450,000 German jobs and over 700 companies relying on trade with the Soviet bloc, economic sanctions were inadmissible. Paris refused to support the sanctions but promised not to undermine them. Britain's *Manchester Guardian* of December 23, 1982, warned that the sanctions against the Soviet bloc were damaging the alliance. "[S]ome Americans," observed the *Guardian*, "talk as though the Kremlin house of cards could be blown over. Europe—more conservatively, more proximately—watches the winds that shake the house." The more conservative London *Daily Telegraph* declared that the dispute over sanctions revealed "snarling and back-biting of a type not seen since NATO began [and that threatened] to bring the alliance to ruin."[53] Why the Reagan administration received no material and little moral response to its pleas was evident enough. For western Europeans, the long-established principle still held—that the interests of

East and West in Europe required respect for the integrity of the European spheres of influence.[54]

The Soviet Pipeline Controversy

Beginning in the summer of 1981, the proposed Soviet Yamal pipeline illuminated dramatically the growing U.S.-European dichotomy in perceptions of danger and possibilities for improved relations with the U.S.S.R. The pipeline emerged as a $15 billion project to carry natural gas from the Yamal Peninsula, northeast of the Urals and above the Arctic Circle, to West Germany, France, and Italy. For western Europeans the pipeline, designed to convey three billion cubic meters of natural gas from Siberia to western Europe each year by 1984, would provide users a much-needed source of energy. West Germany approved the pipeline in July 1980; France, Italy, and Britain quickly endorsed the project. At the western Ottawa summit conference of July 1981, Reagan predictably opposed the pipeline and offered to supply West Germany with energy in the form of coal and nuclear power. The pipeline, he feared, would enhance Soviet power and influence in Europe at the price of Western security. The president, having rejected the possibilities of détente, had no desire to encourage closer ties between Europe and the East. He feared, moreover, that the pipeline would give the Kremlin a stranglehold over western Europe's energy supplies. Such advantage the Soviets could exploit politically by threatening the Western governments with either higher prices or the actual cutting off of gas supplies. Third, the Reagan administration, encouraged by Secretary Weinberger, argued that the $8 billion in annual gas export earnings would enable the Soviet economy to support high levels of military spending.[55] White House adviser Richard Pipes asserted that the United States should compel the Soviet Union "to bear the consequences of its own priorities," adding, "We should not make it easier for the [ruling apparatus] to have its cake and eat it; to maintain an inefficient system . . . and build up an aggressive military force and expand globally. Any attempt to help the Soviet Union out of its economic predicament both eases the pressures for internal reform and reduces the need for global retrenchment."[56]

Western European leaders rejected totally the fears that underwrote Washington's official objections to the pipeline. The Soviet Union was not an ideal supplier, but to Europeans it appeared far more so than the OPEC countries of the Middle East. For them, moreover, the Soviet threat appeared far less threatening than the West's own economic disarray. Western Europe, with its twenty-five million unemployed, regarded the projected pipeline a needed source of employment and trade. Because the pipeline was no less a Soviet than a European interest, Western leaders assured Washington that its construction and use would raise, not lower, the threshold of Soviet aggressiveness. The Soviet need for hard currency was an added and powerful incentive to keep the pipeline open. Even with the expanded European use of natural gas, Soviet sales would account for only 5 or 6 percent of the combined energy needs of West Germany, France, and Italy—only 2 percent of western Europe as a whole. Finally, western Europeans doubted that economic sanctions against the U.S.S.R., in the form of Reagan's crusade against the pipeline, would effect any fundamental change in Soviet behavior. The Soviets already possessed enough weapons to destroy western Europe as well as the United States.[57]

Reagan's decision to bar American companies from furnishing goods for the pipeline faced little opposition in Washington, but U.S. officials disagreed bitterly over the effort to include European subsidiaries of American firms in the ban. Haig and much of the State Department argued that western Europe was committed to the pipeline; additional pressure on them would merely endanger the alliance. Pentagon officials, however, insisted that the United States, even at the risk of alienating the allies, must cripple the Soviet Union even if it required the compliance of subsidiaries with the president's December announcement. For Weinberger the time had come for the United States to strengthen its security by implementing its sanctions unilaterally. Stalled by internal disagreements, Reagan waited until March 1982 before he dispatched a special mission, headed by Undersecretary for Security Assistance James L. Buckley, to Europe to discuss sanctions with the allies. Everywhere the Reagan program faced rejection.[58] Finally, on June 18, the president informed the European community that the United States would impose its sanctions not only on U.S. firms but also on their European subsidiaries. The sanctions would apply as well to non-American firms producing equipment under U.S. licenses.[59] The president's action was such a blatant defiance of international law and so potentially threatening to the western European economies that the governments in Bonn, Rome, Paris, and London announced separately that they would honor their pipeline contracts. Some Europeans wondered why the administration would not similarly threaten U.S. interests by canceling American sales of grain to the Soviet Union. French foreign minister Cheysson accused Reagan of furthering the "progressive divorce" between the United States and its Atlantic partners. "We no longer speak the same language," he complained, "The United States seems wholly indifferent to our problems."[60]

During August 1982, the controversy boiled over when a freighter carrying equipment made by an American subsidiary left France bound for the U.S.S.R. Immediately the U.S. Department of Commerce invoked sanctions that barred the subsidiary and an implicated French-owned company from receiving American products and technology. The European governments ordered companies within their borders to fulfill their contracts with the Soviet Union. It was, said Schmidt, a matter of national sovereignty and the sanctity of contracts. In September, officials of the four countries directly concerned with the pipeline met in London to form a common policy of resistance to the Reagan orders. The dispute, said *The Times* (London) had "torn a nasty hole in the Western Alliance." The *Daily Mail* added, "The Atlantic Alliance is a genuine partnership of free and independent nations, not a superpower plus a gaggle of satellites."[61] The National Association of Manufacturers responded to the controversy by declaring that the United States should not punish a firm because it obeyed the laws of the country in which it operated. Some Reagan critics feared that if the administration attempted additional measures to kill the pipeline, the Europeans would respond with economic reprisals that might endanger U.S. investments in Europe and, indeed, the future of the alliance. It was a contest, some predicted, that Washington could not win. If the unity of the alliance, as Reagan noted, was essential for improved Western relations with the Soviet Union, it was no less true, as West Germany's Hans-Dietrich Genscher observed, that agreement within the alliance on policy toward the U.S.S.R. was essential for Western coherence and ability to act.[62]

Convinced that Washington's opposition to the pipeline seriously endangered U.S.-European relations, the State Department, during the autumn of 1982, arranged an acceptable American retreat based on Europe's willingness to limit Western credits to the Soviet Union. Ultimately Reagan called off the sanctions before the Western governments could debate the requested credit restrictions.

THE ANTINUCLEAR MOVEMENT

Before the end of 1981, Reagan's toughness had unleashed an antinuclear movement that reached from the United States across western Europe. Americans who had never believed in détente were not troubled by its demise. Some spoke freely of the possibility of war. Eugene Rostow, Reagan's chief of arms control, observed, "[W]e are living in a prewar and not a postwar world." Pipes averred in conversation with a Reuters' correspondent that the Soviets could choose between changing their system and going to war. "There is no alternative," he asserted, "[I]t could go either way." Later in 1981 Reagan informed newsmen that "the exchange of tactical weapons against troops in the field" need not bring "either of the major powers to pushing the button." European critics concluded that a limited nuclear war was one limited to Europe.[63] Reagan assured Europeans that the United States regarded any attack on Europe as an attack upon itself. He pointed to the 375,000 American servicemen stationed in Europe; these, he promised, would not be withdrawn. Still, West Germany, potential center of any European firestorm, was especially alarmed over the apparent nonchalance among some in Washington about fighting and winning a nuclear war.[64]

What enhanced the burgeoning antinuclear movement was the conviction, in both the United States and western Europe, that additional nuclear weapons would contribute nothing to Western security or world peace. It was not clear how they would serve any purpose. Leading scientists denied that the United States lacked a credible deterrence against a Soviet first strike. If the Soviets harbored an insatiable determination to dominate the world, why had they not exploited the alleged U.S. window of vulnerability to launch a nuclear attack? The strategic forces of the United States appeared prepared to drop some 10,000 hydrogen bombs on the Soviet Union. But the experience of the Cold War era seemed to demonstrate that destructive power even of that magnitude had exceedingly limited efficacy in controlling international affairs, especially where interests and reason dictated the avoidance of force. The Soviets had blockaded Berlin in 1948, absorbed Czechoslovakia, crushed the Hungarian revolt of 1956, placed missiles in Cuba, and eliminated Czechoslovakia's popular liberal regime in 1968, all during a period when the U.S. lead in nuclear power was overwhelming.

By late 1981 the widespread assumption that the United States had preserved an adequate balance of nuclear power unleashed a concerted American nuclear freeze movement. What aggravated the crusade against a continued nuclear arms race was the apparent danger such weapons posed for the future of civilization. Jonathan Schell's *The Fate of the Earth* (1982), followed by George Kennan's *The Nuclear Delusion* (1982), contributed to the growing concern. Any failure of nuclear deterrence, wrote Schell, would threaten the extinction of human life on the planet. The threat of such destruction lay not in the intentions of government but in the chances of error and miscalculation. "We can live with the threat of accidental nuclear war for ten or twenty or thirty years as we have," wrote Dr. James E. Muller of Harvard University, founder of International Physicians for Prevention of Nuclear War, "but not forever."[65] By the spring of 1982 the American nuclear freeze movement encompassed a wide coalition of professionals and religious leaders. Thousands marched in Chicago in early April, demanding an end to the arms race. In June, hundreds of thousands gathered in New York's Central Park in the largest public demonstration in the city's history. Proponents of the nuclear freeze placed the issue on the ballot in nine states. Already the Catholic bishops of America had moved toward the adoption of their famed antinuclear resolution.

Before the end of 1982, the freeze movement was active in forty-three states and nearly two-thirds of the nation's congressional districts. With an estimated 20,000 energetic volunteer organizers, nearly one million signatures on petitions had been collected in support of city and state resolutions. Soon the campaign would focus on gaining a congressional endorsement. All of this activity, particularly its influence on midterm elections, caught the attention of campaign strategists preparing for the president's reelection.[66]

Dread of a renewed nuclear arms race, unleashed by Reagan's projected military buildup, set off the powerful European peace movement of 1981. Concerned Europeans feared that the superpowers either did not know how to control the nuclear arms race or had no desire to do so. One German peace activist complained, "Talking to the superpowers about disarmament is like talking to drug dealers about stopping drug deliveries."[67] Much of the antinuclear agitation aimed at the dual track decision, of December 1979, for the creation of an effective theater nuclear force in Europe.

Not all Europeans found the decision reassuring. Theater weapons, all under American control, could, in a crisis, "decouple" the American and European defense systems and enable the United States to protect its own territory by limiting a nuclear war to Europe itself. For others the new weapon would saddle Europe with another arms program and predestine those countries that employed the new weapons to become the special objects of nuclear blackmail. The decision to place additional American-controlled weapons in Europe did not necessarily make the threat of European suicide more convincing. If Europe required some deterrent to offset the Soviet SS-20s, that deterrent, some Europeans argued, need not be located in Europe.[68]

Reagan's success in exaggerating and dramatizing the Soviet threat back-fired in sending over two million Europeans into antinuclear, and largely anti-American, demonstrations. The opposition to Euromissiles appeared strongest in West Germany where Hamburg, on June 19, 1981, witnessed the largest protest in postwar Germany. This was not surprising because, as one military observer put it, their villages were only one-megaton apart. On October 10, some 250,000 demonstrators staged a rally in Bonn to denounce NATO plans to modernize its nuclear defenses. One poster read, "Only Schmidt and the Cowboy Need Nuclear Protection." On October 24, 150,000 Britons marched through London, chanting, "Ban the Bomb." One British organizer attributed the demonstration's success to "the feeling that the United States and the Soviet Union . . . [were] determined to collide with each other," adding, "[T]hey are likely to blow us up in the process." In Paris, 100,000 people, many of them conservatives, openly displayed their opposition. Resistance to U.S. missiles seemed strong in the Netherlands and Belgium as well. What would New Yorkers think, declared one Dutch cabinet member, if large installations of nuclear weapons were placed on Long Island? Some European neutralists opposed Soviet weapons no less than American.[69] The marchers—churchmen, youth groups, and citizens of all classes and persuasions—were too numerous, too disparate in age and politics, and too scattered to be dismissed as a fringe movement.

In March 1982, the NATO defense ministers reaffirmed the plan to deploy the U.S. cruise and Pershing II missiles in Europe, beginning in 1983. They still faced the task of convincing their antinuclear publics that Europe's security required the new missiles. Schmidt favored the emplacement of theater weapons if the arms talks stalled, but, he argued, there "might have been fewer demonstrations in Europe if there had been less loose talk out of the United States, telling the Europeans we were not living in a postwar period but in a prewar period. That had a psychologically devastating effect."

POLICYMAKING—REAGAN STYLE

Reagan's critics predicted that his administration would never close the gap between its fears of the U.S.S.R. and its actions. Indeed, the Reagan team framed no policies that conformed to its self-proclaimed global obligations. The foreign policy phrases honed in the early days of the administration were not the determinants of policy at all. No member of the Reagan team defined, with any precision, the occasions when the United States might use force. Reagan found a passing occasion to demonstrate U.S. power and will when Libya, in late 1981, challenged an American naval presence inside the Gulf of Sidra. American pilots ended the brief confrontation by shooting down two Libyan planes. As early as April 1981, the president challenged his policy of toughness completely when he ended Carter's embargo on grain shipments to the Soviet Union. One Soviet expert speculated on the Kremlin's response, "It will confirm their view that there is not yet an American policy toward the Soviet Union—and they are right." No less than Carter, Reagan coexisted quietly with the Soviet presence in Afghanistan, Africa, and the Arabian Peninsula. Critics concluded logically that the Reagan rhetoric was meant, not to undergird a tougher policy, but to create the desired political atmosphere within the country.[70]

Long before the end of 1981, it was apparent that the growing chasm between official words and official actions was aggravating divisions among the pragmatists and the ideologues within the administration. With no clear course of action in the offing, the president received conflicting policy proposals from Haig's State Department, Weinberger's Defense Department, Richard Allen's National Security Council, Jeane Kirkpatrick's UN office, and Republicans everywhere. At times the feuding became so bitter that it suggested a total absence of White House direction. Later Haig complained in his memoirs that the decision-making process was as "mysterious as a ghost ship; you heard the creak of the rigging and the groan of the timbers and even glimpsed the crew on deck. But which one of the crew was at the helm? It was impossible to know for sure."[71]

Actually Reagan's anti-Soviet rhetoric never denied his ultimate intention of seeking improved relations with Moscow. In his inaugural he recognized the American concern for peace. "We will negotiate for it, sacrifice for it," he told the nation, "we will not surrender for it, now or ever."[72] Embracing the need of dealing from strength, Reagan assured his critics that his defense program was designed largely to produce successful negotiations with the Kremlin. "I think that we can sit down and maybe have some more realistic negotiations because of what we can threaten them with," the president told reporters in October 1981. "But they know our potential capacity industrially," he continued, "and they can't match it." Whether the president even then lacked the power to negotiate from strength was doubtful. Carter's alleged "window of vulnerability" had already proved to be a myth.

Negotiation, moreover, comprised other than a weighing of power, especially when available power, whatever its magnitude, conveyed no clear threat of violence. Negotiation entails essentially a search for accommodation over ends, even when the ends are arms reduction.[73]

The president would soon revamp his foreign policy team. Early in January 1982, Reagan replaced Allen as his National Security Adviser with a close personal friend, William Clark, who would report directly to him. Apparently Clark was closer to the president than anyone else in the administration and they shared the same values. And later, George Shultz would replace Haig as Secretary of State.

CHAPTER 3

Reagan Initiatives and Soviet Turmoil

In May 1982, Secretary of State Haig delivered a conciliatory speech before the U.S. Chamber of Commerce, stressing the need for political dialogue with Moscow. That month the president announced that Soviet behavior in Afghanistan was no longer an obstacle to arms negotiations.[1] Throughout the spring of 1982 ineffectual efforts at arms limitation stood at the center of the administration's agenda. The shifts toward moderation in the Reagan foreign policies appeared piecemeal and hesitant. Administration hard-liners insisted that the trims were largely tactical, but the mixture of dogma and pragmatism invited criticism from friends and critics alike.

Many observers questioned the absence of consistency. "The general complaint," wrote Reston in March 1982, "is that the administration has no strategy; no clear interpretation of the world; that it is playing diplomatic chess . . . without any pattern in mind; talking tough, but acting soft and confusing its supporters and adversaries in the process."[2] For many observers the continuing dichotomies in official behavior merely reflected the divisions within the Republican Party. *The New York Times* editorialized in June 1982, "Mr. Reagan wants too many conflicting things at once and has let no one order the priorities. And that is just another way of saying that he had straddled his party's incompatible yearnings—of rightwing ideology and business-like pragmatism—and let them proceed to wreck each other's designs."[3]

CONSERVATIVE CRITICS

Reagan's necessary, if halting, efforts to adjust American policies to the requirements of the times pleased much of the Washington community, as well as observers and commentators everywhere. But for neoconservatives and anti-Soviet ideologues who had dwelled on the evidences of national weakness and failure during the Carter years, the Reagan experience quickly reached the level of disaster. In the process the president had apparently asked them to desert the dreams that they had shared with him at the commencement of his administration. Neoconservative Norman Podhoretz and anti-Soviet columnist George Will lauded the president's military program as the necessary first step toward the restoration of American power in the world. What troubled them, however, was the absence of any political strategy that would move the country toward the achievement of the administration's clearly stated goals. Will condemned Secretary Haig's pronounced tendency to preach toughness and act otherwise. "In Carter's State Department," he complained in mid-January 1982, "rhetoric and policy were both bad, but at least they meshed. Haig's rhetoric does not fit the policies that give an appearance of action without real action. The mismatch is confusing the country." In June, he concluded, "Reagan has had less impact on foreign policy than any modern President (Ford excepted)... [M]ore than any modern president, he has abandoned foreign policy to the Secretary of State. More than any recent Secretary, Haig seems determined to maintain continuity in all the sluggish impulses of the foreign-policy bureaucracy."[4]

For neoconservatives and the new right the evidences of Reagan's failures were almost universal. The president had not achieved the promised strategic consensus in the Middle East. Indeed, neoconservatives complained, his partiality toward Saudi Arabia presaged eventual support for the Arab position on Palestine and the weakening of the U.S. commitment to Israel. For those who believed with Reagan that the nationalist Chinese would one day overthrow the mainland regime, it was disconcerting to have the administration deny advanced jets to the Taiwanese liberators. Podhoretz condemned the president as well for not supporting the resisting Afghans with better arms or backing the Angolan guerrillas trying to expel the Cuban troops who had "helped turn their country into a Soviet satellite." Even in Central America, Podhoretz complained, the president had allowed himself to be thrown on the defensive. The administration had apparently retreated from its intent to stop the Soviet Union, operating through Cuba, from establishing outposts in El Salvador, Nicaragua, and possibly elsewhere in the hemisphere. Will warned those who applauded Reagan's limited involvement in El Salvador. "What will they say," he asked, "when El Salvador has become a staging base for the Soviet-Cuban assault on Guatemala, preparatory to the assault on Mexico?"[5]

Finally, the administration had not employed the country's economic power to aggravate the Kremlin's domestic problems and thereby weaken its control over the Soviet empire. "This administration," Will concluded bitterly, "evidently loves commerce more than it loathes communism." The limited U.S. action in the Polish crisis was further evidence of Reagan's continuing unwillingness to confront Soviet power and influence in the world. As he wrote in *The New York Times Magazine*, May 1982, "What President Reagan's response to the Polish crisis reveals is that he has in practice been following a strategy of helping the Soviet Union stabilize its empire, rather than a strategy aimed at encouraging the breakup of that from within." Podhoretz accused the Reagan administration of merely returning to the détente of the Nixon-Carter years and, like those administrations, failing to hold the Soviets at bay. Reagan's concentration on domestic issues, wrote Podhoretz, had permitted a vacuum to develop "into which have come pouring all the old ideas and policies against which Ronald Reagan himself has stood for so many years."[6] Those who thought the danger real and the need for anti-Soviet victories in Poland, the Middle East, Africa, and Latin America imperative could express their disenchantment with President Reagan's apparent failures. They could not, with equal facility, suggest how Washington might square its actions with its words. Ultimately the world would impose its will on the Reagan administration precisely as it had on Carter's.

FROM NICARAGUA TO LEBANON

By 1982, CIA director William Casey had designed the administration's strategy to eliminate the pro-Soviet forces in Central America. Casey headed the list of those in Washington who believed that the Soviets were on the move. In six years, he argued, the Kremlin had gained major influence in nine countries reaching from southeast Asia, through the Middle East and Africa, to Central America. What U.S. standing and security required, he believed, was a strategy that would free one or more of these countries of their Soviet presence. Casey and Reagan agreed to convert Nicaragua into their test case. The administration launched its Central American offensive in late 1981 by authorizing covert support for the contras, the anti-Sandinista resistance forces in Nicaragua. The administration's objective ostensibly was to interdict the flow of arms from Nicaragua to El Salvador, but CIA officials became skeptical when aid was earmarked for Edén Pastora, a rebel leader operating against Nicaragua out of Costa Rica. Clearly the administration sought the overthrow of the Sandinista government. To aid the administration in carrying out its objectives in Central America, the president established Project Democracy and, in August 1982, assigned the project's covert activities to the National Security Council. The contra war, languishing from the outset, faced a genuine impediment in December 1982, when Congress passed the Boland Amendment that prohibited the expenditures of funds for the overthrow of the Nicaraguan regime. Not until the president appointed L. Anthony Motley, former ambassador to Brazil, as Assistant Secretary of State for Inter-American Affairs, did the State Department accept the CIA's judgment that the contras had credibility and required only U.S. funds and logistical support to gain the necessary triumphs over the Sandinista forces.

During 1982, the administration's counter-revolutionary program for Central America focused on Honduras. That country, bordering both Nicaragua and El Salvador, offered an ideal base of operations against Nicaragua. U.S. officials set out to transform the contras, largely exiled Nicaraguan supporters of ousted dictator Anastasio Somoza, into an effective border force. It began to train and equip the Nicaraguan exiles in camps along the Nicaraguan-Honduran frontier to cross the borders of Nicaragua, undermine the Sandinista regime, and terminate its support for the Salvadoran rebels. At the same time the administration defended the Guatemalan government of President Efrain Rios Montt despite its destructive war against the Guatemalan countryside that drove thousands of peasants across the border into southern Mexico. By late 1982 the contra attacks across the border into Nicaragua were almost daily occurrences. That year there were plots to destroy Nicaragua's only oil refinery as well as bridges and other facilities essential for the Nicaraguan economy. The major military exercise of August 1983, Big Pine 2, ended with the decision to leave almost a thousand U.S. troops in Honduras to guard the assets left behind—radar stations, field hospitals, aircraft, and heavy equipment. Two men advanced the U.S. presence in Honduras: Honduran military commander General Gustavo Alvaraz Martinez, a friend of the United States often accused of running the country, and U.S. Ambassador John D. Negroponte. The buildup of the American presence in Honduras appeared to many, both inside and outside Central America, a prelude to a general war in the area.

As Washington's efforts to destabilize the Sandinista regime continued into 1983 with no success in sight, the president reminded Americans of the consequences of Soviet efforts to build a bridgehead in the center of the hemisphere. On March 10, he addressed a business group in Washington: "It isn't nutmeg that's at stake in the Caribbean and Central America. It is the United States' national security." Yet the president promised his audience that the U.S. role in defending the hemisphere would remain strictly limited. "We will not Americanize this conflict," he said. "American combat troops are not going to El Salvador." In his continuing effort to persuade the American people that an anticommunist Nicaragua was a vital U.S. interest, Reagan, on April 17, told a joint session of Congress, "The national security of all the Americas is at stake in Central America. If we cannot defend ourselves there, we cannot expect to prevail elsewhere. Our credibility would collapse, our alliances would crumble and the safety of our homeland would be put in jeopardy."

Nestor D. Sanchez, deputy assistant secretary of defense for inter-American affairs, added that the Soviet Union, operating through Nicaragua and El Salvador, was "abetting an assault on the security of this hemisphere more dangerous than the postwar threat to Western Europe. The conflict

in El Salvador . . . [represented] merely one step of an attempt to absorb the
closest neighbors . . . into what President Ronald Reagan . . . called 'the most
aggressive empire the modern world has seen.'"[7] Failure to stop the insurgency in Central America, warned Secretary Weinberger, would compel the
United States to withdraw its forces from Europe, Japan, and Korea, leaving
the entire Eastern Hemisphere to Soviet purposes.

United States, Israel, and Lebanon

Events in the Middle East in 1982 compelled the administration to substitute a policy aimed at regional peace for its earlier pursuit of an anti-
Soviet strategy. Reagan had received no European support for his initial
effort to build a strategic program for the region around arms shipments
to Saudi Arabia, Egypt, and Pakistan. Europeans wondered why the United
States would scatter arms to such would-be allies that possessed neither the
will nor the capacity to defend themselves. Repeatedly Europeans reminded
Washington that a comprehensive peace between Israel and the Arab world,
including a settlement of the Palestinian question, was more essential for
regional stability than the building of a military system to keep the Soviets
out.[8] Late in 1981, against extensive Israeli lobbying, Reagan won a close
vote in Congress for the sale of AWACS to Saudi Arabia. He then offered
Israel a new security agreement. In late December, Israel annexed the Golan
Heights, captured from Syria in 1967. Washington, in a mild rebuke, sus-
pended the new strategic cooperation pact with Israel. Immediately Prime
Minister Menachem Begin summoned U.S. Ambassador Samuel Lewis and
castigated the United States for treating Israel like a "banana republic."[9]

Throughout the spring of 1982, U.S.-Israeli relations remained tense. Israel, convinced that the United States was bound morally and strategically
to its survival and thus had no choice but to accept its policies toward its
neighbors, proceeded to build new Jewish settlements in the West Bank. At
the same time Israel faced continual harassment from the Palestinian Lib-
eration Organization (PLO), which had established itself firmly in southern
Lebanon as well as in West Beirut. Searching for a pretext to invade Lebanon
and drive out the PLO, Israel found one in the attempted assassination, on
June 3, of Shlomo Argov, its ambassador to Britain.

Israeli forces, sweeping all before them, advanced far beyond their initial
objective of pacifying southern Lebanon, much to the dismay of Washington. Secretary Haig had applauded the Israeli successes, convinced that Israel
alone could bring peace and order to Lebanon. Although Haig had been at
odds with other members of the administration on matters of policy and
style, it was the gradual rejection of his pro-Israeli stance that led to his
resignation in late June and Reagan's selection of George P. Shultz, an associate of Weinberger in the Bechtel group, as his successor.[10] Whatever the
administration's doubts regarding the wisdom of Israel's policy, it refused

(L to R) Secretary of State George Shultz, Reagan, and Secretary of Defense Caspar Weinberger. Shultz and Weinberger frequently disagreed on arms control issues. *Source:* Ronald Reagan Library.

to exert any pressure that might undermine that country's objective of driving the PLO from Lebanon.

During July, Israeli forces closed in on the PLO-occupied areas of Beirut and proceeded to hammer the city with planes and artillery. The death and destruction shocked the world. The Reagan administration, seemingly powerless to control Israeli policy, found itself implicated in the destruction. The president expressed outrage, but he refused to antagonize Begin's supporters in the United States or compromise his demand that the PLO leave Lebanon—an objective that required an Israeli victory. After weeks of intense diplomatic effort, U.S. negotiator Philip C. Habib, in August, managed to secure an agreement that provided for the withdrawal of both Palestinian and Syrian forces from Beirut.[11]

On September 1, Reagan, for the first time, announced a comprehensive policy for the Middle East. He declared that long-term peace in the region demanded a freeze of Israeli settlements in the West Bank and self-government for the Palestinians, not in the form of an independent state as the Arabs preferred, but in association with Jordan. The formula was not new; it followed essentially the principles that had evolved during the Carter years. Predictably, Israel rejected the Reagan proposal as a sellout of Israel's interests and security. While Israel maintained an unwanted presence in Lebanon, Weinberger acknowledged that the United States had no control over its ally. Israel's refusal to withdraw so isolated Israel at the United Nations that only the U.S. threat of withdrawing from that body prevented the passage of a resolution to remove Israel from membership.

Reagan's decision to assign top priority to the Palestinian problem and to downgrade the quest for an anti-Soviet strategic consensus demonstrated, in large measure, Secretary Shultz's growing influence in Washington. Shultz, a former dean of the University of Chicago Business School, was, like Haig, a conservative—but not an ideologue. He agreed with Haig and other Reagan officials that the United States required a strong military establishment. Unlike Haig, he was not obsessed by ambition and suspicion of others. In pushing for decisions opposed by the hard-line Reagan team, Haig had often ignored the president's injunction that the administration maintain at least the appearance of consensus. From the outset, Shultz, the consummate team player, worked closely with the White House staff and avoided all bureaucratic wars for influence. His working relationship with the president and other top officials was so agreeable that it transformed the image of the country's leadership. In November 1982, *The New York Times* assessed the new secretary's role in Washington: "Trading on close ties to Mr. Reagan and previous experience in Washington, Mr. Shultz set the right priorities. He lowered the secretary's voice and raised his influence."[12]

In September 1982, U.S. Marines landed in Beirut on what appeared to be a simple and peaceful mission—to help Yasir Arafat and his Palestinian followers leave on Greek ferryboats and to maintain some semblance of order among the rival Lebanese factions, Syria and Israel. The president explained the mission on September 28, "They're there along with our allies, the French and the Italians, to give a kind of support and stability while the Lebanese Government seeks to reunite its people which have been divided for several years now into several (armed) factions, and bring about a unified Lebanon with a Lebanese army that will then be able to preserve order."[13] Those objectives seemed sound enough. The president hoped to achieve them by supporting the new Lebanese regime under Amin Gemayel, eliminating Syria's influence from the country, and creating conditions that would permit a total Israeli withdrawal. Unfortunately, Washington, by supporting the Christian Gemayel government against its Moslem detractors, gave Gemayel more confidence than the divisions and anarchy within his country warranted and encouraged him to defy the other political factions. Reagan failed to explain how the United States could be a peacekeeping force when it supported only one of the Lebanese factions in the continuing, bitter struggle for power. The Marines, caught in the crossfire, became the targets of all who opposed the Gemayel regime.

Congress wanted no American war in Lebanon. Still, early in October, it approved a resolution that permitted the president to keep Marines in Lebanon for eighteen additional months. Democratic critics in Congress warned the administration against another Third World entrapment; the position of the U.S. forces in Lebanon had ceased to be simple or reassuring. The president had placed the Marines in a combat zone without giving them the authority or the numbers needed to carry on a war. In April 1983, a terrorist attack on the U.S. embassy killed Marine guards. On October 23, the Reagan commitment to Lebanon faced a crucial test when a suicide car attack on the Marine base killed 241 servicemen—and wounded another 130. Despite such casualties, the Marines had accomplished almost nothing. Their success did not rest on their capabilities but on the capacity of the Lebanese to reach a political settlement.[14]

Reagan met the challenge by tying U.S. credibility throughout the Middle East to the continued presence of the Marines in Lebanon. The Marines, he said, would remain until the situation was under control. "We have vital interests in Lebanon," he said. "And our actions in Lebanon are in the cause of world peace. With our allies, England, France, and Italy, we're part of a multinational peacekeeping force seeking a withdrawal of all foreign forces from Lebanon and from the Beirut area." During the October crisis, the president explained, in the language of falling dominoes, that the Marines were in Lebanon to protect America's global position. "If Lebanon ends up under the tyranny of forces hostile to the West [Syria and its allies]," he warned, "not only will our strategic position in the eastern Mediterranean be threatened but also the stability of the entire Middle East. Lebanon is central to our credibility on a global scale." No longer did the president focus on the maze of feuds within Lebanon. Instead, he transformed the American mission of bringing some order to Lebanon into a confrontation with Soviet expansionism in the region. "Can the United States and the free world," he asked, "stand by and see the Middle East incorporated into the Soviet bloc?" The United States, he added, had the obligation to guarantee the deliveries of Middle Eastern oil to western Europe and Japan, as well as a moral commitment to defend the interests of Israel.[15]

The Reagan administration continued its commitment to Lebanon's President Gemayel even as Syria took up the cause of the Moslem dissidents by placing 50,000 troops in Lebanon. The Gemayel government controlled the grounds of the presidential palace in Beirut, but little else. Nowhere could the Lebanese army deal effectively with the Moslem forces. On May 17, 1983, the United States had negotiated an agreement for the simultaneous withdrawal of Israeli and Syrian forces from Lebanon, leaving Gemayel in control of the country. Secretary Shultz's failure to secure a Syrian withdrawal was predictable; the Syrians were not even present at the negotiations. During November, Gemayel agreed to terminate the May 17 agreement by accepting the Syrian presence in his country. With Syria now the dominant external force in Lebanon, the U.S. peace program, as embodied in the May 17 agreement, was dead as its forces withdrew. Reagan's great miscalculation lay in his assumption that he could put Lebanon together behind a regime that, because of its deep anti-Moslem biases, failed to effect some reconciliation among the Lebanese factions. One Lebanese historian summed up the American dilemma: "Great powers should not get involved in the politics of small tribes."

Israel gained little from its costly Lebanese involvement. Without power to remove the Syrians, Israel emerged from the war with a shattered economy and an inflation rate of 200 percent, its troops bogged down in southern Lebanon and still losing lives. No longer were there any plans for bringing Israel and its Arab adversaries to the peace table. Israel had not disposed of the PLO. Nor had the Arab world curtailed its demand that Israel resolve the Palestinian issue and withdraw from all territory taken in the 1967 war—the West Bank, the Golan Heights, and the Gaza Strip.[16] Such an unsatisfactory outcome columnist Meg Greenfield had predicted as early as June 1982: "What seems indisputable as the firing dies down is that the violence represented failure . . . that what you must do when it is over is what you should have done long before."[17]

THE INVASION OF GRENADA

Suddenly, on October 25, the president announced the U.S. invasion of Grenada—a small island in the eastern Caribbean with a population of 120,000. For years Washington had kept a wary eye on events in the country. Maurice Bishop had gained control of the island's government in 1979 through a bloodless coup and proceeded to establish close ties with Cuba's Fidel Castro. Reagan denied diplomatic relations to the Bishop regime until it severed its ties with Cuba. During a 1982 visit to Bridgetown, Barbados, the president declared that Grenada had joined Cuba, Nicaragua, and the Soviet Union in an effort to "spread the virus" of Marxism in the Caribbean.[18]

Washington opposed Grenada in the World Bank and staged massive naval maneuvers, even a mock invasion, in the island's vicinity. Cut off from U.S. aid, Bishop looked to Venezuela, East Germany, North Korea, Canada, as well as Cuba, with great success. By 1983, Grenada's tourist trade was booming. Bishop brought in thousands of Cubans to complete a huge airstrip and other public projects. In addition, he imported large quantities of Cuban arms.

The Reagan administration condemned the construction of the 12,000-foot Point Salinas airstrip as one designed only for military use, although Barbados, the Bahamas, and Martinique all had longer runways. During 1983, Bishop engaged the administration in verbal war. Then, on October 19, a coup led by Deputy Prime Minister Bernard Coard resulted in a bloodbath and Bishop's death. The triumph of the island's political extremists destroyed whatever legitimacy the revolution had possessed.

In explaining the decision to invade Grenada, Washington revealed that it had received frantic requests to invade from tiny countries around the island. Had the United States refused, declared one senior official, "no one would have taken . . . [it] seriously any more down there. What good are maneuvers and shows of force, if you never use it?" Much of the island's population had little interest in Bishop or his reliance on Cuba. When Bishop's assassination threatened the island with chaos, they welcomed the U.S. invasion and the promises of order and democracy that it offered. American students at the local medical college lauded what the president termed a rescue mission. Grenada's new leadership promised an election in November 1984.[19]

By a huge majority, Americans lauded the surprise invasion, but as a military venture Operation Urgent Fury was hardly encouraging. American forces, consisting of 7,000 officers and soldiers, required three days to over-whelm fifty Cuban soldiers and several hundred construction workers. In the absence of a unified command, army and navy officers failed to attend the planning sessions of the other; attacking units carrying incompatible radios and, at least on one occasion, assaulted each other's positions. The commander of the USS *Guam* refused to refuel Army helicopters unloading wounded soldiers. Still, during succeeding days the Pentagon awarded over 8,000 medals, some to officers who never left the Pentagon or other U.S. bases.[20]

What rendered the Grenada invasion a huge administration triumph was the chasm between the venture's limited costs and the proclaimed magnitude of the achievement in preventing Grenada's incorporation into the Soviet-Cuban bloc. "The events in Lebanon and Grenada, though oceans apart," declared the president on October 27, "are closely related. Not only has Moscow assisted and encouraged violence in both countries, but it provides direct through a network of surrogates and terrorists." A political master-piece, the speech by linking Lebanon, the KAL 007 tragedy, and Grenada shamelessly and successfully buried the Beirut disaster.[21]

Robert C. McFarlane, the president's national security adviser, said to the newsmen, "We got there just in time." Later the president declared that the U.S. invasion had nipped a Cuban occupation in the bud and prevented Grenada from becoming a Soviet-Cuban colony that would export "terror and subversion" throughout Central America. Picking up the theme of Soviet expansionism, Ambassador Jeanne Kirkpatrick argued that the governments of Grenada and Nicaragua were dominated by people "committed not just to Marxism and socialism but integrated into the Soviet bloc." CIA Director William Casey acknowledged the new Soviet threats in Africa and Central America. "How much more alarmed would Churchill be," he said, "if he looked around the world today and saw how the Soviets have grown in strength and how far they have extended their power and influence beyond the Iron Curtain he so aptly labeled." Democrats, the president added, would have invited disaster by failing to invade Grenada.[22]

For Reagan, the United States had never won a needful victory against Communist encroachments in the hemisphere more painlessly and unequiv-ocally. Much of the country seemed to agree. According to an ABC *Night-line* phone-in poll, Americans favored the invasion nine to one. Democratic leaders joined Republicans in lauding the Grenada operation. Neoconservative critic Norman Podhoretz praised the American action in Grenada, asserting that the administration had approached the challenge with the clarity of political and moral purpose that it had not sustained in Lebanon. But he added a word of caution: "Grenada by itself cannot be taken to signify a resurgence of American power, especially given the demoralization evident in our response to the attack on our Marines in Beirut. But if Lebanon shows us a United States still suffering from the shell-shocked condition that has muddled our minds and paralyzed our national will since Vietnam, Grenada points the way back to recovery and health."[23]

Still, countless Americans and Europeans denounced the invasion as an illegal and needless interference in the internal affairs of a small Caribbean country. Responding to the Grenada invasion, thousands of people gathered in Washington, during November, to protest the president's policies in Central America and the Caribbean. Western Europeans were disturbed by the realization that Reagan again linked the U.S.S.R. to the whole of the instability of Africa, the Middle East, and Central America. European officials were more determined than ever to gain some influence in Washington and a more powerful voice in East-West relations. Sir Geoffrey Howe, British Foreign Secretary, responded to the Grenada invasion with the assertion that "there are times when Europe needs a voice independent even of its closest allies." Every Reagan decision delighted some and troubled others; the desired consensus remained as elusive as ever.[24]

THE SOVIET UNION—TURMOIL AND DECLINE

Even as the Reagan administration detected the dangerous presence of Soviet power everywhere in Third World turmoil, the evidence of economic and social decline within the U.S.S.R. were universal. As early as the Carter years, observers of the Soviet system analyzed its highly visible and seemingly irreversible disabilities with astonishing accuracy. Haverford College economist Holland Hunter, in a long 1979 report to the Congress Joint Economic Committee, described not only the serious deficiencies in the Soviet economy but also the institutional resistance to change that rendered needed reform highly remote. The country's centrally controlled command economy added to its pursuit of full employment, created padded rosters, low efficiency, underemployment, unsatisfactory products, and chronic shortages. The Soviet system, by its very nature, thwarted all efforts to introduce efficient processes and improved products. Hunter wrote, "[Market competition] forces old technology off the stage, penalizing with bankruptcy those who fail to adapt . . . , long standing Soviet tradition preserves old capital plant and equipment to an extraordinary extent."[25] Hunter explained why the Soviet system's powerful vested interests found the necessary changes in economic principles and political institutions unacceptable. "A systems approach to technological innovation," he noted, "would concede major initiative to plant management . . . [E]nterprise-level initiative would permit 'localist tendencies' to divert resources from the Party's priorities."[26] Innovation, in short, would threaten the structure of centralized power.

Official American analysts studied the Soviet economy with a heavy bias toward overestimating the Kremlin's expansive power. Beginning in the 1950s, CIA estimates consistently depicted the Soviet economic base as larger than that of the United States. They reported a Soviet investment rate equal to those of West Germany and Japan—twice that of the United States. By the 1970s, U.S. analysts, wedded to the notion of Soviet superiority and misled by exaggerated Soviet statistics, predicted that the Soviet economy would outstrip that of the United States. There were some cautionary American voices. Jack P. Ruina, head of President John F. Kennedy's Defense Advanced Research Projects Agency, returned from Moscow wondering how, behind the Soviet Union's fifteenth-century facade, there could be a sweeping twenty-first-century economy. Swedish economist Anders Aslund described the U.S.S.R. as "a reasonably well-developed Third World country." Some observers placed it in the same category with India. Analyst Robert B. Hawkins, Jr., concluded, "Soviet national income, generally thought to be about half that of the United States, is, in fact, less than a third. That puts the Soviet military burden at as much as 25 percent of GNP." Clearly the Soviet defense bill far exceeded what the country could afford. Without the benefit of sophisticated intelligence-gathering equipment, Senator Daniel Moynihan predicted, in 1979, that the Soviet Union was headed for extinction.[27]

Soviet writers, scholars, and analysts—members of the so-called new thinking—were no less critical of the Soviet system and perceptive in their judgments. They noted that the Soviet economy began to lose its momentum after 1975, falling far behind the advanced nations in productivity, scientific development, and the employment of high technology. Dissident economists, such as Abel Aganbegyan and Tatyana Zaslavskaya, attributed the decline of the Soviet economy not to temporary phenomena (bad weather or ineptitude) but to rigid central planning. Without economic calculations reflecting demand, the command economy could not measure quality or errors in judgment. Nor could it unleash the initiative, energy, and ingenuity required for the production and marketing of better and more varied products.[28] Central planning, with its emphasis on collectivization, undermined the Soviet Union's once-powerful agricultural economy. The Kremlin could control resistance with terror and starvation, but despite the richness of the land, it could not, in the absence of incentives, produce food efficiently or assure its delivery to market. Czarist Russia exported grain, but during the 1970s the U.S.S.R. was compelled to import millions of tons of grain to feed its people. Many urban residents satisfied their food requirements by raising vegetables on small plots.

Without incentives and hopes for advancement, industrial laborers worked lethargically, producing increasingly shoddy goods for noncompetitive markets, relying on subsidies and welfare for their existence. With the stagnation of the economy after 1979, the populace began to experience shortages of food, housing, and consumer goods. The system of special privilege compelled countless citizens to survive through bribery and corruption. The burgeoning cynicism led to moral decay—absenteeism, drug addiction, and alcoholism. Against the power of the state criticism seemed futile. Still, global communication made the Soviet multitudes aware of the contrast between Western progress and Soviet stagnation. Even before General Secretary Leonid Brezhnev's death in 1982, an incipient reform movement began to gather momentum, with intellectuals leading the ever-widening rebellion. But as long as change seemed remote, the reformers remained an embarrassment to the vast majority of citizens who preferred to survive by adaptation to Soviet rule, accepting whatever dispensations it offered. Living in a world of apathy and hopelessness, the masses, to avoid trouble, sustained the regime by endorsing it in sham elections.[29] Yuri Andropov, Brezhnev's successor, recognized the need for reform but was too old and infirm to face the challenge.

By 1980, the discrepancy between the promised socialist utopia and the realities of Soviet life had become a chasm. Clearly the Soviet system had strayed markedly from the precepts of Marx and Engels. The achievement of the Marxist vision of a classless utopia demanded dictatorship, the denial of civil liberties, and the nationalization of everything; from that necessary repression the good life of freedom and plenty would emerge. Unfortunately, the Soviet Communist system became an end in itself. The long-sought "communism with a human face" was no communism at all; socialism, complained Andrei Sakarov, had degenerated into bureaucratic totalitarianism. Marx was not responsible for all the human error committed in his name, but his writings justified a system that disregarded human worth and destroyed the normal incentives for personal achievement.

The accumulating failures of the late Brezhnev years created an ideological vacuum. The stagnation and continued impositions not only reflected the inefficacy of central planning but also destroyed the illusion that life under totalitarian oppression would find its reward in a stateless Marxist utopia. Amid the perennial repressions of Soviet totalitarianism, not even the Communists of eastern Europe accepted the Marxist notion of the "withering away" of the state. The 1968 suppression of Alexander Dubcek's program of economic and political liberalization in Czechoslovakia comprised the Soviet answer to change; there would be no relaxation of centralized planning and control. The Brezhnev Doctrine that year inscribed the principle in concrete that revolution anywhere in the Soviet world would face immediate reprisal.

Nationalism loomed as a more divisive force within the Soviet empire than the persistent decline of the Soviet economy. The U.S.S.R. had been built by conquest and sustained by the power of repression. In the process, the Kremlin undermined the aspirations of large populations for national independence. The constitution of the U.S.S.R. made outward concessions to the pressures for national and ethnic identity by creating a federal union of republics. This was a form without meaning; the Communist Party controlled the economic and political structure of the republics ruthlessly. Still, the Kremlin's capacity to sustain the U.S.S.R. never destroyed the nationalist aspirations among its divergent peoples. The republics with their boundaries and local bureaucracies created a sense of identity among the larger nationalities. Ukraine and the Baltic and eastern Europe states, as well as the central Asian republics, revealed a persistent unwillingness to be part of some Muscovite state. As the Kremlin, after 1975, proved unable to solve the country's pervading economic and social problems, disillusioned citizens looked increasingly to nationality-based local governments for salvation. Moscow faced the time when it would recognize the existing separatism or hold the empire together with greater exertions of force.

Soviet leaders were aware that their economy was lagging seriously behind those of the West. Limited by bureaucratic imperatives to effect meaningful reforms, they relied more heavily than ever on the promise of central planning and affirmation of national greatness through military power. The Soviet armed forces continued to receive privileged access to imported raw materials and technologies, but military production, whatever its quality, could not prevent the persistent deterioration of the civilian economy, the production of noncompetitive goods for command markets, and the diminution of the country's capacity to capitalize on its activities in the Third World.[30]

What Soviet investments from Afghanistan and Yemen to Mozambique, Angola, and Ethiopia contributed to Soviet power and influence was elusive. They unleashed demands for economic support that the Kremlin could not deliver. The failure to assist the starving Ethiopians or to establish a stable regime in Kabul, measured the limits of effective Soviet economic and military power. The requirements of a complex foreign policy, much of it relying on client states with little concern for Soviet interests, created a financial drain that far outstripped the benefits of Third World involvements. If the U.S.S.R. continued to maintain a large, costly military structure, with its huge nuclear component, to underwrite its global position, it was not clear to what purpose or with what success.

The Polish and Afghan Challenges

Troubles in Poland and failures in Afghanistan measured the Kremlin's diminishing external influence. The Polish crisis of 1980 caught the Soviet leaders by surprise, largely because they surmised that Poland's Communist chief, Edward Gierek, had the country's burgeoning discontent under control. The July 1 announcement of increased prices for meat and meat products triggered sporadic strikes. During subsequent weeks the labor troubles began to spread until, in mid-August, a sit-down strike paralyzed the large Lenin Shipyard in Gdańsk. The Gdańsk strike committee became the nucleus of a national free labor union, known as Solidarity. Lech Walesa, leader of the Gdańsk uprising, emerged as spokesman of Solidarity's rebellion against the existing order. Gierek led the counterattack with a television address in which he condemned the work stoppages and threatened reprisals. On August 31, the Polish government signed an agreement with the Gdańsk strikers that recognized the independence of the new labor unions in exchange for the workers' pledge to form no political party or challenge Poland's membership of the Soviet bloc. Only Solidarity's determination, despite its membership of some nine million, to avoid a direct confrontation with the Soviet Union enabled Poland's Communist regime to remain in power.[31]

By early 1981, the situation in Poland had become alarming. In February, General Wojciech Jaruzelski, with Kremlin approval, assumed the premiership in an apparent move to strengthen the government. Still, Solidarity continued to consolidate its gains at the expense of Poland's Communist Party, even as it sought to restrain the ambitions of its more impatient members who were prepared to challenge the Communists for control of the country. Finally, on December 13, 1981, the Jaruzelski regime, to terminate the ever-growing pressures of opposition, proclaimed martial law, seized and arrested thousands of Solidarity activists. Soviet leaders approved the action. Despite its apparent demise, Solidarity had threatened the entire Soviet world system. Its success in undermining the Polish Communist Party exposed Soviet communism's failure to undermine nationalism or establish any allegiance to the U.S.S.R. in the region of eastern Europe. This essential fact deprived the Kremlin of half its influence in the world. Soviet ideology had become discredited or irrelevant for the populations of eastern Europe, as well as those of the Soviet Union. Nothing remained as a remedy for nationalism and anti-Sovietism but the exertion of force.[32]

Meanwhile the Kremlin's unpopular war in Afghanistan revealed the limited efficacy of its vaunted military power. The venture produced 10,000 Soviet casualties a year without demonstrable necessity. Officials in Moscow had refrained from pouring troops into that country in quest of victory; rather they sought only its political stabilization. The Kremlin had anticipated accurately the tenacity of the popular resistance; its mistake lay in overestimating the acceptability of the Kabul government. The embattled Soviet forces were powerless to quell the guerrilla onslaught. Afghanistan had not reached the stage of "Russia's Vietnam," but as a failed venture it offered only the endless draining of resources and public tolerance.[33] History suggested such an outcome. A century earlier, Britain's Sir Henry Rawlinson wrote of Afghanistan, "The nation consists of a mere collection of tribes, of unequal power and with divergent habits, which are held

William Clark, a long-time Reagan confidant, shares a joke with the president on Air Force One as he leaves his role as National Security Advisor to become Secretary of the Interior. *Source:* Ronald Reagan Library.

together, more or less closely, according to the personal character of the chief who rules them." Hostile foreigners alone had the power to provoke unity among them and send them off into holy crusades. Britain, regarding the country—despite its bleakness—as one of strategic importance, fought three wars with Afghanistan and finally gave up the struggle.[34] The Soviets, suffering assured disaster, searched for an honorable escape. Elsewhere in the Third World, the consequences of Soviet involvement compelled the Kremlin to consider whether the limited gains were worth the price.[35]

WASHINGTON'S PRESSURE AND SOVIET NATIONALISM

Soviet weakness, widely recognized in Washington, scarcely diminished the administration's official insecurities, but it reinforced the supposition that the U.S.S.R. could not survive the combined political, economic, and military pressures of the Western world. Some Americans had long regarded the Soviet Union's superpower status a myth. How could a country be a superpower, they wondered, if it could not feed and satisfy the basic needs of its own people? William Clark, as Reagan's national security adviser, termed the Soviet regime merely an evil episode in human history. Pipes advocated a program to accelerate the demise of the Soviet Union by denying it the benefits of Western trade, credits, and technology. One American naval officer observed, "We must pursue policies which aggravate its condition until it bleeds to death from within." Reagan assured the British Parliament, on June 8, 1982, that the march of freedom and democracy would "leave Marxism-Leninism on the ash heap of history." The British understood, he continued, that, given time and strong leadership, the forces of good would triumph over evil. Then on March 8, 1983, the president, speaking before the National Association of Evangelicals, designated the U.S.S.R. "the focus of evil in the Modern World." Nations dared not ignore, he warned, "the aggressive impulses of an evil empire."[36] Impatient Americans favored a massive showdown with the U.S.S.R. to demonstrate its moral and economic failures so dramatically that even Kremlin leaders would have no choice but to acknowledge them and accept, at last, the desired changes in outlook, ambition, and behavior.

Such attitudes were not lost on Soviet leaders. "The Russians I spoke to," Thomas Powers reported after a trip to Moscow, "feel pushed and crowded." Soviet spokesmen complained that the United States had never accepted the Soviet Union's status as a great power with legitimate global interests of its own, never accorded the Soviet view of the world any genuine or consistent attention, never acted on the proposition that the two powers would live together or die together on this planet. Soviet leaders pointed to the endless ring of military bases surrounding the U.S.S.R. from Japan to Norway. What troubled them above all was the American assumption that the United States, in time, could eliminate the Soviet Union from world politics without war. One Kremlin leader reacted to the president's anti-Soviet rhetoric: "He offends our national pride. How can we deal with a man who calls us outlaws, criminals, and the source of evil in the world?" The Russian Orthodox Patriarch wondered how the president could call his country "an evil empire" when it had carried "the full weight of the greatest battle against the Fascist hordes, . . . had never waged war against the United States and does not intend to lift up a sword against it in the future."[37] Kremlin leaders wondered how there could be genuine, long-term coexistence without greater U.S. acceptance of Soviet legitimacy.

Then on September 1, 1983, a Soviet fighter shot down a Korean commercial airliner (KAL 007) that had drifted over Soviet territory. For Washington officials, the incident was further evidence of Soviet paranoia and general unconcern for human life. The State Department termed the disaster "brutal and unprovoked." The president, asking Congress to pass a resolution condemning the Soviet crime, called it a massacre. White House press spokesman Larry Speaks read a statement drafted by the president: "What can we think of a regime that so broadly trumpets its vision of peace and global disarmament and yet so callously and quickly commits *a terrorist act*? What can be said about *Soviet credibility* when they so *flagrantly lie about such a heinous act* [italics in original]?" The United States ordered Soviet airline Aeroflot to close its American offices and withdraw all personnel by September 15. New York and New Jersey denied Foreign Minister Andrei Gromyko landing rights to attend the opening session of the United Nations General Assembly, the first one he missed in twenty years.[38]

On September 28, Andropov condemned Reagan's management of the superpower relationship in perhaps the most comprehensive and categorical top-level Soviet denunciation of any U.S. administration since the early Cold War. The president was risking the prospect of actual war, the Soviet leader declared, in his ideological challenges. "To turn the battle of ideas into military confrontation would be too costly for the whole of mankind. But those who are blinded by anticommunism are evidently incapable of grasping this," Andropov continued, "Starting with the bogey of a Soviet military threat, they have now proclaimed a crusade against socialism as a social system."[39]

When, in November, the strategic arms limitation talks in Geneva continued to stall, the countries of western Europe carried out their threat to accept U.S. Pershing II and cruise missiles. The Kremlin responded by breaking off both the INF and START negotiations. In the absence of agreement, the number of missiles in Europe began to mount.

Meanwhile NATO had planned a command post exercise to test nuclear release procedures, code-named Able Archer and scheduled it for November 2–11. Uninformed of the exercise's purpose, the Warsaw Pact countries anticipated a nuclear attack. On November 7, Grigory Romanov, Leningrad's Party boss, informed a Kremlin gathering, "Comrades, the international situation is white hot, thoroughly white hot." Two days later, the KGB sent out a request for information anywhere that might pertain to a nuclear attack. The Soviet Union was now on a strategic intelligence alert. On November 16, Alexander Bovin, *Izvestia*'s political commentator, accused American leaders, blinded by their hatred of communism, of ignoring the security interests of the Soviet Union and compelling the two countries to walk "the edge of the missile precipice."[40] Days passed, and the attack did not come; the Soviets had exaggerated the danger. Not even the Pershings would have been ready until January. But throughout the days of crisis—although they were aware of the turmoil in Moscow—no U.S. official offered the Soviets any reassurance.

There is some indication that the "war scare" may have had a moderating influence on Reagan's subsequent approach to Moscow. He apparently was surprised to find that "many people at the top of the Soviet hierarchy were genuinely afraid of America and Americans." With a limited grasp of history and a generous interpretation of his own policies, Reagan went on to say, "I'd always felt that from our deeds it must be clear to anyone that Americans were a moral people who starting at the birth of our nation had always used our power only as a force of good in the world."[41]

During an air battle over Lebanon's Bekka Valley in the summer of 1982, the Israeli air force shot down some eighty-five Syrian MiGs without suffering any losses. Pentagon officials, to sustain their inflation of the Soviet threat, responded to this demonstration of U.S. air supremacy by denigrating the performance of the Syrian pilots and pointing to four new superior fighter planes being added to the Soviet air force.[42] Soviet leaders, conscious of their country's economic and technological inferiority, feared further U.S. pressures on the weakening Soviet system.

THE STRATEGIC DEFENSE INITIATIVE—STAR WARS

However, Moscow was not prepared for the president's unprecedented technological challenge when, on March 23, 1983, he announced his Strategic Defense Initiative (SDI) for a space-based defense against incoming missiles. A month earlier during a meeting between Reagan and the Joint Chiefs of Staff, Chief of Naval Operations, Admiral James Watkins, argued that a forward strategic ballistic missile defense would "move battles from our shores and skies." Such battles would be "moral" and palatable to the American people because a missile defense system would protect Americans and "not just avenge them" after a Soviet attack. It seemed realistic, Watkins concluded, to have a long-range program to "develop systems that would defeat a missile attack." Reagan gravitated to Watkins' missile defense idea as a way to alleviate his moral aversion to the reality of nuclear deterrence. As McFarlane and the president's science advisor, George Keyworth II, were drafting Reagan's March 23 speech, Keyworth initially opposed inclusion of a missile defense plan but reluctantly withdrew his objections after McFarlane informed him that inclusion of the proposed missile defense system was a political, not a scientific, decision.

As his speech drew to a close, Reagan told his audience of recent discussions about missile defense with the Joint Chiefs of Staff. Then, after noting the nation's security currently depended on nuclear deterrence, Reagan continued, "Let me share with you a vision of the future which offers hope. It is that we embark on a program to counter the awesome Soviet military threat with measures that are defensive.... What if free people could live secure in the knowledge that their security did not rest on the threat of instant U.S. retaliation to deter a Soviet attack, that we could intercept and destroy strategic ballistic missiles before they reached our own soil or that of our allies?"

Acknowledging this would be a formidable undertaking, he suggested that since current technology offered promise, it was time to begin creating a defensive shield. "I call upon the scientific community in this country, who gave us nuclear weapons, ... to give us the means of rendering these weapons impotent and obsolete. Tonight, consistent with our obligations of the ABM Treaty ... I'm taking an important first step. I am directing a comprehensive and intensive effort to define a long-term research and development program

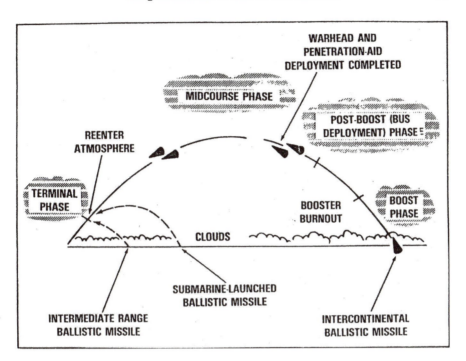

A chart showing how President Reagan's Strategic Defense system might have looked. *Source:* Department of Defense.

to begin to achieve our ultimate goal of eliminating the threat posed by strategic nuclear missiles." By neutralizing all nuclear weapons aimed at the United States, SDI would simply render them harmless.[43] The president's proposal was officially titled the Strategic Defense Initiative (SDI) in January 1984, while critics quickly dubbed it "Star Wars."

While he rarely sought credit for any of his presidency's accomplishments, Reagan claimed ownership of the SDI program and constantly spoke of its beneficial effects on world peace. Two points he often stated were, "I'd be willing to sit down and, in a sense internationalize [it]," if a defensive missile system could be developed and, "We seek the total elimination one day of nuclear weapons from the face of the earth." Meanwhile, the president added that SDI "could be the greatest inducement to arms reduction." While others in the administration might see SDI as a "bargaining chip" in future arms control talks, the president flatly refused to consider it negotiable.[44] SDI was off the table, and Reagan was determined to keep to that way.

The response to Reagan's proposal was decidedly mixed. Undersecretary of Defense Richard Delauer, who endorsed funding ABM research, objected to it being subjected to such a "half-baked political travesty." When cornered by a reporter, Minority Whip Robert Michel of Illinois said the speech might have been "a bit of overkill." *Time* magazine's lead story after the speech suggested Reagan's proposal was representative of a "video-game vision" and its cover pictured Reagan against a background of space weapons resembling a Buck Rogers comic strip about the twenty-fifth Century. Within a week, however, Reagan's missile defense proposal had disappeared because it no longer was considered newsworthy, and the public's attention shifted to more immediate issues.[45] Star Wars raised questions about the status of the 1972 Antiballistic Missile Treaty, haunted future arms control negotiations, and riled some members of the U.S. Joint Chiefs of Staff who resented its subsequent competition for funding.[46]

If Reagan's Star Wars program failed to impress many U.S. military leaders and most scientists, it created consternation in Moscow. Troubled by the Soviet Union's total incapacity to compete with the United States at the higher levels of technology, Yuri Andropov, Soviet leader since November 1982, viewed SDI as a program to bury the ABM treaty of 1972, the only Soviet defense against the ever-widening security and technology gap with the West. In a *Pravda* interview of March 27, Andropov charged that space-based defense would unleash an arms race in offensive and defensive weapons. "Engaging in this is not just irresponsible, it is insane," he said. "Washington's actions are putting the entire world in jeopardy." Andropov condemned the Reagan administration as well for its efforts to undermine the principle of parity by creating new systems of conventional weapons.

Later Mikhail Gorbachev would inform the Twenty-Seventh Communist Party Congress that at no time since 1945 was the world situation as explosive as during Reagan's first term. With that judgment Georgi A. Arbatov, director of Moscow's Institute of U.S.A. and Canadian Studies, agreed.[47]

CHAPTER 4

The Anti-Soviet Crusade Continues

For many American observers the low state of U.S.-Soviet relations had become inexcusable. Marshall Shulman likened the continuing post-Afghan international climate to that produced by the Cuban missile crisis of 1962. Former Ambassador to Moscow Malcolm Toon called relations with the Soviets worse than at any time since World War II. Lawrence T. Caldwell and Robert Legvold, writing in the Fall 1983 issue of *Foreign Policy*, observed that the administration's ideological crusade appeared to the Soviets as a total "rejection of the Soviet Union's right to exist."[1] Perhaps the grimmest assessment came from Soviet expert George F. Kennan. Writing in the October 3, 1983, issue of *The New Yorker*, Kennan observed that public discussion of Soviet-American relations had created the impression that a military showdown remained the only means of settling differences worth considering. "Can anyone mistake, or doubt," he asked, "the ominous meaning of such a state of affairs? The phenomena just described . . . are the familiar characteristics, the unfailing characteristics, of a march toward war—that, and nothing else."

Critics noted that the administration's alleged toughness had achieved no diplomatic successes or negotiated breakthroughs in Moscow or elsewhere.[2] Stanley Hoffmann, in his book, *Dead Ends* (1983), argued that the Reagan ideology was aimed more at Jimmy Carter's flimsy diplomacy than at the challenges of the real world. "It has turned out," he wrote, "to be utterly deficient as a strategy because it fails to address many real problems, it aggravates others, it provides no priority other than the anti-Soviet imperative, and precious little guidance even in connection with the new Cold War."[3] The Soviets, he noted, would neither back down nor go away. It served no national interest to transform animosity into closed communications bordering on nonrecognition. The nature of the Soviet power structure was irrelevant to the requirement of dealing openly and frankly with the Kremlin. "Like Mount Everest," wrote *Newsweek*'s Meg Greenfield, in September 1983, "the Russians are there. And, like Mount Everest, their features are not exactly a mystery. We need to stop gasping and sighing and exclaiming and nearly dying of shock every time something truly disagreeable happens. We have to grow up and confront them—as they are." On January 1, 1984, W. Averell Harriman warned the president that his program of emphasizing power while denigrating diplomacy could lead the country to war. Blaming the Soviet Union for the world's current instabilities was, he wrote, "not a strategy or a policy," adding, "It will not reshape the Russian nation; it will not bring down the Iron Curtain; and, above all, it will not reduce the nuclear threat that hangs over every American."[4]

Actually the president, acting privately, had already set the country on a course that anticipated meaningful negotiations with the Soviet Union. At dinner with Secretary Shultz on February 12, 1983, Reagan lamented that he had been unable to follow other national leaders to Moscow and Beijing. Shultz explained that such ventures would require a major improvement in U.S. relations with the Communist powers. Three days later Shultz arranged a private conversation between the president and Soviet ambassador Anatoly Dobrynin at the White House—Reagan's first serious encounter with a Soviet official. The two-hour meeting covered improved U.S.-Soviet relations, arms control, and human rights in the U.S.S.R., especially the fate of seven Pentecostal Christians residing in the basement of the U.S. embassy in Moscow. Dobrynin agreed to press the issue of the Pentecostals' release, which eventually bore fruit. In Moscow the Reagan-Dobrynin conversation produced no response; the Kremlin was not prepared to take any U.S. overtures seriously. However, Reagan, convinced that his military buildup rendered negotiations promising, could see no contradiction between his, and his administration's, verbal abuse of the U.S.S.R. and his desire for better relations. For the administration's reliance on an offensive nuclear strategy, with nuclear arsenals capable of producing a million Hiroshimas, no longer made sense. No issue in U.S.-Soviet relations required a resolution at the risk of war.

Even as U.S.-Soviet relations worsened throughout 1983, the administration, under Shultz's growing influence, gradually moved toward a more moderate outlook. Following his "evil empire" speech of March 8, in Orlando, Florida, Reagan assured British correspondent Henry Brandon that he sought only to dramatize the differences between the United States and the U.S.S.R. to create the bases of realistic negotiations. Détente was wrong because it attempted to sweep those differences under the rug.[5] That month Shultz sent Reagan a long memorandum suggesting "Next Steps in U.S.-Soviet relations." Thereafter the president began to exchange messages with Andropov. Reagan's letter of July 11 stressed his continuing antipathy toward nuclear weaponry. He reminded the Soviet leader that both shared "an enormous responsibility for the preservation of stability in the world." They could achieve agreement only if they communicated privately and candidly; he was ready, he assured Andropov, to engage in such communication. During the autumn of 1983, Reagan's political advisers, including Richard Wirthlin, warned him that most Americans, bored with the Cold War, disapproved of his handling of foreign affairs. In October, Robert McFarlane, who had succeeded Clark as head of National Security Council, advised the president that the United States could best exploit its military gains by negotiating arms limitations with the Soviet Union. When the Kremlin terminated the Geneva arms talks in November, Assistant Secretary Richard Burt prepared a plan for a more conciliatory U.S. posture toward the Soviet Union. On December 16, Shultz presented the plan to the president, suggesting that he prepare a speech, "not to change ... [their] policy but to stress ... [their] determination to pursue a dialogue and to achieve positive results."

Reagan responded to the mounting pressures, both inside and outside the administration, with his address of January 16, 1984, suggesting a turning point in the country's public approach to the Soviet Union. "We're determined," he said, "to deal with our differences peacefully through negotiations. We're prepared to discuss the problems that divide us and to work for practical, fair solutions on the basis of mutual compromise." If the Soviets wanted peace, there would be peace. "Together," he concluded, "we can strengthen peace, reduce the level of arms, and know in doing so we have helped fulfill the hopes and dreams of those we represent and, indeed, of peoples everywhere. Let us begin now."[6] Still, the Soviets saw little hope in Reagan; his administration simply carried too much anti-Soviet baggage.

Reagan proceeded on course. In his State of the Union message, on January 25, he reminded the Soviets that they and Americans had never faced each other in war. "And if we Americans have our way," he added, "they never will." Speaking at Georgetown University on April 6, the president observed that the buildup of its military power granted the United States the capacity to negotiate successfully. "If the new Soviet leadership is devoted to building a safer and more humane world, rather than expanding armed conquests," he declared, "it will find a sympathetic partner in the West." The great challenge facing both countries was that of reducing the risk of nuclear war because, he warned, "a nuclear war cannot be won and must never be fought."[7] Again in June the president expressed his willingness to meet Soviet leaders at a summit or anywhere else. Columnist James Reston lauded the president's decision to "listen to his aides and pollsters," who were "telling him that this stalemate with the Russians" was "bad election politics, and ... to his allies," who were "telling him that failure to talk to Moscow" was "bad diplomacy."[8]

Reagan's nomination at the Republican National Convention in August was sufficient to assure a second term. The heavy federal deficits and insatiable anti-Sovietism of the first term had polarized the country. Still, his reputation for decisiveness and consistency created an image of strong leadership. A significant minority of voters, many of them Democrats, lauded his presidency even as they acknowledged their considerable rejection of his policies. Against such devotion, Walter Mondale, the Democratic nominee, had no chance. Reagan's complex and contradictory blend of ideology and pragmatism permitted him to escape most troublesome issues. The responsibility for the Beirut disaster, the publication of the embarrassing CIA manual on how to assassinate Nicaraguans, and other lapses that reflected his notorious inattention to detail, the president successfully assigned to subordinates. His rhetorical toughness, combined with an optimistic, romanticized vision of the country, created a national mood of confidence. The improved U.S.-Soviet balance of power elicited widespread public approval. National security adviser McFarlane could advise the press that the Reagan foreign policy performance had reversed "the decline of the West." Polls recorded the public's overwhelming agreement that, under Reagan, the country's world leadership had become more forceful. That same public, the polls revealed even more emphatically, doubted that the world had moved closer to peace. Indeed, analysts continued to complain that Washington had failed to bring the Soviets to the bargaining table or to create a comprehensive program for dealing with the rest of the world.[9]

SEEKING NEGOTIATIONS WITH MOSCOW

Throughout the 1984 campaign the pressures on Reagan to fulfill his promises of negotiation were unrelenting. Senate Republicans Howard H. Baker of Tennessee and Charles H. Percy of Illinois warned the president that the stalled arms limitation talks were becoming a political liability. *The New York Times* regarded ominous the continuing notion that the president intended to launch an arms race to spend the Soviet Union into economic collapse and then attempt to negotiate with the Kremlin from a position of military supremacy.[10] On September 2, Harriman, Clark M. Clifford, and Marshall D. Shulman, writing in *The New York Times*, admonished the administration to stop generating apprehension in the United States and Europe and take seriously the need to avoid war.[11] By autumn the president, responding to the imperatives of his reelection campaign, assured voters that he was indeed a man of peace. *Newsweek* reminded its readers that Reagan's actions had always been far more moderate than his words.[12]

Reagan ended his campaign with visible demonstrations of his determination to pursue closer ties with the Kremlin. In a speech before the United Nations, on October 24, he promised, if reelected, to seek an arms agreement with Moscow. That month he welcomed Soviet Foreign Minister Gromyko to the White House. He reminded Gromyko that the United States was troubled by Soviet expansionism, but he assured the Soviet leader that Washington recognized the Soviet Union's superpower status, accepted the reality of its socialist system, and sought, not military preponderance, but merely the strength to deal with the U.S.S.R. on arms reduction as an equal. Gromyko denied that the U.S.S.R. was expansionist. He warned of the dangers inherent in "mountains of nuclear weapons." To what end, he wondered, were the United States and the Soviet Union inventing and building new ones. Back in Moscow, Gromyko announced that there would be no agreement on strategic weapons that did not dispose of the space defense issue.[13] Clearly the Reagan-Gromyko conversations did not go well. Still, Gromyko's presence in Washington had been gratifying enough. *Le Monde* (Paris) responded with approval, "Reagan's meeting with Gromyko . . . offered proof that his policies have not made contact with the Soviet Union impossible." Italy's *La Stampa* (Turin) added agreeably, "One tends to believe Reagan when he says that he is ready to begin fruitful dialogue with the Soviet Union."[14] Europeans hoped that the president would concentrate on the improvement of U.S.-Soviet relations during his second term. In keeping with that advice, elder statesman John McCloy urged Reagan and Shultz to open negotiations with the Kremlin.[15]

REAGAN AND ARMS CONTROL

Ronald Reagan had never endorsed an arms control treaty—until he met and embraced the Soviet leader Mikhail Gorbachev. He opposed the 1963 Test Ban pact, the 1968 Non-Proliferation Treaty, and the 1972 SALT I and ABM agreements, criticized the Helsinki Accords, and denounced SALT II as "fatally flawed." Moreover, early in his first term, he ended negotiations for a comprehensive test ban treaty. During the 1980 presidential campaign, Ronald Reagan claimed SALT II allowed the Soviet Union a "window of vulnerability" against U.S. land-based nuclear forces. He agreed with the Committee on the Present Danger's (CPC) basic tenets: jettison SALT II, launch a major strategic arms buildup, and create an extensive civil defense program before the Soviet Union's preparations for nuclear war-fighting, surviving, and winning were complete.

Paul Nitze, a CPC founder, had created this doomsday scenario— "window of vulnerability"—because he believed the American people should not be allowed to become compliant. It was not his first such scenario. He was largely responsible for the two others: NSC-68 (1950) which "justified" the Truman administration's arms buildup; and the Gaither Report (1957) which claimed the Soviets were developing an intercontinental ballistic missile (ICBM) capable of a "disarming counter-force attack" on the U.S.; therefore, the Eisenhower administration must accelerate its

ICBM program before 1959, "the year of maximum danger." John Kennedy exploited the so-called missile gap controversy during his campaign, only to discover shortly after becoming president that the actual missile count greatly favored the United States.[16]

These "doomsday scenarios" were necessary, Nitze's CPC colleague Richard Perle later explained, to sustain the nation's security. "Democracies will not sacrifice to protect their security in the absence of a sense of danger," he wrote in *Newsweek* on February 18, 1983, "and every time we create the impression that we and the Soviets are cooperating and moderating the competition, we diminish the sense of apprehension."

The Reagan administration was initially concerned with expanding and modernizing U.S. forces to offset the supposed Soviet military superiority. But under pressure from antinuclear protesters in NATO countries and the nuclear freeze movement at home, in late 1981, Reagan reviewed the ongoing intermediate nuclear forces (INF) negotiations. The INF discussions had been prompted by a NATO decision, late in Carter's administration, to deploy 108 Pershing II and 464 ground-launched cruise missiles (GLCMs) to West Germany, Belgium, Britain, the Netherlands, and Italy in order to offset the Soviet's new SS-20s with their three warheads. Not wanting to bow to pacifist demonstrators in Europe, the Reagan administration offered its "zero option" concept—the U.S. would cancel its scheduled deployment two years down the road in exchange for the Soviet's withdrawal of their intermediate-range missiles carrying some 1,100 warheads.

Meanwhile, in May 1982, Reagan finally outlined his plan for the promised Strategic Arms Reduction Talks (START), which he insisted would bring about "practical phased reduction" of strategic nuclear weapons in two stages. In Phase I warheads would be reduced by a third, with significant cuts in ballistic missiles, followed by Phase II where a ceiling would be put on ballistic missile throw weights and other elements. While the public response was almost enthusiastic, analysts who examine the proposal found, as with the "zero option", it was so one-sided it was nonnegotiable. Phase I would require the Soviets to substantially reduce their land-based ICBMs—their most effective strategic weapons—while the U.S. would retain most of its land-based Minutemen and proceed with its planned emplacement of a hundred new, large MXs missiles in similar silos. In addition, the U.S. could deploy its cruise missiles and modernize its submarine and bomber fleets. During Phase II, the Soviets would be required to reduce by almost two-thirds the aggregate throw weight of their missiles, while the U.S. offered no cuts at all. The proposal was seen by many critics as a nonstarter. "This proposal is so stacked against the Soviets," the sponsor of the House's nuclear freeze resolution Congressman Edward J. Markey complained, "there is little chance they will accept it." Not surprisingly, Moscow ignored the Washington's proposal, and negotiations on strategic weaponry limped along as predicted.[17]

Reagan's "allergy to detail" apparently resulted in his inability on several occasions to grasp the basics of arms control issues. He shocked congressional leaders with the revelation in the fall of 1983 that he had not understood that most of the Soviet's intermediate range nuclear missiles were land-based. He realized now why Moscow had called his 1982 proposal to reduce all land-based missiles by one-half "non-negotiable". Then, later, Reagan acknowledged that he "forgot" the America's long-range bombers and cruise missiles carried nuclear warheads.[18]

During his 1984 reelection campaign, President Reagan faced a dilemma: how to ease tensions with Moscow, deflect the criticism of an active domestic nuclear freeze movement, and appease Senate hard-liners eager to chastise the Soviets for alleged arms control violations. During the late 1970s ardent anticommunists insisted that the Soviets had failed to honor their arms control commitments. Cold Warriors from both political parties, especially Republicans, discovered that the alleged Soviet treaty violations was an issue that played well. The 1980 Republican Party platform—without offering any evidence—claimed that Moscow had not complied with its arms control commitments and condemned the Carter administration for not challenging these violations.

Early on the Reagan administration instructed the U.S. Arms Control and Disarmament Agency and its General Advisory Committee to concentrate on identifying these Soviet arms control violations. Congressional hawks picked up the issue and, as part of Public Law 99-145 passed in the summer of 1985, charged the White House with reporting annually on Soviet noncompliance. The subsequent administration reports to Congress claimed a variety of Soviet violations (and Moscow responded with its own list of U.S. evasions) most of which were "gray-area" complaints. The number of listed Soviet violations increased yearly from seven in 1984 to thirteen in 1985 and eighteen in 1986; however, when these charges were examined by less ideologically motivated analysts the evidence frequently proved ambiguous or no longer relevant. Moscow was guilty, however, of two significant violations: an uncompleted radar site contrary to ABM Treaty terms and a vast experimental biological warfare project—largely undiscovered until after the Cold War—violating the Biological Warfare Convention.[19] This crippling process ignored evidence of Soviet compliance or U.S. noncompliance and created a politically satisfying, but essentially erroneous, image of Soviet arms control commitments.

The president's speech on January 16, 1984, spoke of "reducing the risk of war, and especially nuclear war" through arms control, while raising questions about Soviet compliance and possible evasions of previous treaties. "Reagan's buttery peace appeal to the Russians" followed "with his charge of Soviet cheating," columnists Rowland Evans and Robert Novak crowed, gave "him trump cards for the 1984 campaign the Democrats ... [would] find hard to top."[20]

By late 1984, Washington's emphasis on toughness and power, both divorced from realistic, historically informed policy considerations, had eroded the foundations of consistency. Nothing in Soviet policy had changed. What had occurred was a modest swing toward moderation in Washington's official mood.[21] During December, Shultz, accompanied by Paul Nitze, his special arms control adviser, left for London, Brussels, and Bonn to ease Europe's concerns with more promising notions of the U.S.-Soviet future. The United States, said Shultz, would not permit the search for an effective defense against nuclear attack to become a substitute for arms control negotiations. The secretary's lengthy conversations with Gromyko in Geneva, on January 7 and 8, 1985, did not guarantee future agreements, but they committed both powers to strive for greater cooperation. The Shultz-Gromyko formula included a comprehensive three-talk process, one for long-range missiles and bombers, one for mid-range missiles, and one for space and defensive weapons.[22]

After a lapse of fifteen months, the Geneva arms negotiations reopened in March. The barriers to agreement remained: the deep disagreement over Reagan's Strategic Defense Initiative, the complexities emanating from new technologies, the fragile restraints of existing arms treaties, and the lingering distrust of the U.S.S.R. shared by many of Reagan's chief Pentagon advisers. Observers predicted that the administration would never see merit in any Soviet proposal unless the president, presumed to favor agreement, imposed his own views on the Pentagon civilians, led by Secretary Weinberger, Under Secretary Fred Ikle, and Assistant Secretary Richard Perle, all of whom opposed any concessions to the Soviets.[23]

Washington's attempts to modify the initial START proposal met with interminable bureaucratic delays; eventually it would be delivered in 1991 by George H. W. Bush. The delay was not surprising since the bickering among various American bureaucracies over the specific terms was frequently more intense than the negotiations with Moscow. This intractability prompted a discouraged senior member of the National Security Council to declare, "Even if the Soviets did not exist, we might not get a START treaty because of disagreements on our side." Another high-ranking U.S. official complained, "[If the Soviets] came to us and said, 'You write it, we'll sign it,' we still couldn't do it."[24]

Yet, it seemed apparent that moderates were gaining the ascendancy in the administration's turf wars over foreign policy. Among the conflicting judgments on external affairs were two that took precedence: the supposition that the country's and the world's security demanded improved Soviet-American relations and any achievement on the Soviet front would redound to the credit of the administration. Secretary Shultz operated cautiously at the center of the movement toward moderation, but there were others. White House adviser Michael K. Deaver observed that Nancy Reagan's entreaties were an important element in her husband's conversion. He recalled in his memoirs that she "lobbied the president to soften his line on the Soviet

Jeane Kirkpatrick, U.S. ambassador to the United Nations receives a Medal of Freedom from President Reagan, April 22, 1985. *Source:* Ronald Reagan Library.

Union; to reduce military spending and not to push Star Wars at the expense of the poor and the dispossessed."[25] At times Deaver himself seemed to be a key spokesman for the new moderation. Jeane Kirkpatrick, Reagan's UN representative, recalled Deaver's remark to her at the annual Washington Gridiron Dinner in 1983: "I may as well tell you this, you'll have to find out sometime. This president may have an opportunity to make peace for our time.... [W]hen the time comes, we can't have you and Bill Clark around raising questions."[26] Members of the administration were not always sure that the president was aware of the detailed changes that were occurring. This suggested that the move toward moderation came less from a broad philosophical revolution than from the slow, pragmatic evolution of policy, with the president accepting each new step as the logical extension of what went before. Behind it all was Reagan's long-established desire for arms limitation and the conviction that the United States now possessed the strength to guide and control any advances in the U.S.-Soviet relationship.[27]

GORBACHEV AND THE ROAD TO GENEVA

Fortunately for Reagan and Shultz, they faced, in the early months of 1985, a new, more promising, leadership in Moscow. Mikhail Gorbachev's rise to power within the Soviet Communist Party had been steady. By late

1984 he seemed destined to become Secretary General and thereby head of the Soviet state. Already Konstantin Chernenko, who had succeeded Andropov in February, was too ill to travel. When Gorbachev, with his wife Raisa, visited London in mid-December, Kremlin watchers marked him as Chernenko's successor. Prime Minister Margaret Thatcher, Europe's senior statesman, was impressed. She detected in Gorbachev's predictable elevation new opportunities in European diplomacy. "I can do business with this man," she informed the press.[28] Following Chernenko's death in March 1985, Gromyko, in nominating Gorbachev as Secretary General of the Party, made scarcely a reference to Chernenko. It was the future, not the past, that mattered. From the outset, European leaders recognized in Gorbachev the charm, intelligence, energy, confidence, and authority required to bring new initiatives to Soviet policy. For many in Washington, where all Soviets were alike, this revelation dawned more slowly. At the time of Chernenko's death the disillusionment with the Soviet system was evident—from generals and bureaucrats to intellectuals, laborers, and housewives. Still, the forces for change, contained by censorship and repression, would remain dormant until Gorbachev could release them and give them encouragement and direction.

In April, the Communist Party Central Committee announced its program of perestroika, designed to restructure both the Soviet economy and Soviet foreign policy. Perestroika, Gorbachev declared, would retain, but revitalize, the fundamental principles of socialism by balancing carefully new free market incentives and expanding democracy with central planning and protection of common societal needs. Under perestroika the U.S.S.R. would look within socialism, not outside it, for answers to the country's problems. The new atmosphere of glasnost would encourage openness in every sphere of public life and the search for what was good and true for the improvement of society. For Gorbachev, the new forces of socialism would settle "the historical dispute as to which system is more consistent with the interests of the people." Perestroika might demand painful adjustments, but the only alternative to dynamic and revolutionary change was continued stagnation.

Gorbachev had a better grasp of the realities of international life than did his predecessors. His sparkling performances at press conferences, his knowledge of a wide range of issues, and his confidence in undertaking a redesign of the Soviet role in world affairs separated him from the Soviet past and attracted world attention. His central challenge lay in protecting his country's international status while he rescued it from the costly, overextended, and debilitating global role to which his predecessors had assigned it. Following Afghanistan, Soviet relations with the Western powers had deteriorated almost to the vanishing point. Washington's unrestrained abuse had created an unprecedented mood and anger among Soviet leaders, one exacerbated by their own sense of political and economic vulnerability. They were troubled by Reagan's success in rebuilding U.S. strength and resolve, but they expected European opinion to prevent the deployment of American medium-range missiles in Europe. "Instead," wrote Columbia University's Seweryn Bialer, "they suffered one of their most important defeats in decades when the first Pershings [missiles] were installed."[29] It is not strange that Andropov and Chernenko made little effort to renew the spirit of détente. Soviet propaganda attributed the ongoing international tension to Western militarism and huge military budgets when the U.S.S.R. itself spent some 20 percent of its GNP on defense. Even as Gorbachev continued to absolve the U.S.S.R. of all responsibility for the Kremlin's external troubles, the full spectrum of his "new thinking" on foreign affairs began to emerge.

Gorbachev faced the task of protecting both his domestic reform program and his country's hard-won status as a great power from any negative repercussions that might result from reduced commitments of Soviet resources to the Middle East, Africa, Central America, and eastern Europe. Nothing less would enable him to enlist Washington in his campaign to cut Soviet losses abroad and military spending at home without weakening the foundations of his international authority. If Soviet retrenchment with minimum loss of status demanded Western cooperation, it was essential that Soviet leaders recognize the security interests of other countries as well as their own.

For Gorbachev, Afghanistan headed the list of expendable commitments. The presence of over 100,000 Soviet troops in that country, totally incapable of resolving the ongoing conflict, comprised a massive physical and emotional drain on the Soviet people and a source of endless national controversy. Yet the Kremlin could not sanction the ignominious withdrawal of Soviet forces from that bordering state without affirming the decline of the U.S.S.R. as a world power. The war in Afghanistan demanded a high price of the United States as well. The U.S. Congress, in 1985, provided the CIA $470 million to support the guerrillas.

The only real solution Gorbachev saw for his country's internal and external dilemmas lay in the reduction, if not the elimination, of the nuclear arsenals. He had long questioned the Soviet-Western reliance on nuclear deterrence, both because it rationalized limitless expenditures on weapons and because it legitimized nuclear war should deterrence fail. He understood, moreover, that the U.S.S.R. could never achieve nuclear supremacy over the United States and that an intensified arms race, based on scientific and technological advances, would demand greater human and material resources than the Soviet Union possessed. The United States and the Soviet Union had reached an effective parity of power in the 1970s, giving them the means to destroy each other many times over. In pursuing its continued arms buildup, Gorbachev observed, the United States gained nothing; the U.S.S.R. retained sufficient strength to destroy it in war. "This is why any striving for military superiority," he concluded, "means chasing one's own tail. It can't be used in real politics." The international nuclear environment had become

both dangerous and irrational. The United States and the U.S.S.R., therefore, had no choice but to eliminate their competition in arms and live in
peace.

Within days of achieving the Soviet premiership, Gorbachev found the
world beating a path to his door to hear him expound on the dangers and
irrationality of nuclear weapons and the need for improved East-West relations. In March, he used a *Pravda* interview to challenge the U.S. Strategic
Defense Initiative, a system, he warned, that threatened to undermine the
nuclear balance and unleash a new race in offensive missiles. On April 10,
he addressed a delegation of U.S. congressmen, led by Speaker Tip O'Neill
of Massachusetts. He emphasized the Soviet desire for the return of normal-
ity in U.S.-Soviet relations. Gorbachev appealed to visiting Willy Brandt of
West Germany in late May, and Italy's Prime Minister Bettino Craxi two
days later, to support his opposition to the arms race, now reaching into
outer space. In early October, he visited Paris in a major quest for Western
endorsement of his appeal for coexistence, endangered, he said, by the continued search for new and destructive weapons to be used both on Earth and
in outer space. The U.S.S.R., he declared, had taken the lead in creating a
safer world by unilaterally suspending the further development of medium-
range missiles, terminating all nuclear explosions, proposing deep cuts in
strategic nuclear arsenals, and advocating the total prohibition of weapons
in space. In late October, Gorbachev conferred with leaders of the Warsaw
Pact and, following his return to Moscow, prepared meticulously for the
approaching Geneva summit with President Reagan.

Meanwhile, Reagan officials were surprisingly ineffective in addressing the
mounting concerns of European allies about the president's missile defense
program. Britain's Prime Minister Margaret Thatcher endorsed the Star
Wars research program during her visit to Washington in February 1985.
But leading European experts, no less than many American scientists, predicted that SDI would never produce results commensurate with its promise
and its cost. To gain European support, U.S. officials announced that European firms would be permitted to compete in the bidding for specific defense
projects. In March 1985, Weinberger gave the European governments sixty
days to decide if they wanted to enter a technological partnership with
the United States. The immediate reaction was cool. In London, Foreign
Secretary Howe expressed his government's skepticism toward the project,
attributing it to a Maginot Line mentality. The renewed emphasis on technology, he feared, would overwhelm the need for political decisions. West
Germany's Genscher argued that SDI would damage the strategic unity of
the alliance and undermine the arrangements that had served Europe so
well. In March, Chancellor Helmut Kohl of West Germany announced that
his government had reached an agreement permitting his country to participate in Star Wars research. Eventually the Thatcher government in London accepted a role in SDI research. Opposition leaders in both Bonn and

London accused Kohl and Thatcher of subservience to the United States. David Fairhall, writing in *The Guardian* of May 2, 1985, complained, "Star Wars is like the emperor's clothes. Two years after President Reagan launched his Strategic Defense Initiative, hardly any of his allies dared tell him publicly that nearly everyone thinks it ill conceived."

In Washington, the vast changes in the Soviet Union's world position registered slowly and divisively. In large measure, the problem of recognition lay in the widespread supposition that Gorbachev was too ubiquitous, cunning, and appealing to be trusted. Still, during the late summer and autumn of 1985, both Washington and Europe's capitals had no choice but to shift their attention from continuing stalemate on arms control to the forthcoming Geneva Conference, scheduled for late November. As Gorbachev marched toward the summit amid televised press conferences and meetings with world leaders, U.S. officials, even as they declared Soviet proposals old and unacceptable, acknowledged Gorbachev's success in establishing the Soviet positions as moderate and reasonable. Reagan tried to put the Soviets on the defensive by adding regional conflicts to the summit agenda. Despite the maneuvering, the propaganda, and the struggle for advantage, the European press predicted smiles but meager results. London's *Daily Telegraph* anticipated a change in style but not in substance. Warning against expecting too much, *Die Zeit* (Hamburg) declared that Reagan and Gorbachev could not build an enduring bridge in two or three days.[30]

At Geneva

Outside Geneva's Chateau Fleur d'Eau on a wintry November 19, a coatless Ronald Reagan awaited the approaching Mikhail Gorbachev. The summit itself, the first in six years, was fundamentally a media event. The president, as the official host on this opening day of the Geneva summit, had set the stage for his first meeting with the Soviet leader with great care. He led Gorbachev and their two interpreters to a small meeting room, with a fire crackling in the fireplace, for a private conversation. The people in the neighboring conference room, Reagan began, had given them fifteen minutes "to meet in this one-on-one," saying, "They've programmed us—they've written your talking points, they've written my talking points. We can do that, or we can stay here as long as we want and get to know each other." The private conversation lasted an hour. During a break in the afternoon session, Reagan steered Gorbachev to the chateau's summerhouse for a tete-a-tete before the fire. What concerned Gorbachev was Reagan's known attachment to the expensive and technologically sophisticated SDI. He argued that the 1972 Anti-Ballistic Missile Treaty permitted the two countries one land-based defense system. In broadening the American defense capability, SDI challenged the effectiveness of the Soviet nuclear deterrent. Gorbachev concluded that the Soviets could compete only by building additional offensive weapons. Reagan refused to accept any arrangement that would deny the United States the right to defend itself from nuclear attack.

At the end the two leaders achieved little, yet both regarded the summit a success. Separated by twenty years, they recognized in each other a warmth and sincerity that promised future success. Reagan observed that Gorbachev scarcely resembled his predecessors in his intelligence, knowledge, and openness. Soviet Foreign Minister Eduard Shevardnadze noted, "[W]e had the impression that [the President] is a man who keeps his word and that he's someone you can deal with...and reach accord." The failure to obtain agreement on SDI produced no recriminations. In explaining the U.S. position to the Supreme Soviet, Gorbachev used only moderate language. The two leaders agreed to meet in Washington in 1987 and in Moscow during 1988. Not since the Nixon-Brezhnev summits of 1972 and 1973 had Soviet-American relations appeared more hopeful.

GEOPOLITICS AND CENTRAL AMERICA

To counter the growing congressional and public concern over his Central American policies, Reagan, in July 1983, appointed a special commission, led by former Secretary of State Henry Kissinger, to study the region and make policy recommendations. Although the commission was bipartisan, observers suspected from the outset that it would adopt the rationales that had underwritten the Reagan approach to Central America since 1981. Kissinger obtained what he wanted—the commission's endorsement of a geopolitical view that the struggles for power in that region were essentially extensions of the Soviet-American conflict, demanding military solutions. Others on the commission, especially Robert S. Strauss, insisted that military aid to El Salvador be dependent on progress in human rights. Reagan had long feared that an accent on human rights could undermine the war against the guerrillas; in November 1983, he pocket vetoed the congressional requirement that demanded a periodic certification of human rights gains. When Lane Kirkland and other Democrats on the commission announced that they would resign unless military aid were made conditional, Kissinger agreed to include their demands, although he knew it would be a repudiation of administration policy.[31]

Kissinger's final report, announced in January 1984, proposed a program of economic and military aid designed to build a consensus for U.S. policy in Central America. The commission admitted that the revolutions and pressures for change were indigenous and therefore no danger to hemispheric security. What had made possible the global balance of power at nominal cost was, in essence, the inherent security of the North American continent. Now the advance of the U.S.S.R. into the vulnerable areas of the hemisphere threatened this balance. "From the standpoint of the Soviet Union," warned the commission, "it would be a strategic coup of major proportions to impose on the United States the burden of landward defenses. If they succeeded in doing so they would have out-maneuvered us on a global scale." Nicaragua loomed as a special danger. It was, the report noted, "the indispensable stepping stone for the Cuban and Soviet effort to promote armed insurgency in Central America. With both an Atlantic and Pacific coast, Nicaragua . . . [was] uniquely well-placed" to become the base for Soviet activity in Central America, giving them the presence to subvert the entire region, including Panama. In a warning reminiscent of Vietnam, the report continued, "The triumph of hostile forces in what the Soviets call the 'strategic rear' of the United States would be read as a sign of U.S. impotence. It would signify our inability to manage our policy or exercise our power." What was being tested in Central America was "not so much the ability of the United States to provide large resources but rather the realism of . . . [its] political attitudes."[32]

At the end, the commission recommended a close link between continued U.S. aid and progress on human rights, knowing that the president opposed such linkage and believed the primary purpose of the program was the destruction of the Salvadoran insurgency. In agreement with established policy, the commission never questioned the right of the United States to intervene in the civil wars of Nicaragua and El Salvador. It recommended $8 billion in economic aid over five years, more than either Congress or the administration would endorse. In addition, the Kissinger plan called for a Peace Corps approach to Central America with technicians, teachers, doctors, and other experts. It advocated increased military aid to El Salvador of some $400 million to counter what it depicted as a "direct threat to U.S. security interests." It favored military aid for Honduras sufficient "to build a credible deterrent," as well as the resumption of the aid to Guatemala that the Carter administration had terminated in response to human rights violations.[33] The commission's language of fear raised the stakes in Central America so high that the United States dared accept nothing less than a military victory over the Communist enemy.[34]

Critics in Congress and the press balked at the Kissinger commission's emphasis on the primacy of nonregional threats to Central American stability and hemispheric security. Citing domestic poverty and injustice as the real sources of Central American revolution, some wondered why it had taken so long to occur. For such analysts the commission's recommendations were both potentially costly and unnecessary. The large request for military aid, observed Congressman Michael Barnes of Maryland, chairman of the House Subcommittee on Latin American Affairs, would achieve nothing except "more death, destruction, and suffering." Senator Christopher Dodd of Connecticut agreed, charging that the commission failed "to address the fundamental economic, social and political reform necessary to make any aid program effective within the region . . . There is rhetoric to satisfy every imaginable constituency, but there is no policy." Even the sometimes hawkish Senator Daniel P. Moynihan of New York insisted that the commission had offered no evidence for its assumptions of Soviet-Cuban threats of U.S. security interests in the hemisphere.[35]

What troubled many leading critics was the administration's apparent failure to learn anything from the Vietnam experience. As *The New York Times* editorialized, "The same fears about impotence and credibility were the stuff of a thousand speeches justifying American involvement for a generation in the lost war in Indochina."[36] No critic addressed the issue more forcefully than former Idaho Senator Frank Church. Shortly before his death in early 1984, he complained the United States had ventured into Vietnam to contain China and the Soviet Union, only to discover that these two Communist countries were not the problem in Southeast Asia. He suggested the high price that the country paid for such mistaken judgments:

> It is this idea that the communist threat is everywhere that has made our government its captive and its victim.... This country has become so conservative—so fearful—that we have come to see revolution anywhere in the world as a threat to the United States. It's nonsense. And yet that policy we have followed has cost us so many lives, so much treasure, such setbacks to our vital interests, as a great power ought not to endure. Until we learn to live with revolution, we will continue to blunder, and it will work to the Soviets' advantage. It will put them on the winning side, while we put ourselves on the side of rotten, corrupt regimes that end up losing. And each time one of those regimes is overthrown, it feeds the paranoia in this country about the spread of communism.[37]

Undoubtedly Reagan's approach to Central America enjoyed the support of Republican hard-liners, both inside and outside Congress, as well as those whose faith in the validity of the Vietnam War had never been shaken. But opinion within the country was no more favorable to the administration's Central American policies—and the rationales employed to defend them— than it was to U.S. policy in Vietnam at the moment of its ultimate failure. A Gallup survey of April 1984 indicated that only 29 percent of the people interviewed approved of the president's policies. The same month a *New York Times*-CBS News poll revealed that only one in three persons in the country supported the president. In May, a *Washington Post* poll agreed with these findings. That poll revealed, additionally, that almost half of those interviewed did not know which side the U.S. government supported in El Salvador.[38] Vietnam had destroyed the guideposts to which all administrations from Truman to Ford had attached their containment policies; despite his efforts, Reagan could not rebuild them.

Such widespread rejection of the Kissinger report—and the policies it advocated—in no way altered Washington's official assumption of the threat of falling dominoes in Central America. In mid-April, the president accused Nicaragua of joining the Soviet Union and Cuba in trying "to install Communism by force throughout this hemisphere," adding, "We cannot turn our backs on this crisis at our doorstep." Later that month, the president warned a group of Hispanic Americans at the White House, "If Central America is lost, then our borders will be threatened.... A faraway totalitarian power is committing enormous resources to change the strategic balance of the world by turning Central America into a string of anti-American, Soviet-styled dictatorships."[39]

That the U.S.S.R. was committing "enormous resources" to either the government of Nicaragua or the rebels of El Salvador was doubtful. During May, Mexico's president, Miguel de la Madrid, publicly disputed Reagan's views before a joint meeting of Congress. "We are convinced," he said, "that the Central American conflict is a result of the economic deficiencies, political backwardness and social injustice that have afflicted the countries of this area. We therefore cannot accept its becoming part of the East-West confrontation." Reagan, in response, lectured President Madrid on the importance of U.S. military action against the Soviet-based Communist threat to the hemisphere.[40]

Responding to the administration's ever-mounting concern for Central America, the Pentagon continued to build the necessary military infrastructure, based largely in Honduras, to undergird the forces fighting leftists in Nicaragua and El Salvador. For Washington, this unfolding military activity in Central America was the only alternative to the dispatch of U.S. forces. One officer explained, "If Salvador falls, that's the time the United States would have to decide whether to send troops or withdraw completely and fortify the Rio Grande."

What characterized the entire U.S. military program in Honduras was the absence of public announcements and congressional authorizations that normally accompanied such foreign commitments. The Pentagon, with no formal expression of congressional support, conducted military exercises that permitted it to rotate hundreds, if not thousands, of troops through Honduras, while it maintained its self-imposed limit of fifty-five advisers in El Salvador. Air reconnaissance units based in Honduras flew over El Salvador to aid that government in targeting enemy positions. Initially, U.S. aid to the Nicaraguan rebels had been limited, supporting only tiny bands operating along the border; by 1984, some 18,000 contras, with American encouragement, were conducting full-scale operations in the field. CIA operatives aided the growing army of U.S.-financed counterrevolutionaries in the guerrilla war against the Sandinista government in Managua. Private American groups sent soldiers of fortune into Central America to support the war. Congress contemplated none of this. Congressman Barnes complained, "The U.S. role has just seemed to increase by leaps and bounds while we are constantly being assured that nothing new is happening . . . The U.S. role has expanded in ways that no one would have thought possible a year ago."[41]

Public and congressional doubts regarding U.S. intentions increased when the administration, in early April, became implicated in the mining of Nicaraguan harbors. CIA officials had supervised the mining from a ship off Nicaragua's Pacific coast. Washington acknowledged that the decision to mine the harbors was a scaled-down CIA plan to cripple the Nicaraguan economy, a plan aimed at power plants, bridges, and other key targets. Previously, American officers in Honduras had monitored the rebel ground operations in Nicaragua but had not controlled them.

The mining of Nicaraguan waters involved the United States directly in the war against the Sandinistas for the first time. The Sandinistas took their case to the International Court of Justice at The Hague with the charge that the United States was "directing military and paramilitary actions" against Nicaragua in an attempt to destabilize and overthrow its government. Members of Congress condemned the secret war in Nicaragua. The Senate rebuked the administration for mining the harbors by a vote of eighty-four to twelve. Republican Senator Barry Goldwater of Arizona complained to CIA Director Casey that the mining was a violation of international law. "It is an act of war," he concluded, "For the life of me, I don't see how we are going to explain it." Speaker O'Neill added, "I have contended that the Reagan Administration's secret war against Nicaragua was morally indefensible. Today it is clear that it is legally indefensible as well."

Washington had already informed the World Court that it would not recognize the panel's jurisdiction over Central American disputes. For the British and French governments, no less than for members of Congress, this was an admission of guilt.[42] The president answered his detractors: "[Critics] ignore the most relevant fact: Central America has become the stage for a bold attempt . . . to install communism by force." "To portray Nicaragua as a victim," argued Jeane Kirkpatrick, "is a complete, Orwellian inversion of what is actually happening in Central America." It was Nicaragua, she said, that was violating international law by waging a secret war to overthrow the government of El Salvador.[43]

Jose Napoleon Duarte's triumph, in May, as the first elected president of El Salvador broke the Democratic opposition on the question of aid to that country. Duarte was clearly a man of thoroughly democratic persuasion who had earned wide respect and confidence in Washington. For the administration, Duarte's election was a vindication of its Central American policies, although it was not certain that his election would resolve much in El Salvador. Any effort of Duarte to open negotiations with guerrilla leaders would meet the determined resistance of the political right and the military that still controlled the government. If Duarte failed to negotiate a peace, Washington would continue to remain hostage to El Salvador's right-wing extremists who themselves had little chance of success. Still, with Duarte's election, the president warned his congressional opponents that their failure to vote for the aid bill for El Salvador would undermine the promise of a genuinely democratic regime. With fifty-six Democrats defying Speaker O'Neill, the House authorized both economic and military aid for El Salvador by a vote of 212 to 208.

CHAPTER 5

The Reagan Doctrine

By early 1985 Reagan's crusade on behalf of anticommunist guerrillas had blossomed into the Reagan Doctrine. The president committed his administration to support democratic revolutions everywhere in his State of the Union message of February: "We must not break faith with those who are risking their lives on every continent from Afghanistan to Nicaragua to defy Soviet-supported aggression and secure rights which have been ours from birth."[1] Similarly, Shultz asserted the country's moral responsibility, as leader of the free world, to aid popular insurgencies against Communist domination around the world. Unlike the Truman Doctrine, which justified interventions in defense of governments threatened by Communist expansionism, the Reagan Doctrine proclaimed the right to subvert existing Communist regimes.[2] Actually Reagan had inaugurated his offensive to roll back the frontiers of Soviet influence during his reelection campaign. Addressing Polish-Americans at the White House on August 17, 1984, he rejected "any interpretation of the Yalta agreement" that suggested "American consent for the division of Europe into spheres of influence." Three days later, in an address before the Veterans of Foreign Wars in Chicago, Shultz declared, "We will never accept the idea of a divided Europe." It was left for Casey to rationalize the globalization of rollback in a speech before New York Metropolitan Club in May 1985: "In the occupied countries—Afghanistan, Cambodia, Ethiopia, Angola, and Nicaragua—in which Marxist regimes have been either imposed or maintained by external force ... [there] has occurred a holocaust comparable to that which Nazi Germany inflicted on Europe some forty years ago."[3]

Reagan's new doctrine delighted those on the right who had long clamored for offensive action against the Soviet Union and its alleged clients

Central Intelligence Director William Casey discussing official matters with
Reagan. *Source:* Ronald Reagan Library.

everywhere. George Will lauded the doctrine for its two essential modifica-
tions of the original containment doctrine: its rejection of the sanguine hope
that time would mellow the Soviet regime and its recognition of the hope-
lessly passive nature of containment, with its acceptance of the Brezhnev
Doctrine's assertion that Soviet gains were irreversible. Charles Krauthammer likewise saw in the Reagan Doctrine the antithesis of the Brezhnev Doctrine. "The Reagan Doctrine," he wrote, "proclaims overt and unashamed
American support for anti-Communist revolution." The doctrine, he noted,
had the support of justice, necessity, and tradition: justice because anticommunist revolutionaries were fighting tyranny; necessity because any defeat
for freedom fighters assigned a country irrevocably to Soviet dominance; and
tradition because the United States, throughout its history, had supported
the cause of freedom abroad. All three assumptions left ample room for
doubt and revealed a questionable reading of history. Still, for Krauthammer, it was no longer prudent or moral to neglect the cause of freedom in
deference to national sovereignty. That concern, he complained, had become
the excuse for inaction when oppressed democratic revolutionaries asked for
needed assistance.[4]

For its critics, the Reagan Doctrine suffered from the habitual tendency
to exaggerate the dangers posed by Communist regimes, as well as the need
and available capacity to eliminate them. Robert Tucker questioned the
doctrine's central assumption that all Marxist-Leninist governments lacked

legitimacy and that the United States carried the moral responsibility to support rebellions against them. For him the Reagan Doctrine scarcely represented moral progress. The Sandinista government in Nicaragua, he observed, was far better than many in Central America that the United States had supported. To political scientist Kenneth Thompson, the Reagan Doctrine was hopeless as a guide to policy. "What the Reagan Doctrine requires, in theory," he warned, "is indiscriminate intervention to overturn Communist regimes regardless of calculations of interest and power." In the absence of such calculations, policies would either be abandoned, as in Lebanon, or pursued in the face of public disillusionment, as in Vietnam.[5]

The Reagan Doctrine overrode the traditional limits of statecraft. It unleashed limited war by proxy; there were no commitments of U.S. forces. In practice, the Reagan dictum served as the rationale for U.S. economic and military assistance to the Mujahedeen resistance in Soviet-occupied Afghanistan, to rebel factions arrayed against Vietnam's client government in Cambodia, and, following the repeal of the Clark Amendment in 1985, to Jonas Savimbi's anti-Soviet guerrilla forces in Angola. U.S. action, where it occurred, comprised risk-free funding of low-cost mercenaries, whose devotion to democratic principles and prospects of success remained dubious.[6]

THE NICARAGUAN CONTRAS

Fundamentally, the Reagan Doctrine justified the president's concern for the Nicaraguan contras. As he observed in a speech of March 1, 1985, "They are our brothers, these freedom fighters, and we owe them our help . . . They are the moral equivalent of the Founding Fathers and the brave men and women of the French Resistance. We cannot turn away from them. For the struggle is not right versus left, but right versus wrong."[7] The contras had emerged as the president's special obsession, symbol of the Reagan Doctrine's promise of stemming the Kremlin's global advances. Unfortunately, the contras hardly conformed to the president's portrayal of strength and determination. Few rebel leaders had democratic credentials; some ultimately faced trial and execution for murder and other crimes. The contras succeeded in killing thousands of peasants and rendering other thousands homeless, but the death and destruction brought them no closer to overthrowing the Sandinista regime. They did not control a single town or village. They occupied little of Nicaragua's hinterland, preferring the safer haven of Honduras.[8] Still, their pressures on Managua reduced the Sandinistas to dependent clients of the Soviet Union. The flow of Soviet equipment, including tanks, trucks, artillery, and heavy weaponry, turned the Nicaraguan army into the largest and strongest in the region's history.[9]

Reagan's critics in Congress and the press challenged both the ends and means of the administration's anti-Sandinista crusade. Some questioned the

fears that drove it. Ronald Steel said about Nicaragua, "[It's] an impoverished little country that does not endanger us regardless of who rules it." For
Congressman Lee H. Hamilton of Indiana, who termed Nicaragua "a small,
dirt-poor country with scarce human and material resources," the president
not only exaggerated the importance of Nicaragua to hemispheric security but also suggested no realistic means of eliminating the danger.[10] The
administration's rationales for overthrowing the Nicaraguan government
seemed to convey the threat of eventual U.S. engagement if other means
failed. Yet to reassure a public that had no interest in tough action, the president made clear that under no circumstances would he commit U.S. forces
to that region. Meg Greenfield advised her *Newsweek* readers, in March
1985, to expect little. "[T]his country," she wrote, "is no damned good at
getting its way by means of threats and games of chicken."[11] On the supposition that the U.S. policy in Nicaragua was doomed to failure, Congress, in
May, refused to vote additional funding for the contras. Reagan responded
with an economic embargo against Nicaragua, prompting Daniel Ortega,
Nicaragua's president, to travel to Moscow in quest of assurances that
the Soviet Union would make up the difference. Congress, embarrassed by
Ortega's well-publicized trip, reconsidered its decision and voted $27 million
in humanitarian aid for the contras.

Reagan's personal crusade in behalf of the contras culminated in his dramatic address to the nation on March 16, 1986. He reminded his listeners
that the Soviets and Cubans, using Nicaragua as a base, threatened to become the dominant force in the crucial corridor between North and South
America. "Established there," he warned, "they will be in a position to
threaten the Panama Canal, interdict our vital Caribbean sea lanes, and,
ultimately, move against Mexico." However grave the danger, he promised,
the contras, with needed U.S. support, would eliminate it. Congress, troubled
by the persistent chasm between the specter of Soviet expansionism and the
president's unpromising, risk-free solutions, continued to stall. Wyoming's
Dick Cheney chided the doubters: "You can't have foreign policy carried out
by 435 House members and 100 Senators. There are times when the president needs strong support, and debate has to stop at the water's edge."[12]
Congress, eventually moved by the president's personal obsession and Sandinista indiscretions, voted the contras $100 million in the early summer of
1986.

Joshua Muravchik, writing in *Foreign Affairs*, lauded the congressional
vote. About the sanctioning of the Reagan Doctrine, he wrote, "[I]t constitutes a step, albeit a small and reversible one, in America's continuing search
for a global strategy to replace the one—containment—that was shattered by
Vietnam."[13] One top Carter official agreed. "[F]uture Administrations," he
predicted, "will have more leeway in projecting U.S. economic and military
power without running into the constant argument of Vietnam."[14] Unfortunately, the slow delivery of the funds compelled the Nicaragua Development

Council, a leading contra agency, to launch a direct mail appeal to its list of potential American donors.[15]

Reagan's extended crusade against the government of Nicaragua received no support in Europe. Europeans rejected his admonition that Nicaragua had become a beachhead of Soviet penetration of the Western Hemisphere. They looked askance at his long, divisive effort to wrest $100 million in military aid for the anti-Sandinista rebels. At the Bonn economic summit of May 1985, the Europeans rejected Reagan's plea for support of his trade embargo against Nicaragua. British Foreign Minister Sir Geoffrey Howe warned that an embargo would push the Sandinistas more completely into the Soviet-Cuban camp. Foreign Minister Hans-Dietrich Genscher of West Germany reminded the president that Europeans did not believe in trade sanctions to achieve political ends. So bitter was the reaction to American policy in Nicaragua that the president faced massive anti-American demonstrations when he visited Madrid after the Bonn summit.

Several days later the European Economic Community, under the prodding of France's Claude Cheysson, doubled its aid to Central America, including Nicaragua, in deliberate defiance of the U.S. embargo. Europe's rejection of American policy became complete when the World Court, in June 1986, denounced the United States for backing Nicaragua's anti-Sandinista rebels and violating the U.N. Charter. When Washington ignored the decision, the *Frankfurter Rundschau* complained, "That the U.S. did not even consider it necessary to make an appearance before the World Court in the [*sic*] Hague is more than arrogant flouting of the international court; it sets a negative precedent for other states to follow." Following its victory before the Court of Justice, Nicaragua took its case before the United Nations where only the United States, backed by El Salvador, opposed it.

For international lawyer John Norton Moore, who believed Nicaragua was a second Cuba and the key element in the Kremlin's assault on the hemisphere, it seemed unconscionable that Europe and the United Nations would fail to support the United States. The refusal of the nation's democratic allies to defend it in the Security Council, wrote Moore in October 1986, reflected "an advanced deterioration of the global deterrent system."[16]

Meanwhile, the fundamental Reagan approach to the Third World, anchored to Jeane Kirkpatrick's distinction between authoritarian and totalitarian regimes, began to unravel. Under that distinction the legitimacy of governments lay in their presence of democratic procedures, because democratic governments, responsive to the public will, would not ignore the issue of human rights. Washington's primary concern, therefore, was political progress, not human rights violations.[17] Unfortunately, for Reagan officials, democracy remained a measure of form and structure, not of governmental rectitude. In practice, authoritarian governments, easily categorized as democratic, were immune to condemnation for their oppressions. Washington supported authoritarian governments in Argentina, Chile, Guatemala,

El Salvador, Haiti, the Philippines, and elsewhere that were notoriously repressive. For example, the United States cast the only vote before the UN Human Rights Commission to exonerate Argentina's military regime for the disappearance of thousands of civilians who were abducted, tortured, or murdered by government death squads.[18] Finally, in March 1986, amid the collapse of U.S.-supported governments under the weight of their own misrule, the president announced that the United States would no longer recognize the distinction between authoritarian and totalitarian regimes; it would, he informed Congress, oppose all dictatorships, right and left.[19] The administration encouraged the exile of Haiti's notorious dictator, "Baby Doc" Duvalier, as well as Ferdinand Marcos' departure from the Philippines. Behind such decisions was some admission that Third World struggles were indigenous and that the perpetuation of friendly Third World governments was not essential for American security.

IRAN-CONTRA AFFAIR

Congress, in October, demonstrated its total rejection of the administration's crusade against Nicaragua when it passed a third Boland Amendment to prohibit any federal agency from giving aid to the Nicaraguan contras. During the deliberation, Congressman Edward P. Boland of Massachusetts declared that the amendment would end all support for the war in Nicaragua; there were no exceptions. The amendment, signed by the president, was aimed at the CIA, not the NSC, because traditionally the CIA commanded all covert U.S. operations abroad.[20] In November, Congress cut off all CIA funding for Nicaragua. Republican Senator Charles M. Mathias of Maryland warned the president to limit his objectives in Central America to what Congress would approve. Instead, Reagan turned to the NSC staff, not accessible to Congress, to find nongovernmental funding to sustain the contras until Congress agreed to act. National Security Adviser Robert McFarlane quickly devised a program to secure the necessary aid from both private U.S. sources and foreign governments. McFarlane's most notable success came in Saudi Arabia; the Saudis eventually contributed $32 million to the contra cause.[21]

Lieutenant Colonel Oliver North, a McFarlane deputy, assumed command of the domestic appeal. The Alabama-based Civilian Military Assistance claimed $3 million in contributions for contra nonmilitary aid. Through various conservative organizations in the United States and abroad, General John K. Singlaub, head of the World Anti-Communist League, collected additional millions in nonlethal aid for the contras. In 1985, Singlaub traveled to Taiwan and South Korea, seeking aid for the contras. North assured Taiwan officials that Singlaub spoke for the U.S. government.[22] Meanwhile, the Boland Amendment, despite Casey's assurances that it did not apply to the NSC, continued to trouble the inner circle of the Reagan administration. McFarlane advised North to solicit no more funds for the contras. North turned to Carl R. Channel whose various organizations, such as the National Endowment for the Preservation of Liberty, collected millions for his many causes. North proclaimed to prospective donors the need for help to save the hemisphere from Soviet influence; Channel collected the funds. Major donors received private audiences with the president. Channel later pleaded guilty of defrauding the government.

Under North's direction, Project Democracy evolved into a parallel, largely secret, foreign policy apparatus, with its own sources of income, communications systems, secret envoys, leased ships and airplanes, and Swiss bank accounts. For Casey, North, and their associates, this apparatus carried the burden of sustaining the United States as an effective world power. But to *The New York Times* and other critics, the administration's well-advertised efforts at private funding for the contras comprised merely illegal defiance of the expressed will of Congress.[23] These critics had yet to learn the extent of the defiance.

Iran entered the growing controversy over Nicaragua only tangentially. Some Washington officials had long concluded that U.S. interests demanded the reestablishment of effective and friendly relations with the Iranian government. Late in 1984, a former CIA official informed the National Security Council that Manucher Ghorbanifar, an Iranian arms merchant, had suggested an exchange of U.S. arms for contacts with Iranian officials and the release of American hostages held in Lebanon. If Washington did nothing, Ghorbanifar predicted, in five years the Soviets would control the country.[24]

In June 1985, over the objections of Shultz and Weinberger, the NSC and CIA approved a program that enabled Ghorbanifar to purchase American arms from Israel for shipment to Iran. As the transactions began in August and September 1985, the Iranians released a hostage, Reverend Benjamin Weir. In November, North took command of the arms sales to Iran. He arranged for a trading company, headed by retired General Richard Secord and Iranian businessman Albert Hakim, to deliver the weapons to Iran.[25] At a White House meeting on January 7, 1986, the president's top officials, dominated by spokesmen of the NSC and CIA, adopted a plan whereby the Defense Department would sell weapons to the CIA which, in turn, would sell them to Secord who would deliver them to Iran.

The group agreed not to inform Congress. Shultz later testified, "[I]t was clear to me by the time we went out that . . . all had one opinion and I had a different one and Cap [Weinberger] shared it."[26] The president, recovering from major surgery, signed the necessary finding. In May 1986, McFarlane and North traveled secretly to Teheran to deliver weapons and, through Ghorbanifar, meet high-ranking Iranian officials. They achieved nothing.[27] U.S. officials, without contacts in Teheran, had no choice but to work through Ghorbanifar, although they knew he was untrustworthy.

During January 1986, during a conversation in London, Ghorbanifar suggested to North that they improve Iranian operations by diverting the profits from arms sales to the Nicaraguan contras. By February the diversion was under way. Secord, in possession of the funds, diverted only a small fraction of the profits to the contras. North later defended the diversion: "I thought using the Ayatollah's money to support the Nicaraguan Resistance was a right idea . . . I don't think it was wrong. I think it was a neat idea and I came back and I advocated that and we did it."[28] Vice Admiral John Poindexter, the new national security adviser, approved the diversion, convinced that he had the president's authority to implement the administration's program of aiding the contras. The profits of the Iranian arms sales, he believed, comprised private or third-party funds, no different in nature from other aid flowing to the contras. North and Secord managed the diversion through a wide variety of front organizations.[29]

Throughout the spring of 1986, *The Miami Herald*, *The Washington Post*, *The New York Times*, and other newspapers charged that North and the NSC were violating the congressional ban on aid to the contras. In June, House member Ronald Coleman of Texas introduced a resolution directing the president to provide information regarding the efforts of North and the NSC staff to support the Nicaraguan rebels. Poindexter insisted that the administration was abiding by the letter and spirit of the law. Later he testified that he did not believe that the Boland Amendment applied to the National Security Council. Finally, Poindexter agreed to permit a House Intelligence Committee interrogation of North.

The meeting occurred on August 6 in the White House Situation Room. North insisted that he had given the contras no more than advice on human rights and the need to improve their image; he had not, he said, assisted the contras with fund-raising or violated the Boland Amendment in any fashion. He denied that he had ever worked with Singlaub. Committee members were so impressed with North's testimony that they turned against Coleman's resolution requesting a House inquiry. Poindexter praised North's performance.[30] In September, Costa Rican President Oscar Arias Sanchez threatened to expose the secret Santa Elena airstrip in his country, implicating North and Secord, as well as Costa Rica, in the contra war.[31] Any slip now could sink the administration's illegal operations in Central America.

On October 5, the secret White House operation began to unravel. That day the Sandinistas shot down a plane over Nicaragua carrying supplies to the contras, and captured Eugene Hasenfus. Hasenfus, a native of Wisconsin, was a former Marine and a Vietnam veteran. The president praised Hasenfus for fighting the good cause, but Reston retorted, "If, as the Administration insists, it is perfectly legal to maintain a U.S. embassy in the Nicaraguan capital while permitting private U.S. citizens to supply arms for an attack on that Government, there must be something defective in the U.S. neutrality and arms export legislation."[32] From the administration came the customary denials of any governmental connection with the downed C-123. Shultz insisted that the plane was hired by private individuals. Assistant Secretary of State Elliott Abrams took charge of the damage control efforts of the administration. On October 11, he declared on the Evans-Novak television show that the administration had contributed no support to Hasenfus. "That would be illegal," he acknowledged, "We are barred from doing that, and we are not doing it." On October 14, Abrams informed the House Intelligence Committee, "I will say that no American intelligence or Defense or any other kind of government official was engaged in facilitating this flight or paying for it or directing it."[33] Casey had not told top CIA officials of the Iran-contra affair; now he could not fend off their suspicions that money had passed to the contras. He saw trouble coming; there would be questions of impropriety when the whole business became known. He advised Poindexter to see a White House counsel and North to begin shredding documents and find a lawyer.[34]

On October 15, leaflets appeared in Lebanon that described in detail McFarlane's visit to Teheran in quest of an arms-for-hostages deal. Then on November 3, *Al-Shiraa*, a Beirut weekly, published its version of McFarlane's journey. One day later, Ali Akbar Hashemi Rafsanjani, Iran's dominant leader, acknowledged the trip before the Iranian parliament. Suddenly the U.S. public became aware of the administration's long involvement in Iran and its efforts to trade arms for hostages. Members of the Reagan team were terrified. On November 13, the president told the nation that all the arms sold to Iran "could easily fit into a single cargo plane." At his press conference on November 19, the president, still determined to keep the truth from the American people, assured newsmen that the United States had never condoned Israeli arms shipments to Iran on behalf of the United States.

Edwin Meese, an administration insider and a close presidential associate, was determined to end the mounting confusion. He had listened to Reagan's press conference and knew that the president had made serious misstatements regarding the role of third countries in the shipment of arms. Meese called Poindexter who immediately issued a clarification. When Casey and Poindexter, on November 21, told patent falsehoods to the congressional intelligence committees, the State Department rebelled. Meese, Poindexter, and Chief of Staff Donald Regan now convinced the president to appoint a fact-gathering commission, soon to be headed by former Senator John Tower of Texas. Meese phoned Poindexter and demanded access of every document or other evidence needed to set the record straight. He tipped off Poindexter and North that they had twenty-four hours before the arrival of the aides he was sending to examine NSC files on the Iran affair. To protect the president's deniability, Poindexter destroyed the key finding of December 5, 1985, on arms sales to Iran. North proceeded to shred documents.[35]

North and his staff believed that they had destroyed all evidence of the diversion only to learn that one of the agents had discovered a copy of North's diversion memorandum.[36] Confronted with the evidence, Poindexter acknowledged that North had handled the diversion and that he had done nothing to stop it, believing that the president would have approved. North, Poindexter, and their associates believed themselves empowered to do as they pleased as long as they acted in the president's name.[37] Because they had, in their claims to constitutional immunity, defied Congress as well as the State and Defense Departments, no high officials came to their rescue.

After Reagan acknowledged his role in the Iran arms-for-hostages initiative, few members of Congress cared to challenge his denial that he knew nothing of the diversion. Poindexter and North had established the president's "plausible deniability" so successfully that it enabled him to escape prosecution even while he abandoned them to their fate. The president removed North from the NSC staff and accepted Poindexter's resignation. He dropped the White House chief of staff, Donald Regan, for allegedly failing to control the NSC. Casey, suffering from cancer, entered a hospital shortly after the crisis broke and died several weeks later. In its report of early 1987, the Tower Commission, consisting of Tower, Edmund Muskie, and Brent Scowcroft, upheld Reagan's denial that he knew anything about the diversion. In attacking performance rather than policy, the Tower report condemned only the president's administrative procedures that permitted such broad clandestine operations to continue for so long without his knowledge.

Congress' joint hearings of May and June 1987 were merely a prelude to the dramatic testimony of North and Poindexter in July. The full burden of broken laws fell on them. North had lied to congressional committees, shredded documents, and managed a secret network of money gathering for the contras, all in violation of congressional mandates. With intensely partisan help from Republican members of the committee, however, North quickly shifted the issue of his wrongdoing to a vigorous defense of the president's policy in Central America. He boasted that his lying on behalf of policy had protected hemispheric security against the onrush of Soviet expansionism. "I will tell you right now, counsel, and all the members gathered," he declared, "that I misled the Congress... I participated in preparation of documents for the Congress that were erroneous, misleading, evasive, and wrong, and I did it again here when I appeared before the committee convened in the White House Situation Room and I make no excuses for what I did."[38] Suddenly committee Democrats found themselves hard-pressed to defend their patriotism as the uniformed, decorated, and defiant North upbraided them for the loss of Vietnam and the weakening of American resolve in the face of enemy aggression in Central America. Similarly Poindexter declared in his testimony that no one could trust the State Department, the Defense Department, or Congress to defend the security of the United States. Such singular claims to a higher patriotism could save neither North nor Poindexter from the special prosecutor who eventually secured their indictments, trials, and convictions.[39]

With Iran-contra, the administration's long crusade to eliminate the Sandinistas and subdue the Salvadoran guerrillas came to an end. The United States airlifted 3200 troops into Honduras as a final gesture of support for the contras; within days Honduran students burned the American flag and torched U.S. embassy buildings. Such resentment was predictable. The Reagan policies in Central America repeated all the previous indulgences shown to such pro-U.S. regimes as those of Batista, Somoza, Trujillo, and Ubico; as revealed in Operation Success, the Bay of Pigs Invasion, and the Cuban Missile Crisis; and in the rejection of reform movements out of fear that nationalism was destabilizing and synonymous with Soviet expansionism. But opposition to nationalism, in Latin America as elsewhere, was Washington's fundamental miscalculation. The independent Costa Rican peace process that emerged in 1987 revealed more in common among the Marxist-oriented Sandinistas and the other Central American governments than any one of them could discover in Washington's anti-Soviet crusade. The Central Americans had minds, wills, and interests of their own, something that the Reagan administration had failed to recognize.[40] Nicaragua ceased to be an issue when, in 1990, a free election drove the Sandinistas from power.

Origins of the Affair

When the United States, in 1985, shipped weapons to Iran, the devastating Iran-Iraq War was already in its fifth year. Following Iraq's invasion of Iran on September 22, 1980, the Reagan administration remained officially neutral, but within the administration two factions quarreled over the relative danger of an Iranian or Iraqi victory. McFarlane, North, and much of the NSC staff favored arms for Iran, both to strengthen Israel's security and to facilitate improved relations with Iran in the looming post-Khomeini era. Iran's early successes aroused fears of a revived Islamic revolution, threatening U.S. oil interests. By 1983, Washington's pro-Iraqi faction, led by Weinberger and Shultz, favored a secret initiative to undo the damage wrought by the sale of U.S. arms to Iran. That year the Reagan administration approved secret arms transfers to Iraq from Jordan, Saudi Arabia, Kuwait, and Egypt.[41]

By 1984, the administration was fully committed to a major tilt toward Iraq, demanding only that Iraq refrain from using chemical weapons against Iran. The weapons shipments to Iran in 1985–1986 further divided the administration. Casey, in July 1986, convinced Bush to undertake a secret mission to the Middle East and there urge the Baghdad government to make more efficient use of its air power. While in Jordan, Bush told King Hussein that the Baghdad government should employ its air force more aggressively against Iranian targets. At the same time, CIA officials in Baghdad began to provide the Iraqi military with classified tactical intelligence, as well as equipment to receive intelligence via satellite. With the departure of Poindexter, North, and McFarlane in late 1986, the administration's pro-Iraqi elements were in complete control of U.S. policy. In response to the destructive Iraqi bombing raids advocated by Casey and Bush, Iran, in January 1987, launched its most sustained and bloody operations of the war. Iraq now needed foreign aid more desperately than ever. The Soviet Union proceeded to re-equip the Iraqi military.[42]

The Soviet Union and Iran

Long before 1987, the Iran-Iraq War threatened shipping in the Persian Gulf. Learning that the U.S.S.R. had offered naval assistance to Kuwait, the Reagan administration, determined to defend U.S. strategic interests, sent a flotilla into the Gulf to provide escort to American-flagged Kuwaiti tankers. Again it sought no congressional approval. Having failed to control events in Iran and Afghanistan, Washington dared not suffer another strategic retreat in southwest Asia. The Persian Gulf oil reserves alone constituted a sufficiently high stake to render the defense of the region's oil interests essential. Washington officials predicted that Iranian control of the Gulf would lead to Soviet regional dominance and the transfer of the oil states to Kremlin control. Within weeks, U.S. naval forces found themselves trapped in the crossfire of a Gulf war that they could neither terminate nor escape without a serious loss of credibility. An Iraqi jet almost sank the USS *Stark* with a French Exocet missile, killing thirty-seven crewmen. Tankers without American protection reached the high seas in large numbers while Iranian gunboats dropped mines and attacked freighters and tankers bound for Kuwait, Dubai, and Bahrain in response to Iraqi bombing.

Such damaging operations under the guns of the U.S. warships raised the specter of a clash with Iran that no one wanted. In July 1988, the USS *Vincennes* shot down an Air Iran Flight 655 on a routine flight to Dubai, mistaking it for an Iranian F-14. The after action navy report placed responsibility for the tragic death of 290 passengers on the Iranians for scheduling flights over a combat area. In Washington, the Persian Gulf commitment became more controversial with each passing week; by late 1987 members of Congress were determined to end it. Even Pentagon officials wondered about the long-range implications of the Gulf decision. Indeed, after months of questioning, the administration had trouble in defining any U.S. mission except that of protecting the principle of freedom of the seas. On August 20, 1988, the Iranians accepted, with UN mediation, the Iraqi offer of a cease-fire. For the United States, the buildup of Iraqi power had scarcely begun. John Whitehead, deputy secretary of state, explained the American need of strong ties with Baghdad: "[Soviet] clout and influence is on a steady rise as

the Gulf Arabs gain self-confidence and Soviet diplomacy gains in sophisti-
cation. The Soviets have strong cards to play.... They will continue to be
major players and we should engage them as fully as possible."[43]

The principles of the Reagan Doctrine had found their way into U.S.
affairs in the Middle East.

CHAPTER 6

The Reagan-Gorbachev Détente

In time Gorbachev rescued Reagan from the near-disaster of the Iran-contra affair. However, the progress toward demonstrable improvement in U.S.-Soviet relations came slowly and haltingly. If the diplomatic initiative rested largely with Gorbachev, it was because he was far less politically and ideologically constrained than Reagan. The Third World issues that troubled Washington were not his concern. Yet in an April 23, 1985 speech, the new Soviet leader pointed to what he saw as Washington's hypocrisy—protesting Moscow's intervention in Afghanistan while claiming its "'right' to interfere" in Grenada and Nicaragua.

U.S. officials had long regarded the regional competition between the United States and the Soviet Union a matter of legitimate concern. Such issues had never been negotiable. Soviet Third World involvements had been largely political and had responded to socioeconomic and political processes that created ideological affinities; these, to the Soviets, scarcely comprised aggression. For Washington, however, Afghanistan remained a barrier to improved U.S.-Soviet relations. "It's been six years," the president declared late in 1985, "since the Soviet Union invaded that country, six years of utter hell for the Afghan people who still fight on in the name of ideals upon which our own nation was founded—freedom and independence." To the Kremlin, U.S. support for the Afghan rebels merely hindered a settlement of the Afghan conflict.[1]

GORBACHEV: RETHINKING THE ARMS RACE

Gorbachev understood that achieving a genuine détente with the United States required soothing Western public fears arising from simmering issues focused on nuclear weaponry—the reverse of traditional ideas about the relationship of politics and arms. Later he summed up his thoughts: "The arms race, of course, was both *a result* of the Cold War and *a cause* as it constantly provided new stimuli for continued rivalry. [italics in original]"

From his assumption of power in March 1985, Gorbachev sought to ground his new approach to the arms race and arms control on an American commitment to renounce efforts to gain military superiority and reject any possibility of waging—or devising programs to win—a nuclear conflict. He was determined to break from previous Soviet policy and redefine its basic themes of security, strategic stability and defense sufficiency. If both super-powers would accept the idea of strategic parity, then they could reach a mutual understanding on the amount of arms each nation believed sufficient for relative security. He added, "[The Kremlin does not] want changes in the strategic balance to our favor. We do not want this because such a situation would heighten suspicion of the other side and increase the instability of the general situation." Gorbachev believed that the "level of sufficiency" was "far lower than that the USSR and the United States now possess[ed]." If the new Soviet desire for arms negotiations was unprecedented, Washington's fears of communist expansionism continued to place the administration's opponents of further arms agreements in the ascendancy.

After eight months of discussions that seemed to lead nowhere, Reagan and Gorbachev met at the Geneva Summit in November 1985. As he pre-pared to depart Washington, the president told the American people that the two nations should "seek to reduce the suspicions and mistrust" that had led it "to acquire mountains of strategic weapons." Reagan conceded that it was not an evil opponent but nuclear weapons that posed "the greatest threat in human history to survival of the human race" and declared "a nuclear war cannot be won and must never be fought."

At Geneva, Gorbachev pressed arms control issues, especially limits on the Strategic Defense Initiative and maintaining SALT II and new arms re-ductions but found Reagan refusing to offer concessions on any of contested points. For his part, Reagan found that he could hold his own with the So-viet leader; even more, he saw Gorbachev as a personable politician freed of the Cold War's ideological biases and one with whom he shared "a kind of chemistry." The most significant outcome of the summit undoubtedly was the rapport that developed between the two heads of state.

Upon his return from Geneva, Reagan received a Pentagon report repeat-ing the claims, a few legitimate, that the Soviets were cheating on its arms control commitments.[2] As part of their "hatchet job," the Reagan admin-istration alleged the Soviets violated the 1963 Test ban treaty when over the years some of their underground tests had vented into the atmosphere and been detected beyond the U.S.S.R's borders. While this was techni-cally a violation, the 1963 Limited Test Ban Treaty had anticipated, and discounted, unintentional venting. American tests had also unintentionally vented radioactivity into the atmosphere and been detected beyond its borders, although neither Reagan nor the Pentagon admitted it. If some Cold War hawks claimed that Moscow was "exploiting ambiguities" in the unratified SALT II pact, they had to admit that the Soviets never were over the numerical limits detailed in the treaty.[3]

In clear violation of the 1972 Anti-Ballistic Missile Treaty (ABM), the Soviets had begun to erect a huge radar at Krasnoyarsk in Siberia—an endeavor the Kremlin later acknowledged and halted. Meanwhile, Moscow responded with claims that the two large American radars in Greenland and England were in violation of the ABM agreement. Yet arguably the most serious U.S. violation was the space dimension of the SDI program. Many of these alleged violations could have been quietly resolved in the appropriate adjudicating agency, the Standing Consultative Committee (SCC) established in the ABM treaty, but the Reagan administration scorned the Committee, and it remained virtually dormant.[4] Charges of Soviet compliance violations placated the administration's right-wing political base and supported the ballooning Pentagon budget.

During the months following Geneva, Gorbachev continued to stress the absurdity of strategies that encouraged the costly and potentially dangerous arms race. In a January 1986 address, he offered to withdraw all Soviet intermediate-range missiles from Europe if the United States eliminated its Pershing II short-range missiles. These weapons, he argued, were not essential for the execution of either Soviet or American strategies. At the 27th Party Congress, in February–March 1986, Gorbachev endorsed the need for imaginative thinking to meet the challenges of changing times. He reminded the congress that no country could defend itself against nuclear attack; security, therefore, lay in political settlements, not strategic weapons. "The confrontation between capitalism and socialism," he declared, "can take place only, and exclusively in the form of peaceful competition and peaceful rivalry."[5] Gorbachev's ambitious economic modernization program, endorsed by the 27th Congress, required reduced military spending as well as receding international tensions. For him the Soviet objective was the attainment of mutual security at the lowest possible strategic balance.[6]

It was general knowledge that several senior political members of the Reagan establishment had been pressing the president to withdraw from the unratified SALT II treaty. Whatever the state of Soviet compliance, Europeans opposed any formal dismissal of the treaty. Despite Europe's known preferences, the president, in late May 1986, announced that the United States would no longer be bound by the SALT II formula at the end of the year unless the Kremlin undertook undefined "constructive steps." Europe's reaction was bitter. *Le Figaro* complained that at no time did Washington ask Europe for its opinion. "It's a disaster," fumed Helmut Kohl. Some Europeans regarded the atmosphere more dangerous than at any time since World War II. *The Times* (London) declared that the president had "come close to making one of the most controversial decisions in his six years in the White House. . . . Its impact on the Western alliance could be serious." *The Economist* reported that half the Britons polled distrusted the president's judgment and believed the United States no less a threat to peace than the Soviet Union. In Washington, officials, even while they argued that the president was justified in his response to apparent Soviet cheating, admitted that the administration had failed to anticipate Europe's reaction.[7]

For Moscow and Washington, the continuing arms debate revolved around Euromissiles and the Strategic Defense Initiative (SDI). The Soviets still hoped to reverse their failure to block the deployment of American Pershing II and cruise missiles in Europe. Reagan, promising Americans and Europeans alike an impenetrable fortress in the sky, continued to proclaim his support for SDI against the Soviet complaints that Washington was attempting to regain offensive supremacy and expand the arms race into space.[8]

Gorbachev, recognizing Europe's nuclear anxiety, filled the air with new arms proposals, while Pentagon officials routinely rejected them. *New York Times* columnist James Reston, who favored Shultz's plea for quiet diplomacy to break the deadlock, noted the preference for "ideological confrontation and warrior diplomacy . . . at the Pentagon and the White House." Columnist Andrew J. Glass feared that the Reagan administration would never succeed in assuring the Soviets of its goodwill. "[T]he national security apparatus in the White House," he observed, "remains thoroughly fractionated. With so many hawks and pseudo-hawks flapping about in the Reagan aviary, it will muster all the administration's ability in diplomatic falconry merely to fashion a cogent response to the latest Soviet initiative."[9] Europeans who favored negotiations found hope in the conviction that Reagan, unlike many of his Pentagon advisers, favored an arms agreement as the one means still available to him for reducing international tension and overcoming the legacies of huge federal deficits that he could no longer reverse. Meanwhile, Gorbachev swept the European polls as a man of peace.[10] In late August 1986 Reagan announced that the United States would not exceed the limits imposed by the 1979 SALT II treaty before another possible summit with Gorbachev.[11]

MORE REAGAN-GORBACHEV SUMMITRY

Reagan approached his next meeting with Gorbachev with the knowledge that Soviet power and Third World involvements required a tough, uncompromising U.S. posture. At the same time he recognized that the deep flaws in the Soviet economy and political structure rendered Soviet power tenuous and Kremlin ambitions less than global. Reagan, who personalized his attitudes toward countries and issues, could scarcely sustain his earlier stereotypes of the cheating villains in Moscow after he encountered

President Reagan talking with Soviet Chairman, Mikhail Gorbachev. *Source:* Ronald Reagan Library.

Gorbachev. He recognized in Gorbachev a remarkable leader determined to change the economic and political landscape of the U.S.S.R. for the better.

THE REYKJAVIK MEETING

At the Reykjavik, Iceland, summit in October 1986, the two leaders began with the issue of intermediate-range missiles in Europe. The negotiations proceeded with remarkable speed. Gorbachev agreed to scrap all SS-20s in Europe, retaining only one hundred on the Asian front. In return, Washington could keep one hundred similar missiles in Alaska. But discussions for greater reductions stumbled over Reagan's continued devotion to his newborn missile defense program. He rejected Gorbachev's proposal to confine SDI research to laboratories and to adhere to the 1972 ABM Treaty for ten years, offering instead to sign a treaty to "supersede" the 1972 Treaty and to share SDI technology with the Soviet Union. Gorbachev dismissed Reagan's suggestions as the "same old moth-eaten trash" and responded angrily, "You will take the arms race into space and could be tempted to launch a first strike from space. If you will not share oil-drilling equipment or even milk-processing facilities, I do not believe you will share SDI." When Gorbachev claimed the ABM Treaty had prevented nuclear war for more than a decade, Reagan contended that the treaty only held their people hostage to a balance of terror.

To offset the anticipated public appeal of Gorbachev's conciliatory approach, Reagan's advisors devised a set of extraordinary proposals they were confident the Soviet leader would reject. At the final scheduled session, Reagan presented the "sweeping" U.S. proposals to eliminate all nuclear warheads by 2000. Surprising and startling everyone, Gorbachev responded, "Yes." Gorbachev said he would accept Reagan's proposal to eliminate all nuclear weapons provided Reagan agreed to limit SDI research to "laboratories" for at least five years. Reagan again rejected Gorbachev's offer, saying he would never compromise his missile defense project. At 6:30 P.M., after prolonged discussion, the radical arms reduction proposals were dropped. Reagan closed his briefing book and said, "Let's go George [Shultz], we're leaving." As they walked out of the conference room, Gorbachev asked, "Can't we do something about this?" Reagan replied, "It's too late."[12]

Reviewing the conversations, one is left feeling that Reagan had confused his priorities. He had long talked of his desire to eliminate "nuclear weapons", but when an opportunity loomed he clung to his Strategic Defense Initiative. This system was still largely on the drawing boards, and he had no evidence that it would work and, if it should, when it might be available. "Frankly I have no idea what the nature of such a defense might be," he wrote in a private letter a few months after announcing his plan, "I simply asked our scientists to explore the possibility of developing such a defense." Earlier he acknowledged to reporters that it might be "20 years down the road" before a workable missile defense system arrived. Faced with such uncertainty, he might have been expected to compromise and satisfy his frequently stated desired to rid the planet of the nuclear threat.[13]

Reagan and Gorbachev departed Reykjavik, both disappointed and exhausted. Nonetheless, there was a significant breakthrough when Gorbachev agreed to the continuing American demand for on-site inspections. In the previous Limited Nuclear Test Ban (1963) and the ABM and SALT I pacts (1972), American officials had settled for verification by national technical means—employing satellite reconnaissance, electronic monitoring, and other self-managed intelligence-gathering techniques—while still demanding extensive on-site inspections in exchange for any future arms reductions. After Reykjavik, they would find the Soviets receptive to intrusive inspections.

Upon returning from Iceland, Reagan's aides undertook a propaganda blitz to emphasize that the Soviet's concern over SDI proved that the system was essential. In contrast, Gorbachev dismissed the White House statements as propaganda, stressing that Reagan had backed down from the "sweeping proposals" drawn up by his own negotiating team. When the final summit story was disclosed in the 1990s, Gorbachev was correct in stating that Reagan walked away from an opportunity to reach agreements on reducing or eliminating intermediate- and long-range ballistic missiles.[14]

Western military strategists and political leaders—and most certainly Soviet military chiefs—were shaken by the news of the near-agreement to abolish nuclear weapons. In Washington, Senate arms expert Sam Nunn and former Secretary of State Henry Kissinger feared such an agreement would undermine U.S. and Western security. Margaret Thatcher traveled to Washington to warn the president against trifling with nuclear deterrence. The West's nuclear strategy, based on ballistic missiles, she observed, had underwritten U.S. and European security for almost forty years of record-breaking peace.[15]

What remained feasible was a return to the zero option of intermediate-range missiles. Gorbachev moved into the policy vacuum by separating these missiles, covering only a small portion of Europe's nuclear defenses, from other issues. For David Ignatius, editor of *The Washington Post*'s Sunday "Outlook" section, Gorbachev's nimble approach to arms proposals was becoming dangerous. "As fast as the Reagan administration rejects an offer," he warned, "Gorbachev comes up with a new one. The consistent theme in Gorbachev's diplomacy is to get American nuclear weapons out of Europe. In this, he is striking at the central premise of the Atlantic Alliance—America's nuclear umbrella—and pursuing with greater subtlety the goal the Soviets have held for nearly forty years."[16]

INF and the Washington Summit

On February 28, 1987, Gorbachev surprised Pentagon hardliners by accepting their "zero-sum" proposal, eliminating all intermediate-range nuclear missiles in Europe. Secretary of State Shultz immediately accepted Gorbachev's offer. The Strategic Defense Initiative (SDI) would no longer block progress. Andrei Sakharov had persuaded Gorbachev that Reagan's strategic defense program could never stop a full-scale missile attack with ICBMs carrying decoys and multiple warheads. He argued that SDI should not stand in the way of reducing nuclear weapons, because it was a kind of "Maginot line in space," a line that could not defeat concentrated missile attacks anymore than the French Maginot defense line stopped the German blitzkrieg in 1940.[17]

While Reagan's apostles had claimed that Gorbachev's lack of military funds had ended the Soviet link between missile reductions and SDI, Sakharov's February 1987 criticism, in tandem with others, had lifted the veil on what was "hidden in plain sight." Soviet scientists had long recognized that the SDI program was a "fuss about nothing." As Roald Z. Sagdeyev, the head of the Soviet Institute for Space Research told Strobe Talbott, "We came to realize that we had not helped ourselves by screaming so much about SDI. We had encouraged some Americans to think that anything the Russians hate can't be all bad. And we had overestimated how much damage SDI could do to strategic stability in the short run and even

in the medium term." Consequently, negotiators agreed to a treaty that required the superpowers to destroy 2,611 intermediate-range missiles with
flight ranges from 300 to 3,440 miles or 500 to 5,000 kilometers. These
included U.S. Pershing IIs and cruise missiles and Soviet SS-4s, SS-12s,
SS-20s, and SS-23s. It excluded seventy-two West Germany-based short-
range Pershing IA missiles.[18]

When Weinberger, Perle, and other hard-liners demanded on-site inspections, Gorbachev responded with a verification formula that exceeded their
highest expectations. Schultz put forward an "intrusive verification" plan
where each power would inspect the other's various facilities to determine
the fulfillment of Intermediate Nuclear Force (INF) Treaty terms. Gorbachev's acceptance of the intrusive arrangement forced the Pentagon, the
National Security Agency, and the CIA to reconsider their previous verification demands. They did not want the Soviets prowling U.S. defense plants,
nuclear-armed submarines, and missile sites. As Secretary of Defense Frank
Carlucci admitted, "[V]erification has proven to be more complex than we
thought it would be. The flip side of the coin is its application to us. The
more we think about it, the more difficult it becomes." At every meeting
with Soviet leaders, Reagan had repeated the Russian proverb "Trust but
verify." Now the U.S. willingly accepted less intrusive procedures.[19]

The Washington summit of December 1987 itself was another Reagan-
Gorbachev triumph; the media coverage was huge and favorable. Gorbachev
arrived, Secretary Shultz recounted, "upbeat, positive, animated, and eager." He was concerned about the criticism that Reagan was receiving from
hard-liners, but Shultz reassured Gorbachev, saying, "[T]he vast majority
of American support what President Reagan is doing." The Soviet leader
need not have worried, for he and his wife were so enthusiastically greeted
in the normally blasé capital, that it prompted *Washington Post* columnist
Tom Shales to observe the city was seized by "Gorby fever." Shortly after
arriving in Washington, the Gorbachevs met with a wide-ranging group of
celebrities that included Billy Graham, Henry Kissinger, and Yoko Ono.

The signing of the INF treaty occurred on December 8, with an exchange
of pens and a brisk handshake. "For the first time in history," Reagan declared, "the language of 'arms control' was replaced by 'arms reduction' in
this case, the complete elimination of an entire class of U.S. and Soviet nuclear missiles." For his part, Gorbachev responded that the treaty offered "a
big chance at last to get onto the road leading away from the threat of catastrophe," adding, "It is our duty . . . to move forward toward a nuclear-free
world . . . [that is] without fear and without a senseless waste of resources
on weapons of destruction." Although only some 4 percent of the superpowers nuclear arsenal would be eliminated by the INF pact, it did launch
the process of arms reductions.

The enthusiasm for the INF treaty failed to spur the talks toward a strategic arms reduction treaty. Reagan continued to refuse any compromise

regarding his antimissile program, and Gorbachev still insisted that such research be confined to the laboratory. "We are going forward with the research and development to see if this is a workable concept," Reagan said, "and if it is, we are going to deploy it." Continuing the litany that both leaders had memorized, Gorbachev replied, "Mr. President, you do what you have to do. And if in the end you think you have a system you want to deploy, go ahead and deploy it. Who am I to tell you what to do? I think you're wasting money."

So anxious was the president to cement the new détente that he invited 2300 of his political appointees, with their spouses, to the White House for Gorbachev's farewell ceremony on December 10. As the two leaders again exchanged remarks, Reagan correctly labeled their meeting a "clear success." The Soviet leader responded, "[A] good deal has been accomplished." Demonstrating his political instincts, later that day Gorbachev halted his limousine on Connecticut Avenue and got out to shake hands with people who lined the street. He obviously had "star power," for everywhere crowds waited to greet and applauded him. But there were dissenters.[20]

Critics of the INF Treaty and the new détente were quick to make their views known. Richard Nixon and Henry Kissinger, writing jointly, warned that the treaty weakened the ties between the United States and Europe, increased the Soviet conventional threat, and in no way reduced the Soviet capacity to wage nuclear war.[21] Jeane Kirkpatrick noted that the Reagan team, with no intention to do so, had rendered Europe vulnerable to attack. For William F. Buckley, the INF treaty approached unilateral disarmament, threatening to leave the West naked before the Soviet enemy. The United States, added Kirkpatrick, was trying to get out of the game while the Soviets were playing to win.[22] Perhaps the most hysterical outburst came from Richard Viguerie and Howard Phillips, two of the right's leading activists. As cochairmen of The Anti-Appeasement Alliance, they accused the president of threatening the country with another Munich. Viguerie observed bitterly, "It is with deep regret that we who have supported President Reagan in so many battles during the past 20 years now must begin to publicly separate ourselves from our former leader. We feel alienated, abandoned and rejected." Phillips denounced Reagan as "a useful idiot for Soviet propaganda."[23] Reagan responded to such criticism by pointing to the advances in verification, the need to reject the notion of war's inevitability, and the obligation to use every opportunity to strive for peace.[24]

Soviet Withdrawal from Afghanistan

Early in 1988, Afghanistan again emerged as the central issue in U.S.-Soviet relations. Soviet impatience with the Afghan disaster was wearing thin. The psychological destruction of Soviet troops in Afghanistan was becoming unbearable. For Gorbachev, Afghanistan had become his country's "bleeding wound".[25] U.S. officials remained skeptical that the Kremlin, despite its expressed desire to terminate its Afghan involvement, was actually prepared to withdraw its forces. But on February 8, Gorbachev announced that the Soviets would begin their withdrawal on May 15 and complete it by March 15, 1989. Late in February, Shultz flew to Moscow to arrange for the next summit, scheduled for May. Gorbachev informed him that the U.S.S.R. was prepared to sign the U.S.-sponsored Afghanistan accord at the UN but demanded that Afghanistan, following the Soviet withdrawal, remain neutral and independent. The Kremlin wanted U.S. guarantees for the Communist Kabul regime's continuance. During March, Shultz argued with Shevardnadze in Washington that the Soviets had trapped themselves in Afghanistan and should not expect the United States to make concessions merely to ease a Soviet retreat, especially at the expense of the Afghan guerrillas. On March 28, U.S. and Soviet officials announced that a summit would take place at Moscow beginning on May 29. Shultz now agreed to the Soviet demands on Afghanistan, provided that the Kremlin would halt all arms shipments to the Kabul regime. But Pakistan, along with Afghanistan a principal party to the UN agreement, insisted on the right to continue shipments to the guerrillas. The Soviet-backed government sought the assurance of future Soviet support but finally gave way to Gorbachev's preferences for a total Soviet withdrawal. On April 14, Shultz, Shevardnadze, and the foreign ministers of Afghanistan and Pakistan signed the withdrawal agreement in Geneva.

The CIA spent some $3 billion in support of the Afghan rebels and, in the process, created one of the most powerful networks of Islamist militants in the world. Many left Afghanistan as terrorists. At the same time, it was clear that Washington had no interest in the Afghan cause. The U.S. purpose was to punish the Soviets. With the Soviet withdrawal, Washington stopped all aid to the rebels, although the Communist government was still in power. Not until 1992 did the Moslem rebels take control of Kabul.[26]

The Moscow Summit

Following the Washington summit, the vast majority of the Senate favored the INF treaty, although it appeared to weaken the security link between the United States and NATO. Reagan's assurance that he was negotiating from strength effectively countered the tendency of the critics to associate détente with U.S. decline.[27] Robert Dole, Republican leader in the Senate, endorsed the INF treaty and predicted its approval. Senator Jesse Helms of North Carolina led a small, but determined, opposition that threatened the treaty with "killer amendments" unacceptable to the Soviet Union. Treaty supporters worked hard to secure Senate approval before the president departed for the Moscow summit in late May. On the eve of his departure, Republican leaders asked the opponents to stand aside and permit the necessary vote.[28]

Again the Moscow summit was a huge media triumph. On Sunday, May 29, 1988, the president received a red-carpet welcome at the Kremlin. In greeting the president, Gorbachev declared, "[H]istory has objectively bound our two countries by a common responsibility for the destinies of mankind." On Tuesday, Reagan walked among the people on Red Square. Referring to Gorbachev, Reagan commented to one group, "We decided to talk to each other instead of about each other. It's working just fine." He praised Gorbachev for his reform effort as the possible leading edge "of a world of reconciliation, friendship, and peace." In the Kremlin a reporter asked the president what became of the "evil empire," a phrase he had used in March 1983. Reagan replied, "I was talking about another time, another era."[29]

In April Gorbachev had complained to Shultz that Reagan's public statements continued to be anti-Soviet. Thereafter the State Department and White House collaborated in the preparation of Reagan's speeches—the most memorable of his presidency. On a Tuesday afternoon, he addressed students at Moscow State University, Gorbachev's alma mater, to loud applause:

> Your generation is living in one of the most exciting, hopeful times in Soviet history. It is a time when the first breath of freedom stirs the air and...the accumulated spiritual energies of a long silence yearn to break free...We do not know what the conclusion will be of this journey, but we're hopeful that the promise of reform will be fulfilled. In this Moscow spring, this May 1988, we may be allowed that hope—that freedom...will blossom forth at last in the rich fertile soil of your people and culture. We may be allowed to hope that the marvelous sound of a new openness will keep rising through, ringing through, leading to a new world of reconciliation, friendship, and peace.

On Wednesday, Gorbachev and Reagan signed a statement that looked forward to improved Soviet-American relations, not through abstract principles as Gorbachev preferred, but through realistic negotiations. The U.S. Senate's approval of the INF treaty a few days earlier permitted Gorbachev and Reagan to sign the treaty's ratification documents at the final ceremony.[30] At the end, the summit was long on goodwill but short on achievement. The knowledge that the president was nearing the end of his administration eliminated much of the summit's significance.

Predictably, Reagan's final summit again drew bitter criticism from the right. Buckley countered the president's comforting words by asserting that the Soviet Union, with its human rights violations, remained the evil empire. Charles Krauthammer, of *The New Republic*, had become so distrustful of Reagan's relations with Gorbachev that he hoped the two men would achieve nothing in Moscow.[31] George Will passed his own judgment of the Moscow summit. "For conservatives," he wrote, "Ronald Reagan's foreign policy has produced much surprise but little delight. His fourth and, one prays, final summit is a suitable occasion for conservatives to look back with bewilderment and ahead with trepidation." For Will, the president, in his final White House years, ruined what had been a superb foreign and military policy. His rhetoric and actions had accelerated the country's intellectual disarmament, while his acceptance of arms limitation had eliminated the possibility of a coherent conservative foreign policy, one concerned not with arms reduction but defense of the world's peace and security. What the United States required, added Kirkpatrick, was more rather than fewer weapons.[32]

GORBACHEV'S EFFORTS AT REFORM

Gorbachev's remarkable ascendancy to predominance in the Soviet government had enabled him to project a powerful voice in international affairs. To overcome his country's economic disabilities and thereby sustain its international status, Gorbachev had sought, through perestroika, to revitalize the Soviet system, rendering it more productive and proficient by making it more flexible and amendable to change. For him, such restructuring comprised the Soviet Union's last opportunity for modernization. "If we take fright and stop the process we have begun," he admonished his countrymen, "it would have the most serious consequences, because we simply could not raise our people to such a massive task a second time." Gorbachev initiated glasnost to infuse new ideas and initiatives into the Soviet system. Within months, Soviet intellectuals began to rewrite official Soviet history—the Communist Party, Lenin, Stalin, and the ruling power structure. For many, this successful assault on the country's historic ideological underpinnings destroyed what remained of the system's legitimacy. There was, by 1986, enough public criticism of public policy to give some credence to glasnost, but the impact of the new freedom on the Soviet masses remained negligible. So persistent was the weight of tradition that Gorbachev's efforts at reform faced a pervading public apathy. Soviet citizens unattuned to the spirit of individualism, unprepared to perform in a global environment, and distrustful of the future of reform were not inclined to risk whatever security the old system provided. The Soviet press was reluctant to expose the failures and inefficiencies of the system; its attacks on Party leaders were subdued or nonexistent.

What above all eliminated the possibility of genuine economic modernization was Gorbachev's own constricted view of change. His design for economic and political reform did not include rejection of the doctrines that underlay the Soviet system. "Socialism," he declared, "has not yet spread its wings as it should. We have vast potential which is as yet unused."[33] Most of the "new thinking" ideas for economic modernization had been articulated by Soviet critics at least as early as the Brezhnev years.[34] Gorbachev's predecessors after Stalin tried to combine reform, initiative, even revolutionary change with the perpetuation of Communist ideology and a centrally directed Party structure. They understood that any relaxation of the Soviet system would probably destroy it. Since the Party claimed infallibility, error could occur only as a deviation from doctrine.

For Gorbachev, the required legitimacy for reform lay in Leninism and its embodiment of what was good and humane in socialism. But the Leninist doctrine, which had no relevance to the functioning of a modern industrial and technological economy, had long demonstrated its inadequacy in his country's economic performance.[35] Gorbachev's early assault on the Soviet system was so limited that it scarcely touched the central issues of central planning, private property, free markets, consumer goods, or private business. He anticipated neither democracy nor capitalism. Gorbachev's ideological constraints were profound; his personal enthusiasm and energy could not overcome them. Even his limited reform measures soon produced major budget deficits and sharp increases in inflation.[36]

However limited Gorbachev's reform program, it challenged the old regime sufficiently to unleash a massive bureaucratic and ideological war against it. Openness and restructuring aroused outright hostility among Soviet officials who saw in reform the destruction of their privileges. The whole entrenched structure comprised a serious barrier to reform. By 1988 Gorbachev faced a divided politburo. Yegor Ligachev, whom Gorbachev brought into the Moscow politburo from Siberia as number two in the Communist Party, favored economic reform but not at the price of free markets and political democratization. In the West, he argued, the market system produced too much unemployment, homelessness, and economic inequality.[37] But for Gorbachev's noted supporter, Aleksandr Yakovlev, there would be no reform without democratization and free markets. Only democracy, he believed, would permit a thorough confrontation with the entrenched power structure.

Ligachev's antireform effort culminated on March 13, 1988, when the Russian Republic's leading newspaper *Sovetskaya Rossiya* published a bitter condemnation of perestroika and almost everything that Gorbachev had favored. The author was Nina Andreyeva, a chemist at the Leningrad Technology Institute, but Ligachev and other leading critics contributed to the publication. The essay attacked the reformist disavowal of the past, including the Stalin record. Indeed, it praised Stalin for saving the U.S.S.R. from Hitler and bringing industrialization, collectivization, and the cultural revolution to the Soviet Union. It was disgraceful, it continued, for university students to focus, not on the great victories of the war, but on "the political repressions within the army." The author attacked those who kowtowed "to the 'democratic' chains of contemporary capitalism . . . its real and supposed achievements." What happened, she asked, to the class struggle and the role of the proletariat? What was astonishing was not only the reactionary tone and content of the Andreyeva manifesto but also the absence of any response to it; for many it presumably marked the end of the reform movement. Ultimately Yakovlev prepared an answer, but only when Gorbachev forced a showdown in the politburo and threatened to resign did *Pravda*, on April 5, publish Yakovlev's defense of perestroika. For the moment, Gorbachev and Yakovlev prevailed.[38]

At the Communist Party conference of June 1988, Gorbachev called for radical reform to overcome the mistakes of the previous seventy years. The Communist system, he reminded the Soviet citizenry, had failed. No longer, he knew, could he adapt Party control to the country's economic and political requirements. Now he would transform the government into what Lenin meant it to be, the representative of Soviet society. Gorbachev advocated a new elected parliament, separate from Party rule that would decide all administrative, legislative, and monitoring questions. He sought through elections, to follow in 1989 and 1990, to transfer power to state organizations. Gorbachev hoped that the still-elusive economic reform would follow the gains for democracy. Still, it remained unclear how an ideology-based program could penetrate Soviet society sufficiently to effect the needed changes in attitude toward life and work. The process did little for reform, but it created a democratic, anticommunist opposition that Gorbachev could not control.[39]

Low productivity and unanswered internal disabilities that defied the reform effort could only accelerate the country's declining authority in world affairs. By 1987, Soviet analysts readily acknowledged the slow collapse of the Kremlin's global ambitions. In both capitalist and Third World countries, wrote Soviet external affairs specialist Aleksandr Bovin, "communist parties, with certain exceptions, have been unable to transform themselves into mass organizations and secure the support of the bulk of the working class and working people." Evgenii Primakov, director of the Soviet Institute of World Economics and International Relations, advised the Kremlin to cease all efforts to export revolution. For such Soviet commentators as Vladimir Pozner, the public admission of national restraints would render Soviet viewpoints more credible in the West.[40] Recognizing the steady contraction in the Soviet worldview, journalist Robert G. Kaiser advised Washington, "Mikhail Gorbachev had given us a new opportunity to redraw our image of the East-West confrontation. As he implicitly acknowledges, we are not really dealing with two equivalent giants. Not that we needed his new candor to realize how grave are Soviet weaknesses, or how unfavorable are the trends in that country."[41]

Glasnost added to Gorbachev's troubles by enabling the peoples of central Asia and the Caucasuses to rediscover their rebellious past and identify their current discontent with it. The recovery of historic memory reminded the nationalities that they had once risen against the Russian empire. Now that the U.S.S.R. was headed for an abyss, the past and present rejoined to create the conviction that destiny again lay in the nationalities. As early as December 1986, fighting erupted between Kazakhs and police in Alma-Ata. Gorbachev, in January 1987, recognized the problem of multi-ethnicity within the U.S.S.R. in an address before the Central Committee, but he recommended no revision of Soviet nationalities policy. For him the answer to ethnic discontent lay in the alleged fidelity of the Republics to the country's internationalist ideology. The Alma-Ata uprising was followed by two years of calm in central Asia. Then, beginning in December 1988 and continuing into 1989, violence erupted in the four central Asian Republics of Kazakhstan, Uzbekistan, Tajikistan, and Turkmenistan. In Kazakhstan the uprising resulted from resentment toward the Moscow politburo's efforts at Russianization; elsewhere the clashes displayed economic and social anxieties created by immigrants, largely from the Caucasuses. In February 1988, the soviet of Azerbaijan's autonomous region of Nagorno-Karabakh voted for annexation to Armenia. For the first time, Soviet deputies acted as representatives of the popular will rather than spokesmen of the central government. On August 9, 1989, the bloodiest clash of the Gorbachev era occurred in neighboring Tbilisi, the capital of Georgia, where Soviet troops dispersed a nonviolent crowd demanding independence. The Supreme Soviet suppressed the discontent with only partial success. For Moscow the nationalities problem had only begun.[42]

Not the least of the Soviet problems, after 1988, was the burgeoning spirit of independence among the Warsaw Pact allies. Much of eastern Europe refused any longer to be the sullen occupation zone of the U.S.S.R. The Kremlin had maintained extensive control over eastern Europe through the presence of its military forces, its command of energy and raw materials, and its network of contacts within the regional governments. But that control was no longer what it had been in previous decades. Behind the drive for greater self-determination was the persistent nationalism, as well as the quest for greater economic freedom, which rejected Soviet domination and ideology. Gorbachev appealed to eastern Europeans to accept his promise of a new Communist rule based on the moral and political legitimacy of Lenin. To eastern European economists and writers, however, Leninism required the ideological discipline that justified centralized authority; they looked to western Europe for the models that had given the West its obvious, greater prosperity.[43] Hungary led the assault on Soviet economic restraints. Mátyás Szűrös, secretary of the Hungarian Communist Party, challenged the Soviets openly in the Party's official publication. Because Moscow seemed incapable of creating "uniform solutions" to guide the policies of individual Communist parties and states, he wrote, it should adopt "methods that make optimum allowance for [national] characteristics."[44] Thousands of private companies, operating with the consent of Hungary's Communist government, gave Hungary an expanding economy, with attachments to the International Monetary Fund and a private offshore banking system that made it the Switzerland of eastern Europe. Gorbachev proclaimed Hungary the model for the Soviet bloc.

Poland remained tense. Its Solidarity movement, in quest of greater economic self-determination, continued to threaten the existence of Warsaw's Communist government. The East German regime, traditionally the most loyal to the Kremlin, was drawn westward by the need of West German credits. The Soviets, deeply concerned by such threatening attachments, obtained East German leader Eric Honecker's agreement to postpone a trip to West Germany in the summer of 1984. Even that agreement required five weeks of jockeying between Moscow and East Berlin.[45] Meanwhile, eastern Europeans sought to free themselves from the Soviet-American conflict. War offered only ruin.

The often-expressed eastern European desire for better relations with western Europe came not from intellectuals but from Communist Party leaders. The prime ministers of both Czechoslovakia and East Germany denounced the deployment of Soviet weapons on their soil; leading newspapers in both countries printed letters opposing the Soviet occupation. While the Kremlin criticized western European governments for accepting American theater weapons, Hungary welcomed state visits from three European leaders whose countries had accepted the missiles—Britain's Margaret Thatcher, Italy's Bettino Craxi, and West Germany's Helmut Kohl. Szűrös declared that détente among the countries of Europe should not rest on U.S.-Soviet relations alone. Hungarian leader Janos Kadar added, "[T]he small and medium-sized countries can do a lot for the maintenance of [the] dialogue [in Europe]."[46] On many issues, the countries of eastern Europe, historically at odds with one another, still found common ground with Moscow. They continued to move cautiously, desiring no showdowns with the Kremlin. Twenty years had not erased the memory of the Soviet invasion of Czechoslovakia in August 1968.[47] But, like China, the eastern Europeans were hardly trustworthy allies of the Kremlin. Indeed, two-thirds of the Communist-led peoples of the world looked to the West, not to the U.S.S.R., for support.

Outside the Soviet sphere, even small countries continued to stand up to the Soviets with amazing boldness. The concept of Finlandization assumed that the Soviets would acquire pervading influence over bordering states through the sheer magnitude of their military power, forcing those states to defer to Soviet wishes in a variety of ways. Actually, Finlandization turned out to be an empty myth. The Soviets failed to establish the credibility of their power simply because neighboring countries doubted that the U.S.S.R. had sufficient interest in exerting such influence over them to risk an open conflict through the threatened the use of force.

COST OF REAGAN'S ANTI-SOVIETISM

If changing internal conditions dealt harshly with the Soviet Union, they diminished the global position of the United States as well. The American economy remained the strongest in the world, but its relative decline, beginning in the 1960s, deflated its international role and compelled it to contemplate the fate of the great European states of modern history. President Reagan's initial decision to strengthen the nation economically and militarily with reduced taxes won widespread public approval and produced record-breaking prosperity. Rather than expanding and modernizing the nation's industrial plant, however, the new money underwrote the greatest speculative boom in American history, unprecedented federal deficits, and, ultimately, economic stagnation. What most contributed to the indifferent performance of the industrial sector and the decline in productivity in the 1980s was the heavy federal expenditure on military hardware. Defense appropriations favored aerospace, communications, and high-tech industries over steel, automobiles, machinery, chemicals, and other basic manufacturing. Greater profits seemed to lie more in military research and weapons development than in plant modernization and new industries. Whereas many of the leading American scientists worked on nuclear weapons and delivery systems, Japan's research effort expanded the frontiers of electronics while its new, innovative industries, supported by heavy investment, created the high-quality consumer products that captured the world. Similarly, West Germany, South Korea, Taiwan, Hong Kong, and Singapore devoted their energies and skills to the successful production of attractive goods for the global market. As Japanese and West German productivity soared, the impressive U.S. productivity gains of the early postwar years disappeared.

The decline in competitiveness, added to the reduction in agricultural exports, produced a trade imbalance of $160 billion by 1986. The bottom was not yet in sight. Meanwhile, federal deficits rose from approximately $60 billion in 1980 to over $200 billion by 1985. Defense spending was not the major reason for the annual deficits but rather the uncontrolled growth of entitlement payments. Whatever the reason, the federal debt doubled in those five years, from $914 billion to $1,823 billion. Such increases in national indebtedness in time of peace and prosperity had no precedent in history. Only the influx of foreign capital permitted the country to escape the normal consequences of such overspending. By 1987 the United States owed foreign creditors some $400 billion, a reversal from the positive balance of $141 billion in 1981. The United States had become the world's largest debtor, and the debt continued to grow. Great powers in the past had given up their international primacy to high debts and low economic growth— Spain in the sixteenth century, France in the eighteenth century, and Britain in the twentieth century. Every great power of modern times showed, historian Paul Kennedy wrote in *The Atlantic Monthly* of August 1987, "a significant correlation over the long term between production and revenue-raising capacity of the one hand and military strength on the other." For Kennedy, both the United States and the U.S.S.R. had suffered from imperial overstretch.[48]

Never in history did the strength of the leading powers remain constant over the decades, but the decline had generally been relative. Britain, far richer and stronger than it was during its prime as a world power, saw its world position disintegrate in the twentieth century. Citizens of the United States were far richer in 1988 than they were in 1950, but the country's relative decline eroded its unique capacity to sustain the status of world leader it enjoyed as late as 1960. In large measure, that decline reflected the remarkable success of the nation's postwar policies in rebuilding war torn Europe and Japan. The relative decline of the United States was inevitable, given the artificially predominant status that the United States enjoyed amid the ruins of 1945. That year the United States possessed almost half of the world's production; forty years later that share had slipped to less than 20 percent. Western Europe's GNP exceeded that of the United States; Japan's more than matched that of the Soviet Union.

Washington and Moscow, feeding each other's fears and insecurities, sustained an arms race that kept them in the military forefront, but it was a race that no other nation joined. Such behavior was not without precedent. In the past, countries with broad foreign commitments assigned more and more of their financial and industrial resources to defense even as their economies lost their competitive edge or their share of world production. Having lost their economic, political, and ideological primacy, they had nothing left to perpetuate their world standing except military power. It was scarcely conceivable that the United States would fall to a secondary position as did many of the great powers of history. Its share of world production, even at a reduced 18 percent, remained high. The country's geographical location, its size and resources, and its large and energetic population would sustain its role as a great power but hardly at the level of the Truman-Eisenhower era.[49]

Whatever its relative position in world politics, the United States required a military structure of sufficient magnitude and preparedness to discourage any open assault on the vital interests of the Western world. That deterrent—the greatest in human history—was apparently effective in the defense of external commitments where the world generally could assume an American resort to force. But such commitments no one would challenge. Short of war, the U.S. military establishment could not prevent a myriad of Soviet actions that fell below the threshold of a credible counterstrategy. It was not clear that twice the military power would have made any difference. Threats of retaliation have efficacy only where interests to be sustained by force are clear and strategic advantages unmistakable. All U.S.-Soviet clashes of purpose ended in stalemate simply because the power in the hands of both countries far outstripped the actual interests that they sought to defend. The principle of proportionality ruled out military responses.

Reagan's defense program could not curtail the Soviet-American arms race or terminate Soviet behavior in eastern Europe and the Third World that served as the initial rationale for the higher levels of preparedness. The record demonstrated repeatedly that few interests, places, or occasions would elicit the support of either the American people or the country's allies for a prolonged U.S. military involvement. Defense Secretary Weinberger recognized this reality when he told the National Press Club, in December 1984, that the United States should use military force only in defense of vital interests, only when such action commanded the support of the nation, and then only to win.[50]

Weinberger made no effort to define the nation's vital interests, for good reason. U.S. vital interests were far more limited than those suggested by the administration's anti-Soviet crusade. It achieved nothing to declare interests that no other country would take seriously or that the American people would not sustain at the level of a full national response. Largely unusable in the pursuit of day-to-day national objectives that were considerably less than vital, U.S. armaments could not remove the Soviets from Afghanistan, the Cubans from Angola, or the Syrians from Lebanon. The price of attempting to do so would challenge the country's rationality. Even great powers dared not squander their energies and prestige or act militarily where the requirements of success are questionable. As Ronald Steel warned, "We can dissipate our power by expending it on unattainable ends, demean it by using it unjustly, and trivialize it by applying it capriciously."[51]

As the Reagan defense expenditures moved toward $2 trillion by 1988, the president and his advisers declared that the United States could again "stand tall" in its world relationships. The administration had built its defense program and militant approach to the U.S.S.R. under the supposition that the Kremlin, under previous Washington administrations, had extended its authority dangerously into Africa, Latin America, and the Middle East. Through its alleged control of Ethiopia and Angola, Nicaragua and Cuba, and South Yemen and Afghanistan, it threatened to extend its control to vast regions of the world. In 1988 the president could boast that no territory had fallen to the Communists under his watch. In this triumph of containment there was nothing strange. Throughout the Cold War, the Soviet Union had gained nothing through military expansion; Afghanistan was no exception. Except for its status as a superpower, the U.S.S.R. had achieved nothing tangible from its enormous military expenditures. Nor did the extensive U.S. defense effort of the Reagan years provide Washington with new initiatives for managing international affairs. It was hardly designed to alter the policies of either friends or antagonists around the world. Indeed, the relationship of power to policy was difficult to discern. The very magnitude of American power seemed to militate against its use.

(L to R) Soviet Chairman Mikhail Gorbachev and President Reagan Sign INF Treaty. *Source:* Ronald Reagan Library.

Nuclear weapons had acquired a momentum of their own, backed by the imperative that a nuclear power must exploit the scientific knowledge and technological capabilities at its command. Nuclear arsenals reflected the assumption that a giant war was a constant possibility, requiring the construction and maintenance of huge quantities or such weapons. Washington officials assumed, moreover, that the buildup of the U.S. nuclear arsenal would not only contain Soviet expansionism but also intimidate, disrupt, and eventually compel the U.S.S.R. to accept some resolution of the Soviet-American conflict, largely on Western terms. Yet the possible scenario in which nuclear weapons would be used remained elusive.

No one could predict with any accuracy what impact several thousand nuclear explosions would have on human society. International politics needed, concluded Oxford historian Michael Howard, "to be conducted with the realization that the consequences of using these weapons, on however limited a scale, would be so appalling that no political or ideological objective could even justify such use." Nuclear weapons served, wrote Robert McNamara in September 1983, "no military purpose whatsoever, adding, "They are totally useless—except to deter one's opponent from using them."[52] In the absence of perceived dangers that would render the use of such destructive power feasible, nuclear weapons proved to be quite irrelevant to the task of encouraging Soviet or world conformity with American preferences.[53]

So massive were the constraints on the use of military force that even conventional power lost much of its efficacy for preventing or limiting unwanted international behavior. Few cared to contemplate the destructiveness of another conventional war. The continuing decline of public support for adventurous policies abroad, especially in the Third World, reinforced Washington's reluctance to unleash destructive force. The repeated catastrophe that befell the American armed forces, even when the power of the United States seemed unchallengeable, demonstrated the difficulty that any country, whatever its military prowess, invites when it chooses to fight where interests are unclear or of questionable validity. For too many Americans, official arguments in behalf of Third World ventures failed to carry conviction. That failure permitted the repeated defiance of American will, by Asians and others, to elevate the costs of involvement beyond what Congress and the American people would sustain. Any continuing military operation must convey its own necessity. Decisions that require the interminable explanations of government are generally doomed to failure; the reasons for fighting and dying must be more obvious than that.

However elusive the occasions for armed combat, U.S. power remained an essential element in international stability, especially as a guarantee against large-scale aggression. For forty years American power had underwritten Europe's remarkable postwar equilibrium. The European allies, therefore, never wished to see that power, and the commitment to its use significantly diminished. What troubled them was Washington's propensity to overspend for defense and thereby aggravate the nation's indebtedness and the economic disabilities that flowed from it. With that judgment most American agreed. Congress continued to support high levels of military spending to provide the replacement of essential equipment, as well as an array of new sophisticated weapons. Still, Senate reports suggested that the Reagan program of doubling the military budget increased the country's preparedness only marginally.

THE REAGAN-GORBACHEV DÉTENTE

Gorbachev continued his assault on international tension and the reliance on nuclear arms when he addressed the United Nations on December 7, 1988. In his speech, the Soviet leader declared that the internationalization of communications and economic life demanded cooperation among nations. In a world of universal interests there was no room for foreign relations based on ideology or force. Gorbachev's proclamation that the exercise of restraint in the use of force knew no exceptions suggested a changing Soviet role in eastern Europe, where forty years of Soviet dominance had been based on force. After ranging over the recent progress of international affairs, Gorbachev announced that the Soviet Union would unilaterally reduce the Soviet military forces by 500,000 men. With its Warsaw Pact allies it would withdraw and disband six tank divisions from East Germany, Czechoslovakia, and Hungary. On December 8, *The New York Times* editorialized, "Perhaps not since Woodrow Wilson presented his Fourteen Points in 1918 or since Franklin Roosevelt and Winston Churchill promulgated the Atlantic Charter in 1941 has a world figure demonstrated the vision Mikhail Gorbachev displayed yesterday at the United Nations."[54] Even as Gorbachev, in late 1988, reached the high point of his global leadership, his domestic crisis, unchecked by perestroika, presaged his retreat from the world stage and a passive response to the pressures building across eastern Europe.

For Reagan, the four summits with Gorbachev were the highlights of his presidency. Passing final judgment on those meetings in an address at the University of Virginia in December, the president anticipated the time when summits would become so commonplace that they would no longer attract attention. In their summitry, Reagan and Gorbachev agreed that the nuclear arms race had moved beyond any rational limit and had created a condition where any misstep could set off a calamitous war. Both men accepted the necessity of negotiation. Secretary Shultz made that negotiation possible by organizing the State Department into an effective force for dealing with Soviet issues at all levels. At the same time, his many meetings with Shevardnadze kept the negotiations moving toward tangible objectives such as arms limitation, regional conflict, and human rights. Even then, Shultz would have achieved little except for Shevardnadze's nonideological and optimistic support.

This transformation of U.S.-Soviet relations to a nonconfrontational approach was a remarkable achievement. Yet the new relationship remained more symbolic than real; it never included limitless trust or the negation of military defenses. Reagan advised the American people to limit their expectations. "We must," he cautioned, "continue to fulfill our own responsibility to stand firm and vigilant, to provide the incentive for a new Soviet policy in contrast to the old; for there still remain profound political and moral differences between the Soviet system and our own." If the American people, like Reagan, were not prepared to give the game away, they welcomed the new phase in U.S.-Soviet relations and expected it to run its course.

RESPONSE TO THE NEW DÉTENTE

So far had Reagan's declining Third World interests and the possibilities of a significant U.S.-Soviet arms agreements moved him from his initial posture of opposition to the U.S.S.R. that almost all of his early advisers on the right had left office. On June 1, 1987, Richard Perle gave up his position as assistant secretary of defense, followed by Secretary Weinberger in November. Fred C. Ikle, undersecretary of defense, resigned in January 1988.[55] With the appointment of Frank Carlucci as secretary of defense and

Colin L. Powell as national security adviser, the Reagan administration, for the first time in almost seven years, had three top advisers who were in general agreement. As one administration spokesman phrased it in March 1988, "Over the past three years we have established a broad, active, and quietly developing relationship, almost from a cold start in '85."[56] Pragmatists who dominated the foreign policy establishment understood that the United States not only had no choice but to coexist on the planet with the U.S.S.R. but also wielded no authority to change the Soviet system. They regarded Gorbachev a durable Soviet leader and agreed with him on the need of controlling the arms race. For them the improvement in U.S.-Soviet relations had been welcome.

The division within the country on Reagan-Gorbachev summitry was profound. Limited as it was, the INF treaty exposed all the fundamental doubts in American society regarding the nature of Gorbachev's world. For neoconservatives and members of the New Right the pronounced trends in the Reagan foreign policies after 1986 had been disquieting, if not dangerous. Among anti-Soviet hard-liners, inside and outside Washington, the ultimate Reagan triumphs had emerged with the Reagan Doctrine, followed in 1986 by the vote for contra aid, the warm White House welcome for Angola's Jonas Savimbi, and the destructive bombing of Libyan targets in response to Qaddafi's alleged terrorist activities in Europe. Such Third World triumphs seemed to assure a continued hard line on arms talks and SDI. Writers for whom past decisions meant salvation warned the administration against any departure from its previous noncompromising assault on every source of Soviet danger.

Neoconservatives took Gorbachev in stride by denying that he possessed the power, or even the intention, of modifying the Soviet system. Walter Laqueur averred in the October 1985 issue of *Commentary*, "[B]asic political reform...is not possible under the Soviet system." Gorbachev's economic reforms, added Laqueur, were evidence of the strength, not the failure, of Soviet totalitarianism; glasnost was merely the instrument through which Gorbachev was consolidating his power. Laqueur concluded in July 1988 that glasnost had reached its ultimate and would make no further advances.[57]

For some neoconservatives the Kremlin's external ambitions were equally fixed. In February 1987, Eugene Rostow warned his *Commentary* constituency that the "Soviet program of indefinite expansion achieved by the aggressive use of force...[remained] the central problem...of world politics and American national security." The Reagan buildup, he added, had not prevented the United States from falling further behind the U.S.S.R. "The Soviet Union," he concluded, "is a stronger military power than the United States, and...its military strength is growing more rapidly than ours, despite our rearmament efforts,...[Gorbachev] knows that it is now on the verge of achieving overwhelming strength." With the U.S.S.R.

approaching invincibility, he warned, any improvement in U.S.-Soviet
relations would be illusory. Arms agreements, noted Patrick Glynn as late
as March 1988, would "not only deepen... [American] vulnerability but
seal it for all time."[58] Columnist George F. Will was in the vanguard of the
New Right that condemned the president for his drift toward moderation.
Will repeatedly warned the administration against new initiatives in U.S.-
Soviet relations. In the absence of compatible interests and objectives, he
warned, they could only lead to disaster. Summit agreements, he reminded
Washington, were no measure of successful negotiations because they seldom expressed serious agreement. Will and much of the New Right had no
greater faith than the neoconservatives in Gorbachev's power or intention
to change the established pattern of Soviet repression and expansionism.[59]

Amid the increasingly bitter struggle for influence in Washington, the
continuing anti-Soviet crusade focused on Secretary Shultz. As early as August 1985, several conservative groups, including the Moral Majority, the
Conservative Caucus, the *Conservative Digest*, and the Committee for the
Survival of a Free Congress, all convening in Washington, mounted a campaign to remove Shultz for preempting and sabotaging what they termed the
true Reagan foreign policies of overthrowing the Sandinistas and avoiding
any damaging arms agreements with the Kremlin. Republican congressmen
demanded that the secretary appear before the House Republican Conference to answer the charges against him. Shultz, declared Representative Vin
Weber of Minnesota, had become a liability for the Republican administration. State Department spokesmen assured the critics that Shultz commanded a dominant position in the cabinet and was merely carrying out the
president's policies.[60]

Such efforts to perpetuate the hard-line presumptions of Soviet expansionism, against the ubiquitous evidences of change in both Moscow and
Washington, not only broke the neoconservative ranks but also alienated
Podhoretz and his *Commentary* supporters from their erstwhile political
allies—most notably Daniel Patrick Moynihan. Such earlier neoconservatives as Robert W. Tucker, Daniel Bell, Nathan Glazer, and Seymour Martin Lipset, like Moynihan, no longer contributed to *Commentary*.[61] Kirkpatrick's departure from the United Nations deprived neoconservatives of
a powerful voice in the administration. Assistant Secretary of State Elliott
Abrams continued his fight for the contras, but his limited efforts ended
with the Iran-contra scandal. After Reykjavik, the neoconservative crusade
against Gorbachev and arms control had no chance.

Reagan's critics continued to be stunned by what they termed his "dangerous illusions" of a new Soviet Union. Kirkpatrick accused him of deserting
a lifetime of caution regarding Soviet leaders. "Months ago," she wrote,
"George Shultz argued that Gorbachev was a new type of Soviet ruler. Reagan then resisted this view. Now he believes it." For Kirkpatrick, Gorbachev
remained a classical Leninist, skillful in the pursuit and use of power, totally

committed to the Soviet system and the one-party state, and not unduly critical of the high human cost of past Soviet policy.[62] Similarly George Will accused the president of "liquidating the anticommunist enterprise on the basis of negative evidence." Merely because Gorbachev had never publicly accepted the Marxist theory of the one-world communist state, he wrote, "[W]e are plunging into a restructuring of our strategic policy and sharply revising our moral rhetoric with a swiftness that suggests frivolousness." Former President Nixon joined Kirkpatrick and Will in warning the nation that Gorbachev's charm and agreeable style in no way changed the Kremlin's international goals.[63]

Nonetheless, Reagan departed the White House convinced that the Cold War was over, while Gorbachev awaited initiatives from the new president that would continue easing American-Soviet tensions.

CHAPTER 7

The Vanishing Cold War

When George H. W. Bush entered the presidency in January 1989, the Cold War was receding into history, but he was slow to acknowledge its demise. He was not alone. For many Americans the summitry of the late Reagan years reflected no fundamental change in Soviet-American relations. Former Secretary of State Henry A. Kissinger warned the nation in February to avoid the naiveté of assuming that an American president could make meaningful deals with Soviet leaders at the personal level. Mikhail Gorbachev's moderation was, for Kissinger, no demonstration that the Kremlin had deserted its expansionist ambitions.

BUSH CONSIDERS HIS OPTIONS

The new president agreed. He initially sought to slow down the momentum of U.S.-Soviet relations and emphasized the continued need of vigilance and strength in dealing with the Kremlin. The previous June when Reagan on a summit in Moscow retracted his characterization of the Soviet Union as an "evil empire", Bush responded to reporters, "The Cold War isn't over." The following month he warned against a "euphoric, naively optimistic view about what . . . [would come] next" and was privately concerned by Reagan's "sentimentality" toward Gorbachev.[1]

In December 1988, Reagan and Bush met the Soviet leader in New York. When the president-elect sought assurance that his perestroika and glasnost programs would succeed, an irritated Gorbachev replied, "Not even Jesus Christ knows the answer to that question. . . . I know what the people are telling you." He continued:

(L to R) President George H.W. Bush, General Brent Scrowcroft (USAF, ret.), his National Security Adviser and the President's Chief of Staff John Sununu. *Source:* George Bush Presidential Library.

[N]ow that you've won the election, you've got to go slow, you've got to be careful, you've got to review, that you can't trust us, that we're doing all this for show. You'll see soon enough that I'm not doing this for show, and I'm not doing this to undermine you or surprise you or take advantage of you.

I'm engaged in real politics. I'm doing this because I need to. I'm doing this because there's a revolution taking place in my country. I started it. And they all applauded me when I started it in 1986, and now they don't like it so much. But it's going to be a revolution nonetheless.[2]

After his inaugural, Bush and his Secretary of State, James Baker, agreed that new presidents in the past had gotten into trouble by moving too quickly. It would be better to get a solid grasp of the status of Soviet-American relations before opening formal discussions with Moscow. That month National Security Adviser Brent Scowcroft was even more cautious as he advised the country that the West should keep up its guard because Gorbachev could be a new version of the "clever bear syndrome"—similar to Brezhnev's efforts to lull the West into a false sense of safety while pressing expansionist objectives. Such suspicions of the Kremlin also characterized the outlook of his deputy, Robert M. Gates, as well as Defense Secretary Richard Cheney and Soviet experts in the CIA.

At his first new conference on January 27, the president was quizzed about Scowcroft's earlier pessimistic observation, "I think the Cold War is not over." Bush responded that he did not want to use the phrase "Cold War" because it failed to "properly give credit to the advances" that had "taken place in this relationship." He continued, "Do we still have problems, are there still uncertainties, are we still unsure of our predictions on Soviet intentions? I'd have to say, 'Yeah, we should be cautious.'"[3]

Clearly the new administration entered office intending to move cautiously in U.S.-Soviet relations. Events, however, would soon push Bush and Gorbachev into another close relationship.

SOVIET RULE IN EASTERN EUROPE UNRAVELS

Suddenly in the closing months of 1989 the Soviet world began to unravel, threatening key arrangements that had defined the U.S. role in European affairs. The dramatic and unanticipated assault on the established order began in Poland with the triumph of Lech Walesa's Solidarity movement. Solidarity's earlier attempt to challenge Poland's Communist structure fell to martial law in 1981, but the movement continued to gather strength until, by 1989, it forced the Communist leadership, weakened and discouraged by its own ineffectiveness, into retreat. When the June election placed the Communist regime on the ropes, the Kremlin made no effort to prevent its fall. Thereafter the demise of Communist governments came with amazing speed. All were artificial creations of the Soviet Union, with no popular bases of support.

Nowhere had Soviet ideology successfully challenged the force of regional nationalism. Global television revealed the stark contrasts between the failures of communism and the triumphs of Western democracy. When asked to explain the fall of communism across eastern Europe, Walesa simply pointed to a TV set.[4] The communications revolution had broken the information barrier, providing eastern Europeans the knowledge on which to act. The mere withdrawal of Soviet power exposed all Communist eastern European governments to immediate destruction.

In May, Hungary dismantled its border with Austria, enabling thousands of migrating East Germans to cross the open border and venture on into West Germany. When the East German government attempted to halt the exodus, it succeeded only in unleashing an uncontrollable protest, centering in Leipzig. Long regarded as the most successful of the European Communist states, the German Democratic Republic was decrepit and bankrupt.[5] In October, the opposition movement, New Forum, drove Communist leader Erich Honecker from power. In one long week of early November, Germans scaled the Berlin Wall, dooming East Germany's Communist regime. Meanwhile, in October, the Hungarian parliament abolished the ruling Communist Party and amended the 1949 constitution to prepare the country for the promised parliamentary elections. The spreading upheaval quickly toppled Todor Zhivkov, Bulgaria's Stalinist leader for thirty-five years. In

Czechoslovakia, anti-riot police broke up student demonstrations until, on November 20, anti-government rallies sent 200,000 through the streets of Prague. The country's Communist leaders quickly retreated before such displays of popular disapproval. By the end of December, Czechoslovakia's persecuted playwright, Vaclav Havel, had become president. Rumania's Nicolai Ceausescu defied the winds of revolt until, on December 21, he lost control of his army. Four days later he and his wife faced a summary trial and execution. Soviet troops remained in eastern Europe, but the Soviet bloc ceased to exist.[6] Foreign observers understood that the Soviet satellite empire of eastern Europe was lagging economically, but only the lifting of the Iron Curtain revealed how poor had its economic performance been and how dismal its standard of living. The price of Communist rule had been horrendous, creating economic challenges that lay beyond the immediate power of the new national governments to resolve. Before 1939, Czech prosperity was approximately equal to that of Italy and Austria; after four decades of communism its standard of living, though still the best in eastern Europe, was scarcely a third of Austria's.[7] For forty years countries such as Poland, East Germany, and Czechoslovakia had maintained obsolete, coal-burning factories, turned out shoddy, noncompetitive, subsidized goods, and sustained workers without marketable skills.

For decades the Communist governments of eastern Europe had shielded the effects of pollution from external gaze. The industrial zones poured out poisonous gases and toxic dust in abundance, producing widespread cancer, lung and heart diseases, eye and skin ailments, asthma, emphysema, pneumonia, and shortened lives. One-third of Poland's population lived in areas of ecological disaster.[8] In Bitterfeld, south of Berlin, towering smokestacks released plumes of bright yellow, jet black, and hazy brown smoke, scattering sulfur dioxide over the countryside. Bitterfeld was not the only major polluter of an industrial belt stretching eastward from southern East Germany through Poland and northern Czechoslovakia.[9]

For forty years the state defended the populace from the normal consequences of low productivity with cheap housing and subsidies in profusion. Any shift to a free market would eliminate not only countless nonproductive jobs but also the full spectrum of public subsidies that made life possible. Rising prices outstripped the desired productivity and assured only further destitution. For countless eastern Europeans, whose habits and attitudes rendered them incapable of surviving successfully in a competitive economy, that price of freedom was too high. "The freedom we wanted," wrote Czech scholar Erazim Kohák, "was freedom from care, freedom from responsibility. We wanted to be free of reality's persistent demands." A popular joke observed that the Czechs wanted "to consume like the Germans, be provided for like the Swedes, and work like the Russians."[10] Much of the eastern European populace saw only disaster in free market pricing for food, clothing, housing, and energy. By early 1990, low productivity and empty shelves sent prices soaring, placing many necessities beyond reach. No longer able to afford gasoline, thousands of Polish car owners turned in their license plates.[11] The major cities of eastern Europe quickly spawned large homeless populations. Hungarian officials predicted that, by the end of 1990, the loss of central planning would render 100,000 Hungarians unemployed.

Unfortunately, a populace cast adrift by communism's collapse, and struggling for survival in a dreaded competitive environment, was scarcely prepared to create a democratic, free market paradise. With the exception of Czechoslovakia, the countries of eastern Europe had never been political imitations of the Western states. Their democratic governments were always weak institutionally, with little public involvement. By the end of the 1930s, all except that of Czechoslovakia had instituted centralized governments. The postcommunist regimes confronted barriers to democratic rule even more profoundly. The implications of democracy, with its accent on skills, effort, and personal responsibility, were scarcely appealing to people who had long relied on governmental dispensations for survival. Everywhere the alliances that fought to remove the old Soviet-backed regimes succumbed to public disillusionment. The intellectuals who led the march from communism were too utopian in their perceptions of democracy to seize and maintain power; they were not prepared for the disagreement and tension that characterized the democratic process.

While elites and foreign observers proclaimed the coming triumph of democracy, the reality was confusion, detachment, demagoguery, and often the return to power of former Communists. Political parties that might have created national unity and purpose were nonexistent. Only Hungary produced a coalition government; the other countries spawned largely authoritarian regimes. One Polish leader complained, "Achieving democracy seemed so simple. But, in fact, it's like building a house from the roof down."[12]

Events in eastern Europe marked a sea change in the long ideological struggle between collectivism and liberalism. Francis Fukuyama, a State Department official, attributed the victory of political and economic liberalism to "the total exhaustion of viable systematic alternatives." So complete, he believed, was the ultimate victory for liberalism that it constituted the end of the political struggles that had raged for two centuries. Liberalism had emerged as the ideal that would soon govern the entire industrial world.[13] Still, amid the political and economic turmoil that characterized the eastern European scene, Western liberalism's ultimate triumph was far from certain. There were other alternatives to collectivism.[14]

As eastern Europeans weighed the attractions of Western economic institutions, they contemplated not only laissez-faire capitalism but also various forms of social democracy, with their protections against the ravages of the free market. Indeed, in early 1990 eastern European governments regarded the price of free market reform exorbitant. East Germany's new government made no basic decisions. Change meant lower living standards for most

citizens; for that no one wanted to take responsibility. Still, price liberalization and privatization were the only apparent alternatives to continued
economic stagnation. The International Monetary Fund dictated the move
toward privatization by making it the criterion for Western credits. Poland
ventured slowly into a program of privatization; Czechoslovakia, Hungary,
and Bulgaria followed. It mattered little. Eastern Europeans everywhere continued to experience the resulting pain of unemployment and rising prices.[15]
In February 1990 a leading Polish publisher recorded the impact of economic
change on his country:

> You'd think we could bask in our glorious triumph these days. But the fact
> is that we're facing an absolute catastrophe—especially those of us involved
> in Polish culture. It's a terrible paradox: we are quickly becoming the victims
> of the free market we fought to establish. Prices have shot up enormously
> for everything—food, housing, energy. But salaries are strictly controlled. So
> during the month of January people's standard of living dropped fifteen per
> cent, and this month it still appears to be falling sharply.[16]

Gorbachev's promise of December 1988—to abjure the use of force in
pursuing external objectives—set the standard for Soviet behavior in the
political upheavals of 1989. The U.S.S.R. still possessed military capabilities
only marginally reduced from those of previous years; it commanded the
power to halt the processes of change at their inception. But a half-decade
of rising demands for political and economic self-determination had taken
their toll on Soviet energy and will. For Gorbachev, the price of Soviet
impositions on the peoples of eastern Europe had become both physically
and morally exorbitant. The time had arrived to terminate the Soviet Union's
hegemonic rule.[17]

In repealing the Brezhnev Doctrine that a Communist state could not renounce communism, Gorbachev had invited the eastern Europeans to revolt.
At the end, the Soviet leader encouraged the disintegration of the Soviet empire. As the events in eastern Europe saturated the Soviet press, the collapse
of the Soviet hegemony created no public outcry. For most Soviet citizens
the domination of eastern Europe never served any fundamental, even rec-
ognizable, Soviet interests. Determined to deal with the Kremlin on their
own terms, eastern European leaders, especially those of Poland, Hungary,
and Czechoslovakia, demanded the withdrawal of Soviet forces and termination of the Warsaw Pact as the essential conditions for establishing normal
relations with the U.S.S.R. By March 1990, Soviet forces began to leave.[18]

GERMAN UNIFICATION

Unlike the other states of eastern Europe, the German Democratic Republic had no tradition of nationhood. Self-determination for East Germany recommended German reunification. As the East German Communist regime

crumbled in November 1989, huge demonstrations urged reunification with West Germany. On November 28, West German Chancellor Helmut Kohl seized the initiative by unveiling a plan for a confederation of the two German states that would lead ultimately to a united nation. Polls in the United States and Britain favored German unification overwhelmingly, those in France less so. Those who supported unification presumed that a united Germany would avoid the mistakes of the past. Some argued that unification would enable East Germany to cope with the economic and political wreckage of Communist rule.[19]

The French were not alone in questioning the wisdom of Germany's immediate unification. Many Europeans, among them Germans, feared that a Germany of eighty million people would again dominate Europe. Germany posed no military threat, but its economy seemed sufficient to elevate the country to superpower status, with the possibility that it would become a detriment to itself and the rest of Europe. Some pointed to the apparent revival of German nationalism and wondered whether anything had changed. Gunter Grass, the noted German novelist, warned against reunification. "[N]o one of sound mind and memory," he wrote, "can ever again permit such a concentration of power in the heart of Europe."[20]

Kohl acknowledged the still-existing rights of the four occupying powers—Britain, France, the United States, and the U.S.S.R—over the future of Germany. Britain's Margaret Thatcher announced in January that East Germany should remain independent until the final democratization of eastern Europe, perhaps for ten years. With that judgment French President Francois Mitterand agreed. President Bush favored unification as a right but insisted that a unified Germany be tied to the West economically, politically, and militarily. Whether Germany remained in NATO was, to Bush, a German decision. For forty years Soviet control of East Germany had assured either a divided or a neutralized Germany. With East Germany now independent, Gorbachev asked only that German unification not come before the Soviet Union had received all necessary security guarantees.[21]

Secretary of State James Baker was determined to retain Germany's membership in NATO. In Moscow, on February 8, he reminded Gorbachev that a neutral Germany would be free to develop nuclear weapons. Then he offered Moscow a special assurance: "There would be no extension of NATO's current jurisdiction eastward." West German foreign minister, Hans-Dietrich Genscher, had urged Baker to offer the Soviets this special guarantee on NATO's eastward expansion. Gorbachev informed Baker that any extension of NATO's jurisdiction was unacceptable. The secretary agreed. U.S. Ambassador Jack F. Matlock, no less than Soviet officials, took that promise seriously. But before Baker left Moscow he received White House instructions to pursue a different plan: all German territory would be in NATO, but only German forces would be stationed in East Germany. Gorbachev accepted that arrangement and thereby gave some sanction to

NATO expansion. The two sides never discussed the possibility that Poland, Hungary, or other Central European states might one day enter NATO.[22] At the Ottawa Foreign Ministers Conference of February 1990, the four occupying powers, as well as the two Germanies, accepted the so-called two-plus-four formula under which the two Germanies would negotiate all internal reunification issues. The four powers would resolve all external aspects of German unity.

Kohl moved quickly to exploit the favorable international environment for German unification with a trip to Moscow. There, in Genscher's words, the chancellor made an offer that Gorbachev could not refuse. It included German financial support for the 380,000 Soviet forces remaining in East Germany, forces supported by the East German government at the cost of $400 million a year. If the Soviets withdrew their forces from Germany by 1995, Kohl agreed to reduce the West German army 50 percent by the end of the century. Finally, Kohl promised to honor all East German contracts with Moscow and purchase Soviet uranium on the world market to replace shipments from East Germany.[23]

At the March two-plus-four talks in Bonn, the delegations quickly acknowledged Poland's demands that Germany offer guarantees on the future of the Polish-German border. At the Potsdam Conference of 1945, Poland had received part of Germany as compensation for the loss of eastern Poland to the U.S.S.R. Thereafter it relied on Moscow to protect its new western border. With the collapse of the Soviet hegemony in Eastern Europe, the Warsaw government feared that a united Germany might reclaim its lost territory. Under pressure, Kohl agreed to grant Poland the assurance that a united Germany would make no territorial demands on Poland. At the same time he asked for guarantees that Warsaw would make no demands on Germany for reparations covering the forced labor of Poles during the Third Reich. On March 8, the German Bundestag passed a resolution urging both Germanies to forswear any claims to Polish territory even before formal unification. The four occupying powers agreed that Poland have a voice in any German decision that affected its future.[24]

During March the prospects for German unification seemed propitious. The East German elections that month brought to power a coalition government that favored a rapidly unified Germany, with close ties to the West. On May 18, the two Germanies signed a treaty for currency, economic, and social union, to become effective in July. The remaining barrier to unification lay in the Kremlin's refusal to permit a united Germany within NATO, an arrangement demanded by Britain, France, and the United States, as well as the two Germanies. In April, President Bush rejected the Soviet compromise proposal of German membership in both NATO and the Warsaw Pact.[25] On May 5, the foreign ministers of the two Germanies as well as Britain, France, the United States, and the U.S.S.R. gathered in Bonn. They quickly agreed that German unification must proceed rapidly, but Soviet minister Eduard A. Shevardnadze announced that his government, having lost its Warsaw allies, would bargain hard to protect its security interests in any further negotiations. He asserted that German membership in NATO would seriously affect Soviet security interests, violate the European balance of power, and create, for the U.S.S.R., a dangerous military-strategic situation. Shevardnadze assured the other ministers that the Kremlin wished unity for the German nation, but the Soviet Union, he reminded them, still possessed its victor's rights in Germany.

At Bonn, Baker sought no more than a formula by which the ministers might "terminate and transfer all remaining four-power rights and responsibilities to a fully sovereign Germany." The allies could discuss specific military and security issues, but their resolution, he repeated, depended on appropriate negotiations in other forums, especially between Bonn and Moscow. The four powers, he hoped, would make their final settlement regarding their rights and responsibilities at the foreign minister's meeting, scheduled for July in Paris. To counter arguments that Soviet security required Soviet forces in East Germany, Baker proposed a treaty on reducing conventional forces across Europe. He traveled to Moscow in May to negotiate such an arrangement with Gorbachev but soon discovered that the Kremlin was not prepared to compromise the Soviet Union's military power along its western frontiers. Soviet leaders, moreover, warned the secretary against unleashing the opposition of the Soviet military, conservative politicians, and ordinary citizens to German unification by demanding German membership in NATO.[26]

Speaking in Ottawa on May 30, Gorbachev expressed the hope that the West would not attempt to frame a European security system based on a unified Germany in NATO. At the same time Gorbachev's German policy adviser, Nikolai Portugalov, informed Hamburg's *Die Welt* that his government demanded total military reciprocity with the United States in any German settlement. Moscow's 380,000 troops would remain in East Germany as long as the Western powers maintained forces in West Germany.[27]

Meanwhile, on the eve of the Bush-Gorbachev summit, scheduled to open in Washington on May 31, the president assured a Soviet television audience that the U.S. presence in Europe, with a unified Germany in NATO, comprised no threat to the Soviet Union and would preserve the European stability that the Soviet peoples should welcome. After hours of fruitless discussions in Washington, the president tried a new approach. He reminded Gorbachev that under principles of the Conference of Security and Cooperation in Europe, especially its Stockholm Agreement of 1986, all countries had the right to choose their own alliance. Gorbachev agreed. "The United States and the U.S.S.R.," he responded, "are in favor of Germany deciding herself in which alliance she would like to participate," following a two-plus-four settlement. Bush acknowledged that the United States advocated Germany's membership in NATO, but was prepared to accept any German decision. Again Gorbachev approved. The issue of NATO membership was closed.[28]

During July, following further negotiations with Kohl, Gorbachev consented to German membership in NATO. Kohl agreed to limit German weaponry and military manpower and to permit Soviet troops to remain in East Germany for several years. That month the two-plus-four discussions produced an agreement that guaranteed Poland's existing western border along the Oder-Neisse line. On August 21, the two Germanies signed a Treaty of Unification; the German Democratic Republic was absorbed into the Federal Republic of Germany, an agreement already approved by East German voters in March. On September 12, the former Allied powers of World War II—the United States, Britain, France, and the Soviet Union—terminated the responsibility they had exercised over Berlin since 1945. This act granted full sovereignty to the newly united nation.

The treaty on the final settlement provided for German membership in NATO, set limits on future German troop levels, and prohibited Germany's acquisition of nuclear, biological, and chemical weapons. With the treaty's ratification on October 3, a sovereign and united German came into existence. The U.S. Senate ratified the treaty a week later by a vote of ninety-eight to zero. Finally, on November 14, the Polish-German Border Treaty recognized, as permanent, the line separating Poland and Germany. This German guarantee eliminated at last the perennial antagonism between the two countries.[29] For the Bush administration, the resolution of the German unification and Polish boundary issues was a major triumph. The new, enlarged Germany regained its sovereignty, not as a neutral, unattached power in the heart of Europe, free to impose on its neighbors, but as a country firmly limited in its ambitions and behavior by its membership in NATO.

Kohl's success in setting the agenda for German unification elevated him to a primary position in Europe's political order. Anticipating the resentment that would flow from Germany's unification on almost purely German terms, Kohl sought to balance his window of opportunity with care not to offend Europe's other powers. Still, his very triumph was sufficient to engender bitterness, resentment, and ever fear. Kohl had his way with Britain and France in part because the Bush administration decided early that U.S. interests in Europe demanded cooperation with western Europe's most powerful state. Kohl had his way with Gorbachev as well, largely because of Germany's wealth and power to buy the Soviet forces out of East Germany and provide other forms of financial aid. With unification, Germany moved into a leadership position in Europe, permitting Kohl to dominate the European agenda. German economic power was beginning to cast a shadow over Europe much as Soviet military power had done earlier. Germany's capacity to outstrip Britain and France, as well as the other nations of Europe, seemed to open the vast power vacuum of eastern Europe to German economic expansion, if not ultimate domination. Nicholas Ridley, a member of the

British cabinet, warned that Germany intended to dominate all Europe, as had Hitler. His observation expressed the fears of some Europeans, but it raised a storm of protest in the London government. Ridley resigned and apologized.[30]

Helmut Kohl's triumphant unification of Germany was a dramatic measure of the Soviet decline. For forty years the prevention of a united Germany in the Western bloc was the core of Soviet foreign policy.

THE FALTERING SOVIET ECONOMY

By 1990 the Soviet economy was at the razor's edge. If the collapse of communism created economic havoc across eastern Europe, its impact on the Soviet economy was even severer. For the first time in forty-five years the Soviet economy, in 1990, experienced a fall in both industrial and agricultural production. The drop in industrial output was especially disastrous in the metallurgical and energy sectors, as both oil and coal production fell sharply. Gorbachev's program of glasnost had exposed these failures to public scrutiny. He recognized the country's economic disabilities and the need to improve the Soviet economic system, to render it more humane and acceptable. His ambitious reforms, however, were designed only to reform the Communist system, not to transform the system into one that addressed the consumer demands and desires of the population. He limited his proposals to what the Communist establishment would accept.[31] Meanwhile, the Soviet economy continued on its downward course.

Equally bankrupt was the Soviet political system. By 1990 the Communist Party was a moribund organization, more concerned with its prerogatives than its traditional role of mobilizing society. At the same time, the Soviet authoritarian political system was more and more incompatible with the desire of a better-educated population for policy innovations, civil rights, and individual freedoms. The growing irrelevance of the political structure, even under Gorbachev's leadership, seemed incapable of meeting the country's pervading economic crisis. As early as January 1990, Gorbachev accepted the end of the Communist Party's monopoly on political power, leaving the way open for a multiparty system and, with it, greater flexibility in meeting the country's economic problems. Clearly, the opening of a multiparty system was no panacea. To prevent complete disorder and anarchy, the Soviet leadership adopted a new constitution that fashioned a Western-looking presidential form of government, with a legalized multiparty political system.[32]

In March, Gorbachev chose to have himself elected president by a discredited parliament of which he was not a member. As the discontented again spilled into the streets, Gorbachev could claim no popular mandate for his authority. He pledged to use his new powers to improve the economy, but he had little to offer. The self-imposed limits on his economic initiatives remained enormous. A cartoon of Gorbachev and a sailor standing on the deck of a sinking ship carried this caption: "Captain Gorbachev, the gala to celebrate your vastly increased authority has been moved to the lifeboat."[33]

Unable to resolve the contradiction between his boldness in fostering glasnost and his paralyzing timidity in rejecting perestroika, Gorbachev searched for greater economic efficiency by mobilizing the new professional classes to design and lead the movement for economic reform. He refused, however, to concede his presidential role as the final arbiter. Soviet economic reformers agreed that nothing short of a basically free enterprise, market-oriented economy could gear the economic system to consumer demands and produce the desired national well-being—a truly radical reorientation of the Soviet economy. Without such reforms, declared Gorbachev's senior economic adviser, in April, the Soviet Union had "no future as a highly developed power," adding, "It is all a disaster. You name it. . . . It is in shambles."

The central economic challenge in the Soviet Union lay in the pricing structure that assigned low prices to food and basic consumer goods. To remove price controls on necessities would produce skyrocketing inflation and extensive hardship. Deputy Prime Minister Leonid Abalkin, a leading free market reformer, acknowledged that the opposition to change was so pervading that genuine reform could come only gradually.[34]

Gorbachev already had economic reform programs before him; one prepared by his economic adviser, Nikolai Petrakov, promised significant change and a stronger economy. Gorbachev refused to accept it. Then, on May 22, he and the Council of Ministers announced a comprehensive five-year reform that would end in a "regulated market economy." That phrase left the future of reform in doubt but the government, to the delight of economists, promised to raise prices on food and utilities to establish some equilibrium in the economy and reduce the budget deficit. The announcement was sufficient to overwhelm the Soviet distributive system and trigger a surge of hyperinflation.

Meanwhile, Gorbachev turned to a highly respected economist, Stanislav Shatalin, who during August hammered out a program known as the Shatalin Five Hundred Day Plan. It called for successive steps in the selling of state property and the freeing of prices on nonstaple consumer goods, all directed at the establishment of a free market economy. In October, Gorbachev rejected Shatalin's "500-Day" plan. He understood correctly that it would have destroyed the Kremlin's control of the Soviet economy by shifting too much power, including that of taxation, to the republics. Later that month, Gorbachev announced the postponement of further market reform.[35]

Boris Yeltsin, a provincial Party leader, but not a member of Gorbachev's original reform circle, was convinced that the old Soviet system could not be reformed. He emerged as the country's chief spokesman for free market reform and Gorbachev's chief political rival. He readily adopted the radical 500-day reform program of privatization and free marketization. Economists warned him that he could achieve the needed market reforms only by bringing prices into line with real costs and by closing unprofitable factories. Gorbachev had brought Yeltsin to Moscow in the second wave of reformers, many of whom ultimately broke their ties with the Soviet leader over the issue of economic reform. As early as May, Yeltsin defied Gorbachev directly by winning election as president of the Russian Republic. Recognizing that he was no more than the chairman of the Russian Supreme Soviet Legislature, an honorary title, Yeltsin called for direct election of the Russian president in two years.[36]

Even as Gorbachev struggled to preserve the Soviet political and economic structure, by late 1990 almost every semblance of the U.S.S.R., which had lasted for seventy years, was fading into history. Gorbachev's had been a lost cause; even the existence of his own government was in doubt. It was misleading to view the Soviet Union as a single state therefore decreed by history and tradition to remain united. Actually, the U.S.S.R. was an empire in the process of decolonization. It comprised over one hundred ethnic and language groups, all held together by the raw power of the Communist Party. Independence from Kremlin control was not synonymous with democratic self-determination as it could lead as well to violence, tyranny, and repression. The looming retreat of Kremlin authority unleashed long pent-up nationalist demands for self-determination across much of the Soviet Union. For this Gorbachev was unprepared.

THE RISE OF NATIONALISM

In January 1990, Pope John Paul II warned eastern European states to recognize that their pursuit of self-determination could unleash bitter, internecine ethnic conflicts. Already Bulgaria's long anti-Turkish crusade had deprived the Turkish minority of its traditional rights, among them the use of the Turkish language. So deep were the Slav-Turkish animosities that thousands of Turks fled to Turkey only to find economic conditions there so depressed that they were compelled to return. Still they doubted that the Bulgarians would ever accept them. In Transylvania, the Rumanians never ceased their war on Hungarian culture after they received the territory in 1920. In March 1990, clashes between Rumanians and ethnic Hungarians in the Transylvanian city of Tirgu-Mures, a center of Hungarian culture, left six dead and 300 injured.[37]

Two factors had held Yugoslavia together: Marshal Tito's success, before his death in 1980, in warring against the country's divisive nationalisms, and, second, the country's general prosperity. Serbs, Muslims, and Croats intermarried with little concern for nationality. By eastern European standards, Yugoslavia was open, modern, and cosmopolitan. But by 1990 ethnic and nationalist pressures threatened to tear the country apart. In March 1989, the Serbian government took control of autonomous Kosovo, with its ethnic Albanians, raising fears of Serbian expansionism throughout Yugoslavia. In April 1990, the tiny Slovenia, Yugoslavia's richest province at the edge of the Alps, voted to eliminate Communist rule, demand its independence, and slash its contributions to the Yugoslav government.[38] Also in 1990, the rich northern province of Croatia elected a noncommunist government and demanded greater autonomy from Serbia.

Slobodan Milošević, elected president of Serbia in December 1990, met the challenge by unleashing an effective expansionist nationalism against the other Yugoslav republics. Milošević demonized Serbia's ethnic rivals, especially the Croats who, as Hitler's allies, slaughtered hundreds of thousands of Serbs. The Croats and Slovenes met Serb nationalism head-on with a powerful nationalist resistance of their own. The Serb minority in Croatia, troubled by the rise of Croatian nationalism, feared a repetition of the mistreatment they received from the Croatians during World War II. Without some agreement between Serbs and Croatians, Yugoslavia had no future.

LITHUANIA'S INDEPENDENCE MOVEMENT

Nationalist efforts to escape Moscow's direct authority began in January 1990 with Lithuania's independence movement. Already the secessionist urge had encompassed Ukraine, Georgia, Estonia, and Latvia, but Lithuania was a special case. Taken by the U.S.S.R. under the Nazi-Soviet Pact of 1939, the Kremlin had a stronger claim to Lithuania than to the occupied states of eastern Europe. But Lithuania's strong appeal in the West vastly strengthened its claim to independence. Lithuania gave Gorbachev the choice between permitting it to go in peace or placing his entire foreign policy with the West at risk. Unchallenged, Lithuania could loosen an avalanche of émigré republics, bringing down the fragile Soviet economy, if not the regime itself. Knowing that such secessionism could be his undoing, Gorbachev sought to terminate the process of Soviet disintegration by meeting the Lithuanians head-on. He pleaded with them to trust him and preserve their union with the U.S.S.R.[39] He reminded Lithuanians that their country, far more than those in eastern Europe, was fused to the Soviet economy and political structure, its factories managed by Soviet ministries, burning Soviet oil, producing goods for Soviet customers.

Many members of the Lithuanian workforce were ethnic Russians. Politically, therefore, the departure of Lithuania would be far more perilous for the Gorbachev government than the upheavals in eastern Europe. "My personal fate," Gorbachev acknowledged, "is linked to this choice." How could the Soviets hold their empire together without resorting to imperial massacre? Gorbachev assured the Lithuanians that he would not use force against their right to self-determination.[40]

Unmoved by Gorbachev's appeal, the Lithuanian parliament, on March 11, issued a declaration of independence. Despite Gorbachev's earlier dismissal of force, Soviet military vehicles streamed into Vilnius, the Lithuanian capital. Gorbachev demanded that Lithuania rescind its declaration of independence. Lithuanian leaders assured Gorbachev that the Lithuanian parliament desired no more than a gradual transfer of power and suggested a negotiated settlement. As the crisis deepened, Gorbachev warned Estonia to back off from its threatened challenge to Soviet domination. He then turned on Lithuania, accused it of acting unconstitutionally and illegally, and imposed a crippling economic blockade that compelled the Lithuanians to come to terms.[41]

In May 1990, Yeltsin declared that Russia no longer would be subordinated to the Kremlin's central authority. "Our state, our country," he said, "will only be strong if the republics are strong."[42] Yeltsin warned the Kremlin that Russia might use its constitutional right to secede from the U.S.S.R. if Gorbachev blocked its determination to establish its sovereignty. During subsequent months the intensification of nationalist pressures exposed dangers that defied solution.

GORBACHEV'S AUTHORITY DECLINES

By late 1990, the twin challenges of nationalism and economic collapse, both unanswered and apparently unanswerable, threatened the very existence of the U.S.S.R. Deserted by his reform-minded followers, Gorbachev faced rejection of his leadership on the right as well. Shatalin's plan for the transition to a free market became the catalyst for mounting disenchantment among senior military officers and Party technocrats who directed the defense industries, the still-dominant sector of the Soviet economy, over the many evidences of shrinking Soviet power and prestige. The 500-day plan focused the inchoate resentments at the breakdown of law and order, the damaging economic dislocations, the shortages of food, the continuing threat of Baltic separatism, and the emergence of guerrilla warfare between ethnic groups in the Balkans and the Caucasus. For such critics the country's acceptance of German unification under NATO was a needless reversal of Stalin's great wartime victory. This vanguard on the right could not present an acceptable plan of its own; there was little support for a return to a centrally planned economy or a reimposition of authoritarian political control.[43] The promise of a new order in the U.S.S.R. was too pervading to permit any permanent return of the old guard to power.

Still convinced that state socialism would work, Gorbachev sought refuge among moderates who favored genuine reform but within limitations imposed by the old Communist structure. Unfortunately, moderates of that description were almost nonexistent. With his political authority dwindling, and resentful of the reformers who had deserted him, Gorbachev turned in desperation to the still-powerful Party apparatus, the military forces, the defense industries, and the KGB. In mid-December, 543 Soviet military and industrial leaders called for tough measures to preserve the Soviet Union's Communist structure and geographical integrity. That month hard-liner Colonel Petrushenko proclaimed, "[T]he struggle is now caught between the two camps we have in this country: the democrats and the patriots. The democrats have had their day. We, the patriots, will now dictate the future direction of the country."[44]

To meet the crisis, Gorbachev asked for and received vast new powers to restrict the press and impose rigid controls to protect the Soviet economy against pro-market encroachments. Troubled by Gorbachev's decision to embrace the old guard and accede to various forms of repression, Foreign Minister Eduard Shevardnadze, in December, announced his resignation in an emotional speech to the Soviet parliament. Democracy, he warned, was receding; dictatorship was coming.[45] Of the original team of Soviet reformers, Shevardnadze was among the last to leave.

THE BUSH ADMINISTRATION'S REACTION

Washington reacted to the challenge of a disintegrating Soviet empire with remarkable restraint. It was clear that the Soviet decline offered unprecedented possibilities for imaginative policy, but the administration seemed torn between its desire to support Gorbachev and assumptions that the Cold War was not really ending and that the United States should continue to concentrate on its defenses. The president presumed, moreover, that any improvement in American-Soviet relations mattered far more to the Soviet Union than to the United States. When, on May 12, he unveiled the results of the administration's long policy review at Texas A&M University, he had no new initiatives to offer beyond asking the Kremlin to "tear down the Iron Curtain" and permit the emigration from eastern Europe to continue. He affirmed his purpose of building a more stable relationship with the U.S.S.R. but added that the United States intended to "defend American interests in light of the enduring reality of Soviet military power." But Secretary Baker, following his September conversations with Shevardnadze at his Wyoming ranch in the Grand Tetons, concluded that the administration should strengthen its relations with the Soviet leaders. Similarly *The New York Times* wondered how it could not be in the Western interest to support Gorbachev's decisions to reduce the Soviet armed forces and permit freedoms in eastern Europe—objectives that the West had long demanded and spent trillions to achieve.[46] Not until the Berlin Wall came down in November did the president, as well as Americans generally, understand that Gorbachev was no traditional Soviet leader.

After weeks of temporizing, Bush, in early December, approached the Malta summit with Gorbachev with the acknowledgement that Western interests depended on the success of Gorbachev's leadership. With winds howling and waves crashing in a wild Mediterranean storm, the two leaders met aboard the Soviet cruise liner *Maxim Gorky*. At Gorbachev's invitation, the president opened the discussion with a fifty-minute gambit in which he spelled out a twenty-point program. During subsequent sessions, Bush and Gorbachev defined an ambitious program for cooperation and speedy progress on arms control, enhanced trade relations, and a Washington summit in June 1990 where the two powers would conclude agreements to reduce their arsenals of nuclear weapons. The meeting was congenial, but Bush and his advisers resisted reporters' invitations to declare the Cold War over. At a final press conference, Gorbachev declared, "[T]he world is leaving an era of cold war and entering another. This is just the beginning . . . of a long peaceful period." Bush responded, "Now, with reform under way in the Soviet Union, we stand at the threshold of brand new era in U.S.-Soviet relations."[47]

U.S. AID FOR EASTERN EUROPE?

President Bush's response to the triumph of self-determination in eastern Europe and the looming collapse of the Soviet economy was generally passive, with no soaring rhetoric, exultation, or bold initiatives. The changes, after all, conformed to perennial Western desires. The president refused to make the eastern European revolutions a subject of controversy in U.S.-Soviet relations.[48] With the new governments facing intractable political and economic problems, the president's passivity brought a storm of protest from Congress and the press. Republican Senator Robert Dole of Kansas suggested a diversion of foreign aid funds from Israel and Egypt to the states of eastern Europe. Democratic Congressman and House majority leader Richard Gephardt of Missouri noted that the administration had offered less money to the newly-freed nations than the cost of one major savings and loan bailout. Also, he pointed out that the United States in 1989 spent $125 billion to defend western Europe. Senator Bill Bradley of New Jersey observed that the United States could build valuable goodwill by offering eastern Europe a modified Marshall Plan. Columnist David Broder, on March 21, complained that the Bush administration could do more than encourage voluntary efforts to aid the countries of eastern Europe. Private organizations, such as the U.S. Chamber of Commerce, the American Bar Association, and the International Executive Service Corps were helping. All of this, Broder concluded, was commendable, but it did not measure up to the needs of eastern Europe or the opportunities confronting the United States.[49]

Bush's Washington was not moved. With his public approval soaring to 80 percent, the president's cautious approach to the challenges of eastern Europe and the U.S.S.R. reflected a public mood that recognized no foreign threats and was no longer concerned with events abroad.[50] National indebtedness and opposition to new taxes intensified the administration disinterest in offering large sums of money to eastern Europe. Most Western countries moved quickly with multibillion-dollar programs to aid Europe's fledgling democracies. But the Bush administration, even after being pressed by the Democratic Congress, requested a paltry grant of $500 million for eastern Europe, less than one-twelfth of what Germany provided.

For the State Department, that region no longer mattered. Secretary Baker explained why he opposed a shift in the budget from defense to aid: the American people would pay taxes for defense but not for aid. In July, economist Henry Kaufman concluded that the country's huge deficits and rejection of new taxes simply ruled out any extensive U.S. investments in eastern Europe. "The European Development Bank," he wrote, "will extend credits but not give grants. Thus it is not clear that the Eastern European countries are going to obtain the aid they need."[51]

Repeatedly the president declared that U.S. relations with the Soviet Union hinged on Gorbachev's success. Yet he opposed any aid to the U.S.S.R. and threatened to boycott the new East European Bank if it extended major loans to that country. One Treasury official explained, "For U.S. taxpayers to finance lending to the Soviet Union is not politically acceptable." Czech president Vaclav Havel urged economic aid for the U.S.S.R. with the argument, "You can help us most of all if you help the Soviet Union on its irreversible but immensely complicated road to democracy." Many who recognized the failures of Gorbachev's halfway measures argued that it was all the more important that the United States help the Soviet leader build a bridge across the chaos to a better tomorrow.[52] But when Congressman Richard Gephardt suggested an aggressive program of helping the Soviet Union make the transition from communism to democracy, even if it seemed to the Kremlin's advantage, Republican Senator Alan K. Simpson of Wyoming retorted that two-thirds of the American people opposed substantial aid to the Soviet Union. The administration added that the Kremlin's problem was not shortages but poor distribution and the wasting of money on armaments and foreign expenditures. Others suggested that, in primitive markets, foreign aid and investments offered little promise of success. For such members of the American right as Patrick J. Buchanan, any aid to communist-controlled governments would simply be wasted.[53]

HARD-LINERS DOUBT REVOLUTIONARY CHANGES

To some doubtful Americans the revolutionary changes within the Soviet bloc were no guarantee of Western security. Robert Gates, deputy national security adviser, and other high Washington officials, regarded Gorbachev untrustworthy and incapable of holding power sufficiently to merit the confidence of the United States. One hard-liner, writing as "Z" in *Daedalus*, the journal of the American Academy of Arts and Sciences, warned that Gorbachev had no intention of liquidating the Communist system and its inherent expansionism.[54]

Paul H. Nitze acknowledged in January 1990 that the events of 1989 discredited the communist presumption that Marxist-Leninist ideology was destined for worldwide acceptance. But he advised his readers in *The Washington Post* that the Soviet Communist structure, with its heavy concentration of power, continued to assure Soviet leaders of a sense of identity and purpose, and convince them that they possessed a superior organization for managing and conducting international conflict. This, for Nitze, accounted for Gorbachev's determination to preserve the Communist organization, while deferring the long-term ideological struggle with the West and awaiting the return of conditions that would give Communist parties "a decisive edge in dealing with a potentially fragmented world." Any threat of the reimposition of Communist discipline would demand America's unambiguous opposition even at the price of chaos and disruption within the Soviet Union. The president himself warned in February, "It is important not to let these encouraging changes, political and military, lull us into a sense of complacency. Nor can we let down our guard against a worldwide threat.... Military challenges to democracy persist in every hemisphere."[55]

LITHUANIAN INDEPENDENCE CRISIS

The administration approached the issue of Lithuanian independence cautiously, knowing that the country had neither the interest nor the will to rescue the Baltic state from Soviet force. Bush hoped to achieve a reluctant Soviet recognition of Lithuanian independence. "That," declared one senior U.S. official, "requires a negotiating process that's likely to take months before anyone can tell where it's going, and for the United States to rush in with heavy-handed statements will only make it harder for both sides to work their way through this."[56]

Bush reminded Gorbachev, in late March, of his promise not to use force; he praised the U.S.S.R. for its ongoing constraint. European leaders were even more cautious, fearing that a showdown over Lithuania could unhinge the whole process of bringing self-determination to eastern Europe.[57] Simultaneously, Senator Edward M. Kennedy of Massachusetts, after a trip to the Soviet Union, informed the President that Gorbachev had complained that Western devotion to Lithuania undermined the reform effort in the U.S.S.R. Gorbachev, Kennedy added, faced intense pressure within the Soviet Union to retain Lithuania.

Such reports convinced the White House that further criticism from Washington would merely encourage the Lithuanians and create a crisis in U.S.-Soviet relations. The president understood that the Soviet threat to regional peace receded with Gorbachev's successes, not his failures.[58] On April 11

Bush and Gorbachev meet at Malta on December 1, 1989, to discuss trade and arms control. *Source:* George Bush Presidential Library.

after long effort, Baltic-American leaders received an audience with the president, but Bush denied their request for U.S. recognition of Lithuanian independence. Following the session, White House spokesman Marlin Fitzwater informed the press: "Our policy, we believe, is the correct one, and it does not involve recognition." Bush repeated his support for self-determination, but added, "The U.S. must avoid taking actions that would inadvertently make Lithuania's task more difficult by inflaming the situation." The president had no interest in repeating the fiasco of 1956 when the United States encouraged the Hungarian uprising and then stood by helplessly as Soviet forces crushed the rebellion.[59]

CONTINUING SUPPORT OF GORBACHEV

Although Gorbachev's authority seemed to be disintegrating, the Bush administration continued to acknowledge him as a commanding and necessary figure on the international stage. It anticipated successful negotiations at the coming Washington summit. But for proponents of American anticommunist orthodoxy, Gorbachev and his reform efforts remained an aberration, compelled by adverse circumstances.[60] With economic recovery, they warned, the U.S.S.R. would resume its aggressive behavior and re-create a Cold War world of tension and insecurity. It seemed essential, therefore, that the United States exploit Soviet vulnerabilities to its own advantage, that it confront the Kremlin aggressively and not seek compromises that merely perpetuated old illusions of power. Critics rejected the administration's contention that the United States faced the choice between Gorbachev and the return of Communist hard-liners and thus the wisdom of placing all hopes for the U.S.S.R. on the Soviet leader. Rather, some charged, Gorbachev had become an impediment to reform and therefore dispensable. "Conservatives," observed Representative Dana Rohrabacher of California, "do not see keeping Gorbachev in power a laudable goal. Most see him as communism's last gasp."[61] Meanwhile, the administration's commitment to Gorbachev seemed to prevent it from pressing its advantages against Soviet weakness. Bush brushed aside suggestions that Gorbachev would come to Washington, weakened by his unanswered political and economic troubles. "It is not a question of who is stronger, who is weaker," he said, "[It is a question of trying] to convince him where we differ that our position is correct, just as he will be trying to convince me." *The Washington Post* advised the administration to deal forthrightly with Gorbachev as he addressed the immense task of managing Europe's transition to the post-Cold War era.[62]

THE 1990 WASHINGTON CONFERENCE

Gorbachev arrived in Washington on May 30, beleaguered and profoundly unpopular at home but determined to sustain his image of confidence, enthusiasm, and authority. He jumped out of his limousine to work the crowds on New York Avenue. Observers noted, however, that he was defensive and elusive, especially at his luncheon speech at the Soviet embassy. He responded curtly to suggestions that the Soviet Union had become enfeebled and vulnerable. About the evidences of instability, he said, "[They] are just an indication of the fundamental nature of reform. Talk of weakness is just not serious."[63] He chided those who criticized his regime because of its failures in achieving economic reform. "For Americans," he declared, "it is all so easy. You have all the mechanisms and institutions in place." In the Soviet Union, he complained, there had been nothing resembling a free market economy in decades.

Actually, unlike his Soviet audiences who continually challenged him, his U.S. listeners demonstrated great respect for him. Gorbachev had reason to be delighted at the Washington crowds who gathered to see him. The president welcomed him at a White House ceremony on the South Lawn and then praised him for his role in the momentous events of the previous year. He invited Gorbachev to join him "to further the process of building a new Europe, one in which every nation's security is strengthened and no nation is threatened." Gorbachev, in response, paid tribute to the passing

Cold War and the end of "prejudice, mistrust, and animosity."[64] Despite the continuing ambivalence in U.S.-Soviet relations, the summit was a remarkable success. The two leaders concluded agreements that revealed their countries' mutual interests in trade expansion and weapons reduction. They signed protocols on verification of nuclear testing that permitted ratification of earlier testing limitations. They established a framework for future nuclear arms reductions—the signing of SALT III in August 1991. One agreement reduced the arsenals of chemical weapons of both countries by 80 percent—the Chemical Weapons Convention signed in January 1993.

Several routine agreements provided for increased exchanges of university students, the establishment of cultural centers, joint oceanic studies, cooperation in the peaceful uses of nuclear energy, expansion of civil aviation, and long-term Soviet importation of grain. Reflecting the changing international climate, the familiar diatribes on regional conflicts and human rights violations no longer dominated the exchanges. With the assumption of greater mutuality of interests, the Bush-Gorbachev discussions included transworld issues such as ecology, terrorism, global economic challenges, drug trafficking, health, and peacekeeping.[65]

WHEN DID THE COLD WAR END?

At the Washington summit, U.S. leaders still hesitated to acknowledge the ending of the Cold War. But the NATO summit's London Declaration of July 6, 1990, proclaimed the Cold War's demise. The Atlantic community, in building a new partnership with all the countries of Europe, would now extend to former adversaries "the hand of friendship." The London meeting proposed to Warsaw Pact members a joint declaration which stated, "[W]e are no longer adversaries and reaffirm our intention to refrain...from acting in any other manner inconsistent with the purpose and principles of the United Nations Charter." The declaration invited the Warsaw Pact nations to come to NATO, establish diplomatic liaisons with its members, and enter reciprocal pledges of nonaggression and against use of force. As the Soviet forces withdrew from eastern Europe, NATO would field smaller, restructured active forces, reduce its nuclear deterrents, eliminate all nuclear artillery shells, and diminish its reliance on nuclear weapons. Gorbachev praised the London Declaration for its promise of a peaceful, unified Europe.[66]

At the pan-European Paris summit on November 19, 1990, Gorbachev, Bush and other European leaders signed a treaty for the reduction of conventional forces in Europe (CFE), despite the continued opposition of Soviet army commanders. The CFE pact removed the fear of a conventional war in Europe—the last major obstacle to the ending of the Cold War. While some have called the Paris summit the formal end to Cold War, one might also choose the dismantling of the Berlin Wall in the late autumn of 1989 or formal reunification of Germany in October 1990 as the end of the forty-year contest.

Whatever the date, the end of the Cold War left a general uncertainty of what would fill the vacuum. Throughout the decades of the Cold War the country's special role assumed the presence of an archenemy, recognized as dangerous by much of the external world. But Mikhail Gorbachev's withdrawal from the old East-West rivalry eliminated the face-offs that had, as the *New Yorker* observed, "automatically yielded us a more sharply defined sense of ourselves in relation to a belligerent, untrustworthy Soviet Union." It went on to say,

> They gave us a gratifying self-image, and an important, dramatic place in the world. In contrast, Gorbachev's actions threatened to deprive us of an identity.... [W]e become less the defender of the free world and more a nation among nations. We lose a role, we lose a script, we lose a language by which we have come to be known to others and to ourselves.[67]

Even with future unknown, the world rejoiced that the Cold War had ended with a whimper, not a mushroom cloud.

CHAPTER 8

In Retrospect

Throughout the last years of the Cold War, the Soviet-American conflict rested on the assumption that it remained the supreme phenomenon of international life, dwarfing all other regional and national causes. Washington's view of the world discerned in the U.S.S.R.—a huge country towering over the Eurasian continent, backed by a massive military machine and driven by a crusading ideology, determined to dominate much of the world. Secretary of the Army John O. Marsh described the danger in precisely such terms when he addressed a Richmond audience in April 1984: "This century has seen the birth of a new colossus, one driven by an alien ideology. It draws its strength from the force of arms. It has waged ruthless aggression on its neighbor states. From its Eurasian power base, the Soviet Union now leapfrogs its power to the four corners of the globe, and threatens the peace of an insecure world."

What sustained this presumption of imminent danger was the dual conviction that the U.S.S.R. continued to dominate some areas of U.S.-Soviet military competition, and was in large measure responsible for the specific pressures that threatened the stability of Africa, the Middle East, and Central America. In this global confrontation the United States provided the non-Soviet world its essential defense against the expansion of Soviet power and influence. For some Americans the Soviet-American antagonism remained a zero sum game in which one power would ultimately succumb to the will of the other.

Somehow such depictions of global confrontation scarcely reflected the realities of the existing international order. The fundamental supposition that the military might of the United States carried the essential responsibility for the limitation of Soviet ambition sustained, over time, the country's multitrillion-dollar defense expenditures, but it ignored the role of other nations, whether acting independently or in combination, as factors in international stability. Every country, large and small, defended its interests against predators. Nowhere did the dominoes fall in accordance with the predictions of Communist expansion. Long after the invasion of Afghanistan, the Soviets were not in the Persian Gulf or in possession of Middle Eastern oil but, predictably, were seeking a graceful escape from their torment. The real world of sovereign nations was tougher, more resilient and more resistant to unwanted change than one portrayed by the image of a world endangered by a bipolar antagonism between two superpowers. Indeed, in that world every fundamental trend warred against the concept of bipolarity. The very assumption that two countries dominated world politics was scarcely reassuring to most peoples and governments.

THE CHASM BETWEEN POWER AND PURPOSE

The broadening chasm between national power and national purpose exposed the essential nature of the Soviet-American Cold War. Unlike major international conflicts of the past, that between the United States and the U.S.S.R. revealed no areas where the two powers were mutually and unmistakably in open conflict, rendering war predictable. Through more than forty years of Cold War, Washington officials insisted that the Soviet-American rivalry flowed from the nature of the Moscow regime and its global ambitions, demanding ever-increasing military preparedness. Yet despite the fears that sustained their ponderous rivalry, the Soviet danger remained so imprecise that no one could define it. Rhetorically, the Soviet threat was global, but nowhere—not in Europe, the Middle East, Asia, Africa, or Latin America—did the Soviets reveal any ambition or interest of sufficient importance to merit a resort to military force or a showdown with the United States. Nowhere did the Kremlin threaten direct military aggression against any region regarded vital to the security of the United States and its Western allies. George Kennan reminded a Washington audience, in November 1983, of the absence of specific dangers in the Soviet-American conflict. "There are no considerations of policy—no aspirations, no ambitions, no anxieties, no defensive impulses," he said, "that could justify the continuation of this dreadful situation."

For some analysts the world of the 1980s was similar to that of 1914, with the leading powers arming for a war that nobody wanted and over issues that few considered critical. "We are trapped," wrote Thomas Powers in the January 1984 issue of *The Atlantic Monthly*, "in a tightening spiral of fear and hostility. We don't know why we have got into this situation, we don't know how to get out of it, and we have not found the humility to admit we don't know. In desperation, we simply try to manage our enmity from day to day."

During the Reagan years, the Soviet-American rivalry in the Third World carried the chief burden of national insecurity and superpower conflict. There subversion and revolution seemed to offer the Kremlin untold opportunities to extend its influence at the expense of the West. Revolutions, invariably indigenous and historic, permit little gain to those who support them. The very nationalistic impulses and objectives that unleashed the postwar upheavals across the Afro-Asian world erected formidable barriers against external influences, whether they emanated from the United States or the Soviet Union. Confronted with such determined resistance, Washington and Moscow could not establish any control over Asian or African affairs commensurate with their efforts. Thus Washington's counterrevolutionary program, aimed at the containment of Soviet expansionism, never engaged the U.S.S.R. because the success or failure of Third World revolutions never constituted any interest, Soviet or American, whose pursuit was worth the risk of war. The Kremlin's reluctance to expose its troops to death and destruction in regions beyond the Soviet Union's periphery measured its limited interests in the Third World.

Soviet challenges to American will in Asia, Africa, and the Caribbean had little relevance to Soviet strategic capabilities; the Kremlin, in practice, limited its ambitions to what its exports of weapons and advisers could achieve. For Gorbachev, even this Soviet investment had become excessive and counterproductive. Too often it supported Marxist governments that lacked legitimacy, faced persistent and costly guerrilla insurrections, drained the Soviet economy, and appeared incapable of resolving acute economic and political problems. Such aid, in prolonging unwanted revolutionary activity, antagonized neighbors and diminished Soviet influence in key non-Marxist developing countries that offered far greater commercial, diplomatic, and geostrategic rewards.[1] Gorbachev, moreover, regarded the U.S.-Soviet rivalry in the Third World unnecessarily damaging to desired superpower cooperation.

With each passing year, the United States and the U.S.S.R. faced a growing diffusion of international resistance, marked by the determination of nations to define and defend their interests and to stand against the pretensions of others. Whatever its comparative power, no country can long exert its will against a world of sovereign states without coming up against the preferences of nations that, even under the threat of violence, will concede very little. Countries can exert their will only against the insecure; the world in general had no reason to fear either the United States or the Soviet Union. Soviet dominance never extended beyond the reach of Soviet armies; similarly the United States controlled its own territory and little else. Outside that limited realm, Washington could argue; it could not compel.

Facing profound disagreements on basic definitions of national interest, Washington less and less sought or received European support for its global decisions. Throughout the Third World states behaved no less independently. Even where the United States stationed large armies over long periods of time, as in South Korea and the Philippines, it gained little influence. High levels of economic and military aid brought few concessions from Israel, Egypt, and Chile. Countries inside and outside Europe dealt with the United States and each other largely on their own terms. For them the Soviet-American conflict was generally irrelevant.

In only one respect did the United States and the Soviet Union maintain their global predominance, and that was in the area of nuclear and conventional military power. It was their capacity to ruin the world, not manage it, that sustained the illusion of a globe overshadowed by the Cold War. In every other respect the international activity and competition that mattered was not between them at all. In world trade and investment the leading players were the United States, the countries of western Europe, and Japan, with the U.S.S.R. lagging far behind. In the UN General Assembly, Third World blocs almost eliminated both the United States and the U.S.S.R. as dominant forces in the organization. Long before the 1980s, Washington and Moscow faced a solid nonaligned bloc of more than one hundred countries that neither could control. Jeane Kirkpatrick, while chief U.S. delegate to the United Nations, characterized the American position in the world body as "essentially impotent, without influence, heavily outvoted, and isolated." On some important issues, the United States, deserted even by its European allies, was reduced to a minority of one. If the votes in the General Assembly did not reflect the actual distribution of military and economic power in the world, they did reveal the almost total absence of Soviet and American ideological influence among the world's nations.

The Cold War's perennial failure to dominate the behavior, outlook, and material progress of international society limited its impact on world politics. Common interests in trade, investment and other forms of international activity governed international life far more than did the fears of Soviet aggression and war. The flourishing of world commerce after mid-century was totally without precedent. By most standards of human progress, the forty years of Cold War comprised the most pervading, most prosperous, golden age for modern societies in history.

The prodigious investment in human and physical resources assumed a fundamental international security that, despite the recurrence of limited crises, permitted the evolution of the complex, technology-driven Western civilization that emerged during the age of the Cold War. The forces underwriting international stability seemed dominant enough to sustain the material gains of the age, symbolized graphically by the changing skyline of every major city in the Western world. Even as the perennial Cold War rhetoric warned insistently that the country and the world were in danger of global Communist conquest, every modern nation built with the confidence that its civilization was secure, and none more so than the United States itself.

WHAT PROMPTED THE END OF THE COLD WAR?

Citizens and historians have long questioned—after more than forty years of Cold War rivalry—what was responsible for its end? Among the causes most often put forward has been that of the technical and economic challenges posed by the Reagan administration's extensive arms buildup. It was, and is, argued that Soviet Union's economic malaise, caused by its efforts to match the U.S. military spending, prompted Kremlin leaders to surrender.

An undercurrent of thinking during the Reagan presidency, especially during the first term, held that expanding America's defense spending and exploiting its technological advantages, especially the Strategic Defense Initiative, would cause the competitive Soviet economy to falter and bring the Cold War to an end. This view gained brief support in the immediate afterglow of the Soviet Union's collapse when Tom Wicker, a critic of the administration, agreed that Reagan's SDI program and the extensive military buildup had forced the Soviets to reexamine their international and domestic policies.

For English author Paul Johnson the vulnerability of the Soviet Union demonstrated the magnitude of the Reagan triumph. The Reagan rearmament program had demoralized the Soviet elite and forced it to embark on the "risky and potentially disastrous road to reform." For Reagan's secretary of defense, Caspar Weinberger, what produced the U.S.S.R.'s collapse was the capacity and willingness of the administration to outspend the Soviets and thereby exhaust their resources and capabilities. Peter Schweizer, another Reagan bureaucrat, averred that the Pentagon's buildup convinced the Kremlin that it lacked the financial resources to sustain its global Cold War with the United States. "Reagan's policies," he concluded, "were absolutely critical to the demise of their system." Unfortunately for former Cold War hawks and neoconservatives, this view is not sustained by available data.[2]

Another writer speculated, "Gorbachev's fear of SDI's potential [was] the driving force behind his willingness to accept deep and unprecedented cuts in the Soviet Union's nuclear arsenal." However, in the early 1970s Soviet scientists had recognized the enormous technical difficulties of creating a shield against missiles, each carrying independently targeted multiple warheads, in the near term. At that time they demonstrated that adding inexpensive decoys to each of its missiles could overcome even sophisticated antimissile defenses, thus prompting the Kremlin's endorsement of the 1972 Anti-Ballistic Missile Treaty. Foreign Minister Gromyko angrily denounced Reagan's SDI program because he believed that an extensive American ABM system could enhance its ability to launch a first strike, a threat that the administration's rhetoric appeared to enhance. He urged threatening a "tit-for-tat" weapons response. Additionally, the Kremlin feared the SDI program would initiate the placing of nuclear weapons in space and create another arms race.

Senior Soviet scientists Yevgeny Velikhov and Andrei Kokoshin, around the same time, provided a very different point of view. Calling the SDI an improbable venture, they contributed significantly to strategic debates in the mid-1980s by choosing to ignore the demand for weapons parity and emphasizing the idea of an "asymmetric response." This policy involved a realistic appraisal of SDI's limits and the relative ease of introducing inexpensive countermeasures to defeat it.[3] Gorbachev agreed and ceased his concern.

The Soviet Union's economic malaise, while undoubtedly deepened by 25 percent of GNP being continuously set aside for the military-industrial complex, has been more properly attributed to the rigid "command economy" system established in the 1930s. Production and investment decisions were in the hands of a centralized bureaucracy that could ignore market factors, competition, and individual or collectives initiatives. Contemporary Western observers, moreover, underestimated the Soviet military-industrial complex's dominant role in controlling Soviet expenditures and its ability to resist Soviet leader's efforts at reform. "Soviet defense spending under Brezhnev and Gorbachev was primarily a response to internal imperatives [and was] not correlated with American defense spending," according to Lebow and Stein, "Nor is there any observable relationship between the defense spending and changes in the political relationship between the superpowers."[4] This was because the Kremlin had no reason to fear the United States. The Reagan buildup never conveyed a threat of war; it dangled in a policy vacuum. If anything, the expanded defense program enabled the Soviet military establishment to sustain its pressures on the Kremlin.

The persistent claim of the Cold War hawks and neoconservatives that America's foreign policy—grounded on the pursuit of military superiority—achieved victory in the Cold War is, in Professor Robert English's considered assessment, "greatly oversimplified." He suggests the Reagan military buildup, coupled with the administration's aggressive rhetoric, actually "made the accession of genuine reformist leadership much more difficult. The effort to tilt the military balance sharply in the West's favor certainly heightened Soviet perceptions of deepening problems and a need for a change." The contention, however, that the military buildup and the Star Wars program caused the Soviet system to collapse, English argues, reflects "a lapse in basic counterfactual reasoning, if not an even more deterministic triumphalism."[5]

WHO ENDED THE COLD WAR: REAGAN OR GORBACHEV?

Leaving Washington hours after George H.W. Bush was sworn in, Reagan declared flatly, "The Cold War is over." Weeks ahead of most policymakers, the American public grasped that the Cold War was over after hearing Gorbachev's December 1988 speech at the United Nations. Public opinion polls revealed that 54 percent of Americans now considered the Soviets to be either "no threat" or "only a minor threat", while 60 odd percent believed the Soviets now were essentially focused on their own security, and only 28 percent thought they were still seeking world domination. Frances Fitzgerald summed it up best: "Gorbachev launched a political revolution in the Soviet Union. Few in Washington understood what he was doing or where he was going, and the Cold War was over before the American policy establishment knew it."[6]

Ambassador Jack F. Matlock, Jr., Reagan's former expert on Soviet affairs, has argued that individuals who give the American president full credit for ending the Cold War do so "out of a sense of partisanship".[7] And those who extend total credit to Gorbachev fall into the same trap. How to apportion the credit is still in the hands of the historical jury, yet it is possible to reach an interim judgment.

Reagan's Contribution

Not until the middle of the 1946, when he became president of the Screen Actors Guild during a strike against producers, had Reagan become concerned about communism, especially Hollywood's communists. He was deeply affected reading Whittaker Chamber's account *Witness* where he apparently picked up the notion of the Kremlin being the focus of evil in the world—and later wound it up in his "Evil Empire" speech. After he stood against communism during the House Un-American Activities Committee hearing the following year, Reagan became convinced that he was one of the truly blacklisted victims because his roles virtually disappeared. "There is no question," he told Cannon, "my career suffered from [my] anticommunism."

"I know of no leader of the Soviet Union... including the present leadership," President Reagan declared in his initial press conference on January 29, 1981, "[who denied that] their goal must be the promotion of world revolution and a one-world Socialist or Communist state.... [And since these leaders] have openly and publicly declared that the only morality they recognize is what will further their cause... [and] reserve unto themselves the right to commit any crime, to lie, to cheat... [to gain that goal; thus, when you] do business with them... keep that in mind."

Reagan's strong conviction that Communism was inherently immoral and evil was matched by his fascination with the dramatic biblical story of Armageddon—the world's final struggle between good and evil. As he apparently understood the account, "Russia would be defeated by an acclaimed leader of the West who would be revealed as the Antichrist. He, too, would fall, and Jesus Christ would triumph in the creation of 'a new heaven and a new earth.'" The Armageddon story that Reagan envisioned as a nuclear holocaust never reconciled him to the possibility of nuclear war; indeed, he declared often, "A nuclear war can never be won, and must never be fought." It was prudent, Reagan believed, to seek means to avert or mitigate such a possibility by the elimination of nuclear weaponry, which he eventually came to believe could be accomplished by missile defenses designed to provide a nationwide shield.

The president did shift away from his initial diplomatically inconsiderate and provocative anti-Soviet rhetoric during his second term, especially after meeting Gorbachev. In his final years in the White House, Reagan came to think of Mikhail Gorbachev as a friend and proclaimed a "new era" in American-Soviet relations. Reagan had changed, according to his biographer Lou Cannon, "even though he did not recognize any ideological odyssey."

"The purpose of a negotiation is to get an agreement," the president once declared, yet he found it difficult to even marginally compromise the Star Wars program that was, at best, very far in the future. This rigidity, together with his administration's rigid adherence to the institutionalized precepts of the Cold War, prevented the formulation of realistic policies to substantially reduce nuclear weapons.[8] "It became a cruel irony of fate that President Reagan's desire to banish the nuclear specter on the one hand opened up the prospect for nuclear disarmament," Raymond Garthoff has rightly observed, "while foreclosing it with the other through stubborn dedication to the quixotic pursuit of his SDI illusion."

Nevertheless, former Pentagon official Richard Perle attributed the passing of the Cold War to U.S. nuclear and conventional military superiority that compelled the Soviet leadership "to choose a less bellicose, less menacing approach to international politics," saying, "We're witnessing the rewards of the Reagan policy of firmness." To Harvard historian Richard Pipes, Ronald Reagan was the champion of those who believed the Soviet Union "a totalitarian state driven by a militant ideology and hence intrinsically expansionist." For Pipes, no less than for hard-liners generally, it was the "policy of containment, reinforced by a technological arms race, economic denial, and psychological warfare, that brought down the Soviet Union and communism." Pipes was convinced that the hard-liners had emerged triumphant.[9]

But Pipes' consequent assault on those who favored a more modest response to Soviet behavior ignored the close relationship between official public condemnation and silence in the absence of affordable policy choices. Hard-line official rhetoric committed the United States to nothing—and for good reason. Library shelves were replete with writings of leading Soviet experts, both American and European, who described and analyzed the continuing internal weaknesses of the U.S.S.R., without reference to the United States or the Reagan administration. The president acknowledged the internal Soviet decline as early as 1982 and was wise enough to avoid a consequently unnecessary war, with the dreadful prospect of countless casualties. Except for Grenada, he never committed U.S. military forces in response to his countless portrayals of Soviet expansionism—and readily accepted détente when Gorbachev offered it.

Reagan clung to his conviction, much to the dismay of skeptical neoconservatives, that the Soviet leader's efforts at domestic reform and international cooperation were genuine. Moreover, he willingly met and negotiated with the Soviet leader. By continuing to negotiate with Gorbachev in spite of the abusive criticism of so many supporters, Michael Beschloss placed Reagan in his pantheon of courageous presidents.[10]

Gorbachev's Contribution

The Soviet leader provided a charismatic, imaginative leadership during the "crisis" of the mid-1980s that redirected Moscow's relations with the West. If the crisis within the Soviet Union created an opportunity for domestic and foreign policy reform, for a liberalization of policies, it should also be recognized that the crisis also provided an opening for powerful reactionary forces. These reactionaries could have instituted repressive policies to deal with dissent at home and heightened confrontational ones abroad. Unquestionably, with the hard-liners in charge the Cold War could have been prolonged for at least a few more decades. Although often not realized in America, Gorbachev's selection as General Secretary in March 1985 was a close run affair. While making no secret of his desire for reforms, he withheld his more radical ideas and was elected by an unorganized majority of conservatives.[11]

Gorbachev represented a new generation, especially the intellectuals who espoused a "new thinking" regarding foreign affairs. Since he was not burdened by the horrific experiences of World War II, it was easier for him to put aside the "old thinking" steeped in the Stalinist concept of a hostile capitalist encirclement and the prospect of a final, apocalyptic conflict with the imperialist nations. He could thus greatly expand on Nikita Khrushchev's program of "peaceful coexistence." During 1986, Gorbachev frequently met foreign leaders and their representatives seeking to deflate their fears of the Soviet Union and through these discussions he came to understand "the other world" and to formulate his bold foreign initiatives. The impact of the Chernobyl tragedy—when a deadly nuclear reactor explosion and fire resulted in thousands of deaths and devastated the surrounding countryside—greatly affected the new leadership's policies. Not only did this event reveal the inefficiency and corruption of the Stalinist system and the hard-liners' efforts to cover up such events, it graphically demonstrated the nuclear dangers and pressed the urgency of arms control.

Preparing for the October 1986 Reykjavik meeting with Reagan, Gorbachev unveiled a policy that dealt with strategic weaponry grounded on "reasonable sufficiency." Surprising many observers and angering his own military officials, he offered substantive concessions in an attempt to eliminate all nuclear weapons. While Reagan's refusal to accept minor restrictions on the SDI program prevented an agreement, the American president did recognize that the Russian leader was sincere and someone intent in restructuring Soviet policies. Indeed, according to a close observer, Gorbachev had "already decided, come what may, to end the arms race." He was willing to take this gamble because he was convinced, to quote his words, "Nobody is going to attack us even if we disarm completely." The hard-liners would continue to protest his proposals and concessions because they wanted to maintain a strictly numerical parity, but he stuck to his objective and succeeded in halting the arms race.[12]

The subsequent unraveling of the Soviet empire was an *unintended* side effect of Gorbachev's reforms; termination of the Cold War was not. Reagan deserves credit for recognizing Gorbachev's sincerity and his determination to greatly alter earlier Soviet policies. And for this, Reagan felt the wrath of anticommunist hawks for "doing business" with a Communist leader. But it was Gorbachev himself who concluded the superpowers had become "mesmerized by ideological myths," which ruled out any meaningful discussions of a possible accommodation of political issues for more than four decades. Even the long-time Soviet ambassador to Washington, Anatoly Dobrynin, acknowledged in his memoirs that Moscow's Cold War policies were "unreasonably dominated by ideology, and [that] this produced continued confrontation."[13]

Mikhail Gorbachev broke the Cold War's ideological straitjacket that had paralyzed Moscow and Washington's ability to resolve their differences. Though politically weakened, Gorbachev conceded nothing to U.S. military superiority. Never did he negotiate from a position of weakness. In doing so, he faced greater political, even physical, risks. After considering all of this, it is difficult to avoid the conclusion that without Gorbachev, the end of the Cold War could have played out very differently and very dangerously.

NOTES

PREFACE

1. The CIA especially had no luck in anticipating the collapse of the Soviet Union in 1989. See Tim Weiner, *Legacy of Ashes: The History of the CIA* (New York: Doubleday, 2007).

2. See Robert Service, *Comrades! A History of World Communism* (Cambridge: Harvard University Press, 2007); Robert D. English, *Russia and the Idea of the West: Gorbachev, Intellectuals and the End of the Cold War* (New York: Columbia University Press, 2000); and Melvyn Leffler, *For the Soul of Mankind: The United States, the Soviet Union, and the End of the Cold War* (New York: Hill and Wang, 2007).

3. A brilliant treatment of this subject is found in Jason Flanagan, "Defining the Enemy: A Study in Twentieth Century Presidential Rhetoric," Ph.D. dissertation, University of Queensland, 2006.

CHAPTER 1

1. This introduction was drawn from Joseph M. Siracusa and David G. Coleman, *Depression to Cold War: A History of America from Herbert Hoover to Ronald Reagan* (Westport, CT: Praeger, 2002), 225–243.

2. At the end of 1999, when the treaty expired, U.S. troops withdrew from Panama, and control was passed back to the Panamanian government.

3. James Mann, *About Face: A History of America's Curious Relationship with China, from Nixon to Clinton* (New York: Vintage, 1998), 78–79.

4. Ibid., 93–94.

5. Thomas Parker, *The Road to Camp David: U. S. Negotiating Strategy Towards the Arab Israeli Conflict* (New York: P. Lang, 1989); and William B. Quandt, *Peace

Process: American Diplomacy and the Arab Israeli Conflict Since 1967, rev. ed. (Washington, DC: Brookings Institution, 2001).

6. Lawrence Walsh, *Firewall: The Iran-Contra Conspiracy and Cover-up* (New York: W. W. Norton, 1997); and Warren Christopher, Oscar Schatcher, and Abraham A. Ribicoff, *American Hostages in Iran: The Conduct of a Crisis* (New Haven, CT: Yale University Press, 1985).

7. Gary Sick, *The October Surprise: America's Hostages in Iran and the Election of Ronald Reagan* (New York: Random House, 1991).

8. Hedrick Smith, Adam Clymer, Leonard Silk, Robert Lindsey, and Richard Burt, *Reagan: The Man, the President* (New York: Macmillan, 1980): 99–100, 234ff.

CHAPTER 2

1. Reagan quoted in George C. Herring, "The 'Vietnam Syndrome' and American Foreign Policy," *Virginia Quarterly Review* 57 (Autumn 1981): 612.

2. For a superb contemporary evaluation of the Reagan foreign policy team, see Hedrick Smith, *New York Times*, May 25, 1980.

3. Van Cleave interview in "The Week in Review," *New York Times*, Oct. 12, 1980.

4. Interview with Richard V. Allen, *New York Times*, June 29, 1980.

5. *Newsweek*, Dec. 22, 1980, 53.

6. John A. Marcum, "The United States at the UN: The Kirkpatrick Era," *Worldview* 24 (June 1981): 20.

7. Reagan quoted in *Newsweek*, Feb. 9, 1981, 45.

8. Opening Statement at Confirmation Hearings, Jan. 9, 1981, U.S. Department of State, Bureau of Public Affairs, *Current Policy No. 257*.

9. *New York Times*, May 3, 1981.

10. Walter LaFeber, *Inevitable Revolutions: The United States and Central America* (New York, 1983), 240; *New York Times*, Mar. 23, 1980, 8.

11. *New York Times*, July 13, 1980, 14.

12. *New York Times*, April 2, 1981, 3.

13. Reagan quoted in Alexander Cockburn, *Wall Street Journal*, Mar. 12, 1981.

14. Joseph M. Siracusa and David G. Coleman, *Depression to Cold War: A History of America from Herbert Hoover to Ronald Reagan* (Westport, CT: Praeger, 2002), 260.

15. Ibid., 261–264.

16. Ibid.

17. Karen de Young, *Washington Post*, Mar. 8, 1981; *Newsweek*, Mar. 16, 1981, 34–38; Mar. 30, 1981, 20–21.

18. David Douglas Duncan quoted in *New York Times*, Jan. 3, 1982.

19. Robert W. Tucker, "America in Decline: The Foreign Policy of 'Maturity,'" *Foreign Affairs* 58(3) (1980): 480, 484.

20. *Newsweek*, June 15, 1981.

21. Kiguel Schapira, "Wanted: A Foreign Policy," *World Press Review* (Jan. 1982).

22. Roger Fisher, *New York Times*, Mar. 30, 1980.

23. See Editorial, *The New York Times*, Mar. 22, 1981.

24. Bernard Gwertzman, *New York Times*, June 21, 1981.

25. Gwertzman, *New York Times*, Mar. 14, 1982.

26. Steven R. Weisman, "Reaganomics and the President's Men," *New York Times Magazine* (Oct. 24, 1982): 83–85.

27. Drew Middleton, *New York Times*, Jan. 3, 1982; Richard Halloran, *New York Times*, Apr. 11, 1982.

28. Middleton, *New York Times*, June 21, 1981 and Feb. 14, 1982.

29. "A New Direction in U.S. Foreign Policy" (Apr. 24, 1981), U.S. Department of State, Bureau of Public Affairs, *Current Policy No. 275*, 2.

30. Seweryn Bialer and Joan Afferica, "Reagan and Russia," *Foreign Affairs* 61 (Winter 1982–1983): 71.

31. Steven Rattner, *New York Times*, Apr. 13, 1980.

32. John M. Berry, *Washington Post*, Feb. 14, 1981.

33. Leslie H. Gelb, *New York Times*, Aug. 23, 1981.

34. Kennan warned that the administration's demonizing of the Soviets as "total and incorrigible enemies . . . dedicated to nothing other than our destruction—that, in the end, is the way we shall assuredly have them, if for no other reason than that our view of them allows for nothing else, either for us or for them." *New York Times*, Nov. 18, 1981.

35. *Worldview* 24 (May 1981): 4.

36. Cockburn, *Wall Street Journal*, Mar. 12, 1981.

37. *Economist* quoted by James Reston, *New York Times*, June 7, 1981.

38. See, for example, Stanley Hoffmann's excellent survey, "The Western Alliance: Drift or Harmony?" *International Security* 6 (Fall 1981): 105–125.

39. McGeorge Bundy quoted in Theo Sommer, "Europe and the American Connection," *Foreign Affairs* 58(3) (1980): 630.

40. Peter Jenkins quoted in *World Press Review* 28 (Sept. 1981), 44.

41. For the Soviet view, see David G. Coleman and Joseph M. Siracusa, *Realworld Nuclear Deterrence: The Making of International Strategy* (Westport, CT: Praeger, 2006), 104–106.

42. Leslie H. Gelb, *New York Times*, Aug. 9, 1981.

43. Viola quoted in *World Press Review* 28 (Oct. 1981): 5l.

44. De Gaulle quoted by Leslie Gelb, *New York Times*, July 26, 1981.

45. Henry Kissinger, *The White House Years* (Boston: Little, Brown, 1979), 1132, 1150–1151; Anatoly Dobrynin, *In Confidence: Moscow's Ambassador to America's Six Cold War Presidents* (Seattle: University of Washington Press, 2001), 251–252; "Schmidt's Calculability's," *Economist* 273 (Oct. 6, 1979): 54.

46. Quoted in James O. Goldsborough, "The Roots of Western Disunity," *New York Times Magazine* (May 9, 1982): 58.

47. *Sunday Times* (London) quoted in *New York Times*, Feb. 22, 1981.

48. Quoted in *World Press Review* 29 (Apr. 1982): 12.

49. *Newsweek*, Mar. 22, 1982, 42.

50. For Fontaine's views, see *World Press Review* 29 (Apr. 1982): 27.

51. *Times Herald Record*, Dec. 24, 1981.

52. Schmidt's statement in Norman A. Graebner, "Western Disunity: Its Challenge to America," The Reynolds Distinguished Lecture Series, Davidson College, Fall 1982, 34.

53. *Manchester Guardian* quoted in *World Press Review* 29 (Feb. 1982): 14.

54. Ronald Steel, *New York Times*, Jan. 3, 1982.

55. For the Ottawa Conference, see Leslie H. Gelb, *New York Times*, July 19, 26, 1981.

56. Pipes quoted by Stephen S. Rosenfeld, *Washington Post*, Oct. 8, 1982.

57. Reston, *New York Times*, Feb. 7, 1982.

58. For the debate within the administration, see Bernard Gwertzman, *New York Times*, Feb. 21, 1982.

59. For the Reagan announcement and the bitter European reaction, see *World Press Review* 29 (Aug. 1982): 4.

60. Flora Lewis, *New York Times*, June 27, 1982.

61. Steven Ratner, *New York Times*, Aug. 29, 1982.

62. Hans-Dietrich Genscher, "Toward an Overall Western Strategy for Peace, Freedom, and Progress," *Foreign Affairs* 61 (Fall 1982): 42.

63. Richard J. Barnet, *New Yorker* (Oct. 17, 198): 153.

64. Ibid., 156.

65. Four distinguished American students of strategy—McGeorge Bundy, George Kennan, Robert McNamara, and Gerard Smith—argued in *Foreign Affairs* (Spring 1982) that the United States, to limit the possibilities of nuclear war, should reverse its policy of three decades and promise never to use nuclear weapons first.

66. Armando Orique in *World Press Review* 29 (Mar. 1982); see Douglas C. Waller, *Congress and the Nuclear Freeze: An Inside Look at the Politics of a Mass Movement* (Amherst: University of Massachusetts Press, 1987), xviiiff.

67. Barnet, *The New Yorker* (Oct. 17, 1983): 156.

68. Flora Lewis, *New York Times*, Nov. 15, 1981.

69. Judith Miller, *New York Times*, Aug. 23, 1981; also Steve Breyman, *Why Movements Matter: The West German Peace Movement and U.S. Arms Control Policy* (Albany, NY: State University of New York Press, 2001), especially 93–95.

70. Anthony Lewis, *Daily Progress*, May 6, 1981.

71. Alexander M. Haig, Jr., *Caveat, Realism, Reagan and Foreign Policy* (New York: Macmillan, 1984).

72. Also see Siracusa and Coleman, *Depression to Cold War*, 249–250.

73. *Public Papers of the Presidents: Ronald Reagan, 1981* (Washington, DC: GPO, 1981), I, 957, 958.

CHAPTER 3

1. *New York Times*, May 14, 1982.

2. *New York Times*, Mar. 23, 1982.

3. Editorial, *New York Times*, June 27, 1982.

4. *Times Herald Record*, Jan. 124, 1982.

5. *Newsweek*, Mar. 1, 1982, 80.

6. Norman Podhoretz, "The Neo-Conservative Anguish Over Reagan's Foreign Policy," *New York Times Magazine* (May 2, 1982): 96–97.

7. Nestor D. Sanchez, "The Communist Threat," *Foreign Policy* 52 (Fall 1983): 43–44.

8. Peter Jay, "Europe and America: Europe's Ostrich and America's Eagle," *Atlantic Community Quarterly* 18 (Summer 1980): 141–142.

9. Robert Lacey, "How Stable Are the Saudis?" *New York Times Magazine* (Nov. 8, 1981): 35–38, 118–121.

10. David K. Shipler, *New York Times*, Mar. 28, July 25, 1982.

11. Eric Pace, *New York Times*, July 4, 1982.

12. Bernard Gwertzman, *New York Times*, Oct. 10, 1982.

13. "The Week in Review," *New York Times*, Jan. 1, 1984.

14. Thomas J. Friedman, "America's Failure in Lebanon," *New York Times Magazine* (Apr. 8, 1984): 32–33.

15. "The Week in Review," *New York Times*, Jan. 1, 1984; Bernard Gwertzman, *New York Times*, Oct. 9, 1983, E1, 6; Hedrick Smith, *New York Times*, Oct. 30, 1983, E1.

16. Marvin Howe, *New York Times*, Aug. 29, 1982.

17. Meg Greenfield, *Newsweek*, June 28, 1982, 84.

18. Ronald Reagan, "Remarks . . . Following a Luncheon Meeting with Leaders of Eastern Caribbean Countries," in *Public Papers of the Presidents, Ronald Reagan, 1982,* Book 1 (Washington: GPO, 1983), 448.

19. J. Thomas, *New York Times*, Oct. 30, 1983; Bernard Gwertzman, *New York Times*, Oct. 30, 1983, 1.

20. Nicholas von Hoffman, "Terrestrial Wars," *The Spectator* (Apr. 13, 1985): 8–9; Norman A. Graebner, "The Uses and Misuses of Power: The 1980's," *Dialogue: A Magazine of International Affairs* 1(1) (Mar. 1988): 29; Daniel Patrick Moynihn, *On the Law of Nations* (Cambridge: Harvard University Press, 1990), 122, 127–131. (For Moyniham, the Grenada invasion was illegal.)

21. Lou Cannon, *President Reagan: The Role of a Lifetime* (New York: Public Affairs, 1991), 391–393.

22. Hedrick Smith, "The Week in Review," *New York Times*, Oct. 30, 1983, F1; Stuart Taylor, Jr., *New York Times*, Nov. 6, 1983, 20; William Casey, quoted in "The Week in Review," *New York Times*, Oct. 30, 1983; Francis Clines, "The Week in Review," *New York Times*, Feb. 5, 1984.

23. Michael D. Barnes, "Grenada: The Invasion Was Right," *Washington Post National Weekly*, Nov. 21, 1983, 32; Editorial, *New York Times*, October 30, 1983; Podhoretz, *New York Times*, Oct. 30, 1983.

24. John Wylee, "The West at a Crossroads," *World Press Review* 31 (Feb. 1984): 35.

25. Holland Hunter, "Soviet Economic Problems and Alternative Policy Responses," *Soviet Economy in a Time of Change*, A Compendium of Papers Submitted to the Joint Economic Committee, Congress of the United States, vol. I, Oct. 10, 1979 (Washington, DC: GPO, 1979), 27.

26. Ibid., 31.

27. Daniel Patrick Moynihan, "The Soviet Economy: Boy, Were We Wrong!" *Washington Post*, July 11, 1990, A19.

28. Marshall Goldman, *What Went Wrong With Perestroika* (New York: Norton, 1991), 48–49.

29. On the reluctance of the masses to oppose the Soviet regime see Leszek Kolakowski, "Amidst Moving Ruins," *Daedalus* 121 (Spring 1992): 55.

30. Christopher Mark Davis, "The Exceptional Soviet Case: Defense in an Autarkic System," *Daedalus* 120 (Fall 1991): 116–119.

31. Adam Ulam, *Dangerous Relations: The Soviet Union in World Politics* (New York: Oxford University Press, 1983), 276–279.

32. Ibid., 311–314.

33. Ibid., 266–267.

34. *The Economist* 339 (June 8, 1996): 41.

35. Dr. Alexei Dmitriev on the Soviet price of Afghanistan in Tony Parker, *Russian Voices* (New York: Holt, 1991), 386–387.

36. Remarks to Members of the British Parliament, June 8, 1982, *Public Papers of the Presidents: Reagan, 1982*, I (Washington, DC: GPO, 1983), 747–748; Remarks at the annual convention of the National Association of Evangelicals, Mar. 8, 1983, *Public Papers of the Presidents*, 363–364.

37. Graebner, "The Soviet-American Conflict," 583; *Christian News*, Apr. 18, 1983, 1.

38. Reagan's Address to Congress, Sept. 5, 1983, *American Foreign Policy: Current Documents, 1983* (Washington, DC: GPO, 1985), 544–547.

39. Strobe Talbott, *The Russians and Reagan* (New York: Vintage, 1984), 122, Appendix.

40. Alexander Bovin quoted in *World Press Review* 31 (Jan. 1984): 53.

41. Ronald Reagan, *Ronald Reagan: An American Life.* (New York: Pocket Books, 1990), 588–589.

42. Andrew Cockburn, *Dangerous Liaisons: The Inside Story of the U.S.-Israeli Relationship* (New York: HarperCollins, 1991), 273–275.

43. Edward Reiss, *The Strategic Defense Initiative* (New York: Cambridge University Press, 1992); McGeorge Bundy, *Danger and Survival: Choices About the Bomb in the First Fifty Years* (New York: Random House, 1988), 571; Ronald Reagan, *An American Life* (New York: Simon & Schuster, 1990), 571–572.

44. Interview with the *New York Times*, Feb. 11, 1985, in *Public Papers, Reagan, 1982*, I, 150; Inaugural Address, Jan. 21, 1985, *Public Papers, Reagan, 1982*, 57; Lou Cannon, "Reagan Predicts Serious Talks on Arms Curbs in Next Term," *Washington Post*, Nov. 7, 1984, A38.

45. Frances Fitzgerald, *Way Out There in the Blue: Reagan, Star Wars and the End of the Cold War* (New York: Simon & Schuster, 2000), 197, 207–208; Walter Isaacson, "Reagan for Defense," *Time* (Apr. 4, 1983): 18–19; Michael A. Learner and William Cook, "Star Wars: Will Space be the Next Battleground," *Newsweek* (Apr. 4, 1983): 16–22.

46. John Tirman, "The Politics of Star Wars," in John Tirman, ed., *The Empty Promise: the Growing Case Against Star Wars* (Boston, MA: Beacon, 1986); Union of Concerned Scientists, *The Fallacy of Star Wars* (New York: Vintage, 1984); and Richard Dean Burns and Lester M. Brune, *The Quest for Missile Defenses, 1944–2003* (Claremont, CA: Regina Books, 2003), 77–100.

47. John Newhouse, "Annals of Diplomacy: The Abolitionist I," *The New Yorker*, January 2, 1989, 39, 48–49; Christopher Andrew, *KGB: The Inside Story of its Foreign Operations from Lenin to Gorbachev* (New York: HarperCollins, 1990); Christopher and Oleg Gordievsky Andrew, *Comrade Kryuchkov's Instructions* (Stanford, CA: Stanford University Press, 1993). For Arbatov's views of U.S.-Soviet relations see the *Washington Post National Weekly*, May 28, 1985, 6.

CHAPTER 4

1. Lawrence T. Caldwell and Robert Legvold, "Reagan through Soviet Eyes," *Foreign Policy* 52 (Fall 1983): 5.

2. Leslie H. Gelb, "The Week in Review," *New York Times*, May 1, 1983, E1.

3. Stanley Hoffmann, *Dead Ends: American Foreign Policy in the New Cold War* (Cambridge, MA: Ballinger, 1983), 154–155.

4. *New York Times*, Jan. l, 1984, E13.

5. Henry Brandon, *Special Relationships: A Foreign Correspondent's Memoirs from Roosevelt to Reagan* (New York: Atheneum, 1988), 401.

6. Address on U.S.-Soviet Relations, January 16, 1984, *Public Papers of the Presidents: Ronald Reagan, 1984*, I (Washington, DC: GPO, 1986), 42.

7. State of the Union Address, Jan. 25, 1984, *American Foreign Policy: Current Documents, 1984* (Washington, DC: GPO, 1986), 28; Address at Georgetown University, Apr. 6, 1984, *American Foreign Policy*, 8.

8. James Reston in *New York Times*, June 17, 1984, E21.

9. See, for example, Oswald Johnston, "Reagan Foreign Policy: A Lesson in Fate?" *Los Angeles Times*, Feb. 6, 1984, A1, 8.

10. Editorial, *Los Angeles Times*, July 1, 1984, E20.

11. Hedrick Smith, *Los Angeles Times*, June 17, 1984, E1.

12. *Newsweek*, Aug. 27, 1984, 37.

13. John Newhouse, "Annals of Diplomacy: The Abolitionist—II," *New Yorker* (Jan. 9, 1989): 51.

14. *Le Monde* quoted in *World Press Review* 31 (Nov. 1984): 20.

15. Leo Wieland, *Frankfurter Allgemeine Zeitung*, quoted in *World Press Review*, 35–36.

16. Frances Fitzgerald, *Way Out There in the Blue: Reagan, Star Wars and the End of the Cold War* (New York: Simon & Schuster, 2000), 88–96; Douglas C. Waller, *Congress and the Nuclear Freeze* (Amherst, MA: The University of Massachusetts Press, 1987), 14.

17. Fitzgerald, *Way Out There In The Blue*, 153–154; Waller, *Congress and the Nuclear Freeze*, 94–97, 99.

18. Leslie Gelb, "The Mind of the President," *New York Times Magazine* (Oct. 6, 1985): 21ff.; Lou Cannon, "Dealings with the Soviets Raise Uncomfortable Questions," *Washington Post*, July 2, 1984, A13.

19. Gloria Duffy, *Compliance and the Future of Arms Control* (Stanford, CA: Center for International Security and Arms Control, 1988), 105ff.; Judith Miller, Stephen Engelberg, and William Broad, *Germs: Biological Weapons and America's Secret War* (New York: Simon & Schuster, 2001), 165–182.

20. Raymond L. Garthoff, *Détente and Confrontation: American-Soviet Relations from Nixon to Reagan*, rev. ed. (Washington, DC: The Brookings Institution, 1994), 146n.10.

21. For similar observations, see Leslie H. Gelb, *New York Times*, Nov. 4, 1984, 34.

22. David Fouquet, *Christian Science Monitor*, Dec. 13, 1984, 13, 15; George Shultz, "U.S.-Soviet Agreement on the Structure of New Arms Control Negotiations," *American Foreign Policy, Current Documents, 1985* (Washington, DC: U.S. State Department, 1986), 73.

23. Charlotte Saikowski, *Christian Science Monitor*, Jan. 3, 1985, 3, 5.

24. Quoted in Fitzgerald, *Way Out There In The Blue*, 445.

25. Michael K. Deaver, *Behind the Scenes* (New York: Morrow, 1987), 39.

26. Jeane Kirkpatrick, *Washington Post*, May 24, 1988, A23.

27. See David K. Shipler, *New York Times*, May 29, 1988, E1, E3.

28. For Gorbachev in London, *New York Times*, Dec. 16, 1984, 1, 5.

29. Seweryn Bialer quoted in *Los Angeles Times*, Feb. 6, 1984, 8.

30. Editorial, *New York Times*, November 3, 1985, E20.

31. Mary McGrory, "Struggles over a Kissinger Report That Will Change Nothing," *Washington Post National Weekly*, Jan. 23, 1984, 23.

32. Seymour M. Hersh, *New York Times*, Jan. 8, 1984, 1, 16.

33. *New York Times*, Feb. 4, 1984.

34. Joanne Omang, "The Play of Light and Shadow Hides the Truth in El Salvador," *Washington Post National Weekly*, Apr. 16, 1984, 16.

35. *Newsweek*, Jan. 23, 1984, 28.

36. Editorial, *New York Times*, Jan. 15, 1984, E22.

37. David S. Broder, "Frank Church's Challenge," *Washington Post National Weekly*, Feb. 6, 1984, 4.

38. David Schribman, *New York Times*, Apr. 29, 1984.

39. Bernard Gwertzman, *New York Times*, Apr. 15, 1984, 1, 12.

40. See James Reston, *New York Times*, May 20, 1984, B23.

41. Fred Hiatt, "The U.S. Military Buildup Continues," *Washington Post National Weekly*, Apr. 30, 1984, 16.

42. Philip Taubman, *New York Times*, Apr. 18, 1984, 1, 12.

43. For a legal defense of the Reagan policy, see John Norton Moore, *The Secret War in Central America: Sandinista Assault on World Order* (Frederick, MD: University Publications of America, 1987).

CHAPTER 5

1. *New York Times*, Feb. 24, 1985.

2. George P. Shultz, "Shaping American Foreign Policy: New Realities and New Ways of Thinking," *Foreign Affairs* (Spring 1985): 713.

3. Also see Joseph M. Siracusa and David G. Coleman, *Depression to Cold War: A History of America from Herbert Hoover to Roanld Reagan* (Westport, CT: Praeger, 2002), 263.

4. George Will, *Washington Post*, Dec. 12, 1985, A19.

5. Robert W. Tucker, "Intervention and the Reagan Doctrine," *Intervention and the Reagan Doctrine* (New York: The Council on Religion and International Affairs, 1985), 16–17.

6. *Newsweek*, Dec. 23, 1985, 32–34.

7. *Chronology of the Cold War, 1917–1992*, compiled by Lester Brune and edited by Richard Dean Burns (New York: Routledge, 2006), 483.

8. Dickey, Christopher, *With the Contras: A Reporter in the Wilds of Nicaragua* (New York: Simon & Schuster, 1987), 10–11.

9. *The Sandinista Military Build-Up*, Inter-American Series 119 (Washington, DC: Dept. of State, 1985); and *The Soviet-Cuban Connection in Central America and the Caribbean* (Washington, DC: Dept. of State and Dept. of Defense, 1985).

10. Lee Hamilton, "Central America in Perspective," in *The Crisis in Central America* (Washington, DC: The Washington Institute for Values in Public Policy, 1987), 35, 39.

11. *Newsweek*, Mar. 11, 1985, 86.

12. Cheney quoted in Steven V. Roberts, *New York Times*, May 25, 1986, E1.

13. Joshua Muravchik, "The Nicaragua Debate," *Foreign Affairs* (Winter 1986–1987): 366.

14. Quoted in Bernard Weinraub, "The Reagan Legacy," *New York Times Magazine* (June 22, 1986).

15. *Newsweek*, July 21, 1986, 5.

16. John Norton Moore, *The Struggle for Peace in Central America: And the Deterioration of the Global Deterrent System* (Washington, DC: Washington Institute for Values in Public Policy), 2, 42.

17. Elliott Abrams, director of the State Dept.'s Bureau of Human Rights and Humanitarian Affairs, in *Foreign Policy* 52 (Fall 1983): l22, 124; *Foreign Policy*, 53 (Winter 1983–1984): 175.

18. For American acceptance of extensive human rights violations by friendly governments in Argentina, Guatemala, and El Salvador and the official rationale for the acceptance, see Charles Maechling, Jr., "Human Rights Dehumanized," *Foreign Policy*, 52 (Fall 1983): 118–135; On U.S. refusal to hold the government of El Salvador accountable for its murders of Americans as well as thousands of its own citizens, see Guillermo M. Ungo, "The People's Struggle," *Foreign Policy*, 52 (Fall 1983), 51–63.

19. Flora Lewis, *New York Times*, Mar. 16, 1986, E25.

20. Theodore Draper, "The Rise of the American Junta," *New York Review of Books* 34 (Oct. 8, 1987): 47–48.

21. Draper, *A Very Thin Line: The Iran-Contra Affairs* (New York: Hill & Wang, 1991), 79–82; "The Rise of the American Junta," 48–49.

22. Draper, *A Very Thin Line*, 86–88.

23. Editorial, *New York Times*, Aug. 11, 1985, E22.

24. Draper, "The Rise of the American Junta," 50.

25. Draper, *A Very Thin Line*, 166–169, 246, 289.

26. Ibid., 249–257.

27. Ibid., 319–327.

28. Ibid., 274

29. For Secord's extended and complex contra operations in Central America, see *Washington Post*, Dec. 7, 1986, 1.

30. Draper, *A Very Thin Line*, 333, 344–345.

31. Ibid., 348.

32. James Reston, *New York Times*, Oct. 12, 1986, E23.

33. Draper, *A Very Thin Line*, 352–357. Abrams was later tried and sentenced to prison for lying to Congress and then later attempting to mislead it on the matter of collecting funds for the contras from Brunei; Draper, *A Very Thin Line*, 370–373. For Abrams' defense, see Elliott Abrams, *Undue Process: A Story of How Political Differences Are Turned into Crimes* (New York: Free Press, 1992).

34. Draper, "The Fall of the American Junta," 54.

35. Draper, *A Very Thin Line*, 458–459, 474–483, 496–501.

36. Ibid., 299–302. North had prepared the fateful diversion memorandum in April 1986 for the benefit of Poindexter and the president. Under questioning,

Poindexter first denied that he had seen it then acknowledged that he might have destroyed it. Apparently the president never saw it.

37. For constitutional aspects of the Reagan administration's conduct of external relations, see Draper, *A Very Thin Line*, 580–595.

38. Quoted in Draper, *A Very Thin Line*, 346, 568.

39. Also see Siracusa and Coleman, *Depression to Cold War*, 270.

40. George Black, *The Good Neighbor: How the United States wrote the History of Central America and the Caribbean* (New York: Pantheon Books, 1988), 179–180.

41. Murray Waas and Craig Unger, "In the Loop: Bush's Secret Mission," *New Yorker* (Nov. 2, 1992): 65–69.

42. Ibid., 72–80.

43. Whitehead quoted in Waas and Unger, "In the Loop," *New Yorker*, 82.

CHAPTER 6

1. Gorbachev quoted in *Pravda*, April 24, 1985; *New York Times*, Dec. 29, 1985, 5.

2. David Hoffman, *Washington Post*, Nov. 10, 1985, A37.

3. Mikhail Gorbachev, *On My Country and the World* (New York: Columbia University Press, 2000), 196; Raymond Garthoff, *The Great Transition: American-Soviet Relations and the End of the Cold War* (Washington, DC: The Brookings Institution Press, 1994), 236, 242–243; Gloria Duffy, *Compliance and the Future of Arms Control* (Stanford, CA: Center for International Security and Arms Control, 1988), 52–54; Lou Cannon, *President Reagan: The Role of a Lifetime* (New York: Public Affairs, 2000), 670.

4. Duffy, *Compliance and the Future of Arms Control*, 89–103.

5. Gorbachev quoted in David K. Shipler, *New York Times*, Mar. 9, 1986, E3.

6. Philip Taubman, *New York Times*, Apr. 6, 1986.

7. For compliance, see John Newhouse, *New Yorker* (Jan. 9, 1989): 59–61.

8. Michael Mandelbaum and Strobe Talbott, *Reagan and Gorbachev* (New York: Vintage, 1987).

9. James Reston, *New York Times*, Apr. 6, 1986, E23.

10. European polls in 1986 consistently revealed Gorbachev's popularity; see for example Michael R. Gordon, *New York Times*, June 7, 1987, 7.

11. *New York Times* Aug. 29, 1986.

12. Garthoff, *The Great Transition*, 252–267; Frances Fitzgerald, *Way Out There in the Blue: Reagan, Star Wars and the End of the Cold War* (New York: Simon & Schuster, 2000), 332–340; George P. Shultz, *Turmoil and Triumph: My Years as Secretary of State* (New York: Scribner's, 1993), 751–755; also see David Callahan, *Dangerous Capabilities: Paul Nitze and the Cold War* (New York: HarperCollins, 1990), 472–478.

13. *Public Papers of the Presidents: Ronald Reagan, 1983* (Washington DC: government Printing Office, 1984), I, 465; letter, June 20, 1983, in Kiron K. Skinner, Annelise Anderson, and Martin Anderson, eds. *Reagan: A Life in Letters* (New York: Free Press, 2003), 425.

14. Garthoff, *Transition*, 285–289; Fitzgerald, *Way Out There in the Blue*, 347–329; Shultz, *Turmoil*, 755–773; see also Mikhail Gorbachev, *Reykjavik: Results and Lessons* (Madison, CT: Sphinx Press, 1987).

15. David K. Shipler, "The Week in Review," *New York Times*, Oct. 26, 1986, E1.

16. David Ignatius, "Outlook," *Washington Post*, Apr. 19, 1987.

17. Fitzgerald, *Way Out There in the Blue*, 409–411, 412–415; Anatoly Dobrynin, *In Confidence: Moscow's Ambassador to America's Six Cold War Presidents* (Seattle: University of Washington Press, 2001), 620.

18. Andrei Sakarov, *Moscow and Beyond* (New York: Alfred A. Knopf, 1991), 21–42; Strobe Talbott, *Master of the Game: Paul Nitze and the Nuclear Peace* (New York: Alfred A. Knopf, 1988), 306; Garthoff, *Transition*, 327n.64; Shultz, *Turmoil*, 1009–1015; Fitzgerald, *Way Out There in the Blue*, 426.

19. Newhouse, *New Yorker* (Jan. 9, 1989): 65-66; Lou Cannon, *President Reagan: The Role of a Lifetime* (New York: Public Affairs, 1991), 694; Fitzgerald, *Way Out There in the Blue*, 444–445.

20. *Washington Post*, Oct. 31, 1987, A1, A17; *Washington Post*, Dec. 9, 1987, A1; Rowland Evans and Robert Novak, *Washington Post*, Dec. 11, 1987, A27; Cannon, *President Reagan*, 695–698, Shultz, *Turmoil*, 1009–1011.

21. *Daily Progress*, Nov. 1, 1987. A5.

22. *Washington Post*, Oct. 12, 1987, A19.

23. For a critique of Phillips and Viguerie, see James J. Kilpatrick, *Washington Post*, Dec. 15, 1987, A23.

24. *Washington Post*, Dec. 4, 1987, A1.

25. For the impact of the Afghan war on the Soviet soldiers, see Tony Parker, *Russian Voices* (New York: Holt, 1991), 82–84.

26. Mary Anne Weaver, "Blowback," *Atlantic Monthly* 277 (May 1996): 24–36.

27. Steve Smith, "The Superpowers and Arms Control in the Era of the 'Second' Cold War," in Michael Cox, ed., *Beyond the Cold War: Superpowers at the Crossroads?* (Lanham, MD: University Press of America, 1990), 175–177.

28. *New York Times*, Jan. 24, 1988, 1, 12; Shultz, *Turmoil*, 1081–1085; Fitzgerald, *Way Out There in the Blue*, 453.

29. Lou Cannon and Gary Lee, *Washington Post*, May 30, 1988, A1, A21.

30. Don Oberdorfer, *Washington Post*, June 1, 1988, A1.

31. *Washington Post*, June 7, 1988, A23.

32. *Washington Post*, May 29, 1988, C7.

33. John Newhouse, *New Yorker* (Jan. 9, 1989): 53.

34. For limitations on Gorbachev's reforms, see Robbin F. Laird, "The Gorbachev Challenge," in Robbin F. Laird, ed., *Soviet Foreign Policy* (New York: Academy of Political Science, 1987), 1–9; Erik P. Hoffmann and Robbin F. Laird, *The Politics of Economic Modernization in the Soviet Union* (Ithaca, NY: Cornell University Press, 1982); Erik P. Hoffmann and Robbin F. Laird, "The Scientific-Technological Revolution," in *Soviet Foreign Policy* (New York: Pergamon Press, 1982); Erik P. Hoffmann and Robbin F. Laird, *Technocratic Socialism: The Soviet Union in the Advanced Industrial Era* (Durham, N.C.: Duke University Press, 1985).

35. William Pfaff, *Barbarian Sentiments: American in the New Century* (New York: Hill and Wang, 2000), 123.

36. Marshall Goldman, *What Went Wrong With Perestroika* (New York: Norton, 1991), 89, 94, 128–137, 142–143.

37. Yegor Ligachev, *Inside Gorbachev's Kremlin: The Memoirs of Yegor Ligachev* (New York: Pantheon Books, 1993).

38. Goldman, *What Went Wrong with Perestroika*, 180–183.

39. Pfaff, *Barbarian Sentiments*, 118–123; Walker, *The Cold War*, 307–308.

40. Erik P. Hoffmann, "Soviet Foreign Policy from 1986 to 1991: Domestic and International Influences," in Robbin F. Laird, ed., *Soviet Foreign Policy* (New York: Academy of Political Science, 1987), 265, 270.

41. Robert G. Kaiser, "The Soviet Future That Failed," *Washington Post National Weekly*, Oct. 8, 1984, 6.

42. For a history of these national uprisings, as well as discontent in the Baltics, see Helene Carrere d'Encausse, *The End of the Soviet Empire*, trans. Franklin Philip (New York: Basic Books, 1993), 8–9, 33–43, 52–55, 73–75, 96–111, 120–122.

43. Pfaff, *Barbarian Sentiments*, 80–81, 96–97.

44. Szűrös quoted in Charles Gati, "It's Still Moscow's Parade, but Not Everyone Is Marching in Step," *Washington Post National Weekly*, July 23, 1984, 25.

45. For an overview of Soviet-satellite tensions in 1985, see Robert Miller, "Europe's Yalta Legacy: The Politics of Division," *World Press Review* 32 (Apr. 1985): 35–36.

46. David Binder, *New York Times*, Sept. 2, 1984.

47. J.F. Brown, *Eastern Europe and Communist Rule* (Durham, N.C.: Duke University Press, 1988), 449.

48. Paul Kennedy, *The Rise and Fall of the Great Powers: Economic Change and Military Conflict from 1500 to 2000* (New York: Random House, 1987), 514–535; see Joseph Nye, "Understanding U.S. Strength," *Foreign Policy* 72 (Fall 1988): 106.

49. Kennedy, *The Rise and Fall*, 488–489.

50. On Weinberger's proposal and the experience of the Vietnam War, *Time*, Apr. 15, 1985, 40–42, 45.

51. Ronald Steel, "Behaving Like a Great Power," *Vanity Fair* 47 (Feb. 1984): 36; Richard J. Barnet, "Annals of Diplomacy: Alliance II," *New Yorker* (Oct. 17, 1983): 165.

52. George Kennan emphasized this: "[T]here is no issue at stake in our political relations with the Soviet Union . . . which would conceivably be worth a nuclear war." Quoted by Stanley Hoffmann, "Kennan's Passionate Realism," *Atlantic Monthly* 250 (Dec. 1982): 96.

53. David G. Coleman and Joseph M. Siracusa, *Real-world Nuclear Deterrence: The Making of International Strategy* (Westport, CT: Praeger, 2006), ix–xii.

54. Martin Walker, *The Cold War: A History* (New York: Holt, 1994), 308–309.

55. Sidney Blumenthal, *Washington Post*, Nov. 23, 1987, B1, B8.

56. *New York Times*, July 10, 1988, E30.

57. Walter Laqueur, "Is There Now, or Has There Ever Been, Such a Thing as Totalitarianism?" *Commentary* (Oct. 1985): 34; Laqueur, "Glasnost & Its Limits," *Commentary*, (July 1988): 23.

58. Eugene V. Rostow, "Why the Soviets Want an Arms-Control Agreement, and Why They Want It Now," *Commentary* (Feb. 1987): 20, 26.

59. Will's warnings in *Newsweek*, Mar. 18, 1985, 90.

60. On the early crusade against Shultz, see *Newsweek*, Feb. 3, 1986, 19–20.

61. John Ehrman, *The Rise of Neoconservatism: Intellectuals and Foreign Affairs, 1945–1994* (New Haven: Yale University Press, 1995), 165–172, 176–177.

62. Kirkpatrick, *Washington Post*, Dec. 14, 1987, A15.

63. *Newsweek*, Dec. 21, 1987, 78.

CHAPTER 7

1. Michael R. Bechloss and Strobe Talbott, *At the Highest Levels: The Inside Story of the End of the Cold War* (Boston: Little, Brown and Company, 1993): 9.

2. Quoted in ibid., 11.

3. *Newsweek*, May 15, 1989, 22; Department of State, *Bulletin* 89 (April 1989): 2, 4–5; Beschloss and Talbott, *At The Highest Levels*, 12–13, 17–19; Robert M. Gates, *From the Shadows: The Ultimate Insider's Story of Five Presidents And How They Won the Cold War* (New York: Simon & Schuster, 1996).

4. *Newsweek*, Dec. 25, 1989, 40; *The Economist* (London), 330 (Feb. 12, 1994), Survey, 4.

5. For the failures of the East German government, see Charles S. Maier, *Dissolution: The Crisis of Communism and the End of East Germany* (Princeton: Princeton University Press, 1996); Tony Judt, "New Germany, Old NATO," *New York Review of Books* 44 (May 29, 1997): 40–41.

6. *Newsweek*, Dec. 25, 1989, 40; also see Martin Walker, *The Cold War: A History* (New York: Holt, 1994), 310–313.

7. *Newsweek*, Dec. 25, 1989, 40.

8. Craig R. Whitney, *New York Times*, Jan. 7, 1990, E3 and April 8, 1990, 14.

9. *Washington Post*, Apr. 16, 1990, A1, A20.

10. Erazim Kohak, "Ashes, Ashes . . . Central Europe after Forty Years," *Daedalus* 121 (Spring 1992): 207; Whitney, *New York Times*, Jan. 7, 1990, E3; *The Daily Progress* (Charlottesville), Mar. 2, 1990, A6.

11. See Lonnie R. Johnson, *Central Europe: Enemies, Neighbors, Friends* (New York: Oxford University Press, 1996).

12. *Newsweek*, Sept. 10, 1990, 36.

13. Francis Fukuyama, "The End of History," *National Interest* 16 (Summer 1989): 3–4. His views were rejected by members of the right. See James Atlas, "What Is Fukuyama Saying?" *New York Times Magazine* (Oct. 22, 1989): 42.

14. See Robert Skidelsky, *The World After Communism: A Polemic for Our Times* (New York: Macmillan, 1995); *Parameters* 19 (Dec. 1989): 93–97; E. J. Dionne, Jr., *Washington Post*, Oct. 10, 1990, A3.

15. Girard C. Steichen, "Bulgaria Slips Deeper into Economic Crisis," *The Christian Science Monitor*, Mar. 5, 1991, 5.

16. *New Yorker*, Feb. 19, 1990, 33.

17. On Gorbachev's leadership, see Stanley Hoffmann, "A Case for Leadership," *Foreign Policy* 81 (Winter 1990–1991): 20–22.

18. Alexander Dallin, *Washington Post*, Jan. 15, 1990, A19; Meg Greenfield, *Newsweek*, Feb. 5, 1990, 75 and Mar. 12, 1990, 63; *Washington Post*, Jan. 19, 1990, A14.

19. *New York Times*, Dec. 1, 1989, Y9; Judt, "New Germany, Old NATO," 40; Henry Ashby Turner, *New York Times*, Feb. 11, 1990, E25; Elizabeth Pond, *Washington Post*, Feb. 25, 1990, B2.

20. *Newsweek*, Feb. 26, 1990, 17–18; Jim Hoagland, *Washington Post*, Mar. 22, 1990, A23 and Apr. 1, 1990, A1, A32; *New York Times*, Jan. 7, 1990, E25.

21. *Washington Post*, Jan. 20, 1990, A15; *Washington Post*, Feb. 3, 1990, A20; *Washington Post*, Feb. 7, 1990, A19; *New York Times*, Feb. 21, 1990, 1.

22. On NATO expansion, see Philip Zelikow and Condoleezza Rice, *Germany Unified and Europe Transformed: A Study in Statecraft* (Cambridge, MA: Harvard University Press, 1996); Michael R. Gordon, "The Anatomy of a Misunderstanding," *New York Times*, May 25, 1997, E3.

23. *Newsweek*, May 28, 1990, 27; Stephen S. Rosenfeld in *Washington Post*, Nov. 1, 1996, A25.

24. *Boston Globe*, Mar. 1, 1990, 18; *Daily Progress*, Mar. 6, 1990, A5; *Washington Post*, Mar. 9, 1990, A25; Mar. 15, 1990, A29; and Mar. 22, 1990, A1, A35. For Brandt's assurancee to the Poles, see *New York Times*, Mar. 11, 1990, 14.

25. *Washington Post*, Apr. 12, 1990, A38.

26. For the Bonn meeting, see Serge Schmemann in *New York Times*, May 6, 1990, l, 20; *Newsweek*, May 28, 1990, 27.

27. William Claiborne, "West Urged Not to 'Dictate,'" *Washington Post*, May 31, 1990, A1; For Gorbachev's Canadian visit, see *Washington Post*, A1, A28; Rowland Evans and Robert Novak, *Washington Post*, June 1, 1990, A19.

28. James A. Baker, III, *The Politics of Diplomacy: Revolution, War and Peace* (New York: Putnam, 1995), 253; Mikhail Gorbachev, *Memoirs* (London: Doubleday, 1995), 722; Michael Boll, "Superpower Diplomacy and German Unification: The Insiders' Views," *Parameters* 26 (Winter 1996–1997): 119–120.

29. Judt, "New Germany, Old NATO," 40; Elizabeth Pond, *Beyond the Wall: Germany's Road to Unification* (Washington: Brookings Institution Press, 1993); Tadeusz Pieciukiewicz, "Security in Central and Eastern Europe: A View from Warsaw," *Parameters* 26 (Winter 1996–1997): 127.

30. Craig R. Whitney in *New York Times*, July 15, 1990, E1, E3; Richard Cohen in *Washington Post*, July 18, 1990, A23.

31. *Chicago Tribune*, Apr. 10, 1990, 8; *Atlantic Monthly* 265 (Feb. 1990): 20–24; *New Yorker*, Jan. 13, 1992, 21.

32. James H. Billington, "The Crisis of Communism and the Future of Freedom," *Ethics & International Affairs* 5 (1991): 87–97; *Washington Post*, Jan. 14, 1990, A1 and Feb. 8, 1990, A10; *New York Times*, Mar. 13, 1990, E1; *Washington Post*, Feb. 5, 1990, A1, A15; Stanislav Kondrashov, *Washington Post*, Feb. 15, 1990, A25.

33. *Newsweek*, Mar. 26, 1990, 13; *Washington Post*, Mar. 16, 1990, A1.

34. *Chicago Tribune*, Apr. 10, 1990, 8.

35. Marshall Goldman, *What Went Wrong with Perestroika* (New York: Norton, 1991), 214–121.

36. *New Yorker*, Jan. 13, 1992, 21; *Washington Post*, May 31, 1990, A29.

37. *New York Times*, Jan. 14, 1990, l3; Glenn Frankel, *Washington Post*, Jan. 14, 1990, A26; Mar. 22, 1990, A30; and Mar. 25, 1990. A18.

38. Zlatko Dizdarevic, *Christian Science Monitor*, Dec. 28, 1993, 19; *New York Times*, Feb. 14, 1993, E5; Jan. 29, 1990, A15; and Apr. 14, 1990, A1.

39. *Daily Progress*, Mar. 24, 1990, A6; Stephen S. Rosenfeld, *Washington Post*, Mar. 30, 1990, A25; *New York Times*, Jan. 14, 1990, E3; *Newsweek*, Jan. 22, 1990, 32–33 and Feb. 19, 1990, 29.

40. *New York Times*, Jan. 14, 1990, E3; Editorial, *Washington Post*, Jan. 14, 1990, B6; *The Atlantic Monthly* 265 (Mar. 1990): 32–40.

41. *New York Times*, Jan. 14, 1990, E3; *Newsweek*, April 2, 1990, 26; *Washington Post*, Apr. 3, 1990, A12; Apr. 4, 1990, A33; Apr. 5, 1990, A1; Apr. 10, 1990, A1; and Apr. 14, 1990, A1.

42. *Washington Post*, May 31, 1990, A1, A19.

43. Walker, *The Cold War*, 315.

44. Martin Malia, *Bulletin of the American Academy of Arts and Sciences* 44 (Nov. 1990): 9–12; Bill Keller, *New York Times*, February 2, 1991, l, 12; *The Economist* 318 (Jan. 26, 1991): 41–42; Michael Dobbs in *Washington Post*, Dec. 20, 1990, A25; Goldman, *What Went Wrong with Perestroika*, 202.

45. On Shevardnadze, see *The Economist*, 318 (Jan. 19, 1991): 39–41; Eduard A. Shevardnadze, *The Future Belongs to Freedom* (New York: Free Press, 1991).

46. Coit D. Blacker, "The New U.S.-Soviet Détente," *Current History* 88 (Oct. 1989): 324; Editorial, *New York Times*, Sept. 17, 1989, E22; *New York Times*, Dec. 1, 1989, Y30.

47. *Newsweek*, Dec. 11, 1989, 28–32, 39; Editorial, *New York Times*, Dec. 1, 1989, Y30; *New York Times*, Dec. 4, 1989; Elizabeth Drew, "Letter From Washington," *New Yorker*, Jan. 1, 1990, 80–83.

48. Michael Mandelbaum, "The Bush Foreign Policy," *Foreign Affairs* 70 (1990–1991): 5–8.

49. Editorial, *Washington Post*, Jan. 18, 1990, A22 and, Mar. 28, 1990, A23; Broder, *Washington Post*, Mar. 21, 1990, A21.

50. *Daily Progress*, Apr. 8, 1990, A3.

51. *Washington Post*, Jan. 27, 1990, A13, A15; On the State Department, *Washington Post*, Mar. 16, 1990, A34; Henry Kaufman, *Washington Post*, July 10, 1990, A19.

52. *Washington Post*, Mar. 16, 1990, A34; On Havel, see *Boston Globe*, Feb. 23, 1990, 12; *New York Times*, Feb. 11, 1990, E25.

53. *New York Times*, Mar. 18, 1990, E3; Editorial, *New York Times*, Jan. 21, 1990, E20; *Daily Progress*, Jan. 23, 1990, A4; Editorial, *New York Times*, Jan. 21, 1990, E20.

54. Editorial, *New York Times*, Jan. 14, 1990, 22.

55. Paul H. Nitze, "Gorbachev's Plan For a Communist Comeback," *Washington Post*, Jan. 10, 1990, A19; Feb. 7, 1990, A18; and Feb. 13, 1990, A1, A9.

56. *Washington Post*, Mar. 13, 1990, A21.

57. Ibid., Mar. 23, 1990, A19 and, Mar. 29, 1990, A31.

58. Ibid., Mar. 30, 1990, A1, A20; Stephen S. Rosenfeld, *Washington Post*, Apr. 6, 1990, A15.

59. Tom Wicker, *Daily Progress*, Apr. 2, 1990, A4 and Apr. 12, 1990, A1; *Washington Post*, Apr. 12, 1990, A33 and Apr. 14, 1990.

60. Bill Keller, "Gorbachev's Need: To Still Matter," *New York Times*, May 27, 1990, 1, 10; William G. Hyland, *The Cold War Is Over* (New York: Random House, 1991); Walter Laqueur, ed., *Soviet Union 2000: Reform or Revolution?* (New

York: St. Martin's Press, 1991); Caspar Weinberger, *AARP Bulletin* 31 (Feb. 1990): 16.

61. Stephen S. Rosenfeld, "Lighten Up, Fellows," *Washington Post*, May 25, 1990, A21; Dan Balz, "Conservatives: Victory or Vigilance?" *Washington Post*, May 26, 1990, A1, A14.

62. William Safire, "Gorbachev's Strength Is Weakness," *Daily Progress*, June 3, 1990, A5; Ann Devroy, *Daily Progress*, May 28, 1990, A19; Editorial, "With Mikhail Gorbachev," *Daily Progress*, May 29, 1990, A22; T. R. Reid, "Giving Gorbachev Credit," *Daily Progress*, May 27, 1990, A1, A25.

63. David Remnick, *Daily Progress*, June 1, 1990, A21.

64. Ibid., A23; Jim Hoagland, "Still a Serious Leader," *Daily Progress*, May 31, 1990, A23; *Daily Progress*, June 1, 1990, A22.

65. Lawrence T. Caldwell, "Soviet-American Relations: The Cold War Ends," *Current History* 89 (Oct. 1990): 308, 346; Raymond L. Garthoff, "The Bush Administration's Policy toward the Soviet Union," *Current History* 90 (Oct. 1991): 315.

66. For the London Declaration, see *Current History* 89 (Oct. 1990): 334; Garthoff, "The Bush Administration's Policy toward the Soviet Union," 314.

67. *New Yorker*, Mar. 13, 1989, 25.

CHAPTER 8

1. Eric P. Hoffmann, "Soviet Foreign Policy from 1986–1991," in Robbin F. Laird, ed., *Soviet Foreign Policy* (New York: Academy of Political Science, 1987), 261.

2. Tom Wicker, "Plenty of Credit," *New York Times*, Dec. 5, 1989, A35; Cal Thomas, *The Daily Progress*, Aug. 26, 1993, A4; Paul Johnson, "Europe and the Reagan Years, *Foreign Affairs* 68(1) (1989): 34–37; Caspar Weinberger, *Fighting For Peace* (New York: Warner, 1990); Peter Schweizer, *Victory: The Reagan Administration's Secret Strategy That Hastened the Collapse of the Soviet Union* (New York: Atlantic Monthly Press, 1994).

3. Robert G. Kaufman, *Henry M. Jackson: A Life in Politics* (Seattle: University of Washington Press, 2000), 439; Aleksandr' G. Savel'yev and Nickolay N. Detinov, *The Big Five: Arms Control Decision-Making in the Soviet Union* (Westport, CT: Praeger, 1995), 21–22, 163ff; Robert D. English, *Russia And the Idea of the West: Gorbachev, Intellectuals And the End of the Cold War* (New York: Columbia University Press, 2000), 179, 218.

4. Richard Ned Lebow and Janice Gross Stein, *We All Lost the Cold War* (Princeton, NJ: Princeton University Press, 1994), 372.

5. English, *Russia and the Idea of the West*, 33–34.

6. France Fitzgerald, *Way Out There in the Blue: Reagan and Star Wars and the End of the Cold War* (New York: Simon & Schuster, 2000), 17–18, 466–471.

7. Jack R. Matlock, Jr., *Reagan and Gorbachev: How the Cold War Ended* (New York: Random House, 2004), 323.

8. Lou Cannon, *President Reagan: The Role of a Lifetime*, 2nd ed. (New York: Public Affairs, 2000), 241, 246–250; Lou Cannon, "Reagan at the Crossroads Again, 1986," in Kenneth W. Thompson, ed. *Leadership in the Reagan Presidency: Seven*

Intimate Prespectives (Lantham, MD: Madison Books, 1992), 125; Fred Barnes, "The Reagan Presidency: Moments," in Thompson, in Kenneth W. Thompson, ed. *Leadership in the Reagan Presidency: Seven Intimate Prespectives* (Lantham, MD: Madison Books, 1992), 99.

9. Perle in Charles W. Kegley, Jr., *The Long Postwar Peace* (New York: Harper-Collins, 1990), 104; Richard Pipes, "Misinterpreting the Cold War: The Hardliners Had It Right," *Foreign Affairs* 74(1) (1995): 154–160; Raymond Garthoff, *The Great Transition: American-Soviet Relations and the End of the Cold War* (Washington, DC: Brookings Institution Press, 1994), 524.

10. See Michael Beschloss, *Presidential Courage: Brave Leaders And How They Changed America, 1789–1989* (New York: Simon & Schuster, 2007).

11. English, *Russia and the Idea of the West*, 196–198.

12. Ibid., 206, 212–217, 241.

13. Mikhail Gorbachev, *Perestroika: New Thinking For Our Country And the World* (New York: Harper & Row, 1987), 211; Anatoly Dobrynin, *In Confidence: Moscow's Ambassador to America's Six Cold War Presidents* (Seattle: University of Washington Press, 2001), 472.

SELECTED BIBLIOGRAPHY

GENERAL ACCOUNTS

Becker, Jasper. *The Chinese: An Insider's Look at the Issues Which Effect and Shape China Today*. New York: Oxford University Press, 2000.

Blacker, Coit D. *Hostage to Revolution: Gorbachev and Soviet Security Policy, 1985–1991*. New York: Council on Foreign Relations Press, 1993.

Boyle, Peter G. *American-Soviet Relations: From the Russian Revolution to the Fall of Communism*. New York: Routledge, 1993.

Brands, H. W. *The Devil We Knew: Americans and the Cold War*. New York: Oxford University Press, 1993.

Bulletins Of the International Cold War History Project, # 1, Spring 1991 to 2004 and beyond. Washington, DC: Woodrow Wilson Center. Declassified documents from various former communist nations can be found at http://wilsoncenter.org/index.cfm?topic_id=1409&fuseaction=topics.home.

Cahn, Anne Hessing. *Killing Détente: The Right Attacks the CIA*. University Park, PA: The Penn State University Press, 1998.

Carney, John T., and Benjamin F. Schemmer. *No Room for Error: The Covert Operations of Special Tactics Units From Iran to Afghanistan*. New York: Ballantine Books, 2003

Cohen, Warren I. *America in the Age of Soviet Power, 1945–1991*. Vol. 4 of *The Cambridge History of American Foreign Relations*. New York: Cambridge University Press, 1993.

Cohen, William S., and George J. Mitchell. *Men of Zeal: A Candid Inside Story of the Iran Contra Hearings*. New York: Viking, 1988.

Fitzgerald, Frances. *Way Out There in the Blue: Reagan, Star Wars and the End of the Cold War*. New York: Simon & Schuster, 2000.

Gaddis, John Lewis. *The Long Peace: Inquires into the History of the Cold War*. New York: Oxford University Press, 1987.

Garthoff, Raymond L. *The Great Transition: American-Soviet Relations and the End of the Cold War*. Washington, DC: Brookings Institution Press, 1994.

———. *A Journey Through the Cold War*. Washington, DC: Brookings Institution Press, 2001.

Gorodetsky, Gabriel, ed. *Soviet Foreign Policy, 1917–1991: A Retrospective*. Portland, OR: Frank Cass, 1994.

Hyland, William G. *Mortal Rivals: Superpower Relations from Nixon to Reagan*. New York: Random House, 1987.

Keddie, Nikki R., and Mark J. Gasiorowski, eds. *Neither East Nor West: Iran, the Soviet Union and the United States*. New Haven, CT: Yale University Press, 1990.

Kovrig, Bennett. *Of Walls and Bridges: The United States and Eastern Europe*. New York: New York University Press, 1991.

LaFeber, Walter. *America, Russia, and the Cold War, 1945–1996*. 8th ed. New York: McGraw-Hill, 1997.

Larson, Deborah Welch. *Anatomy of Mistrust: U.S.-Soviet Relations during the Cold War*. Ithaca, NY: Cornell University Press, 1997.

Lundestad, Geir. *East, West, North, South: Major Developments in International Politics Since 1945*. Trans. by Gail Adams Kvam. 4th ed. New York: Oxford University Press, 1999.

McCormick, Thomas J. *America's Half Century: United States Foreign Policy in the Cold War and After*. 2nd ed. Baltimore: Johns Hopkins University Press, 1995.

Matlock, Jack F., Jr. *Reagan and Gorbachev*. New York: Random House, 2004.

Meneges, Constantine C. *Inside the National Security Council: The True Story of the Making and Unmaking of Reagan's Foreign Policy*. New York: Simon & Schuster, 1988.

Painter, David S. *The Cold War: An International History*. New York: Routledge, 1999.

Patterson, Thomas G. *Meeting the Communist Threat: Truman to Reagan*. New York: Oxford University Press, 1988.

Powaski, Ronald E. *The Cold War: The United States and the Soviet Union, 1917–1991*. New York: Oxford University Press, 1998.

Prados, John. *Presidents' Secret Wars: CIA and Pentagon Covert Operations from World War II through the Persian Gulf*. Rev. and expanded ed. Chicago, IL: I. R. Dee, 1996.

Sakwa, Richard. *The Rise and Fall of the Soviet Union, 1917–1991*. New York: Routledge, 1999.

Seppain, Hélène. *Contrasting US and German Attitudes to Soviet Trade, 1917–91: Politics by Economic Means*. New York: St. Martin's Press, 1992.

Smith, Tony. *America's Mission: The United States and the Worldwide Struggle for Democracy in the Twentieth Century*. Princeton, NJ: Princeton University Press, 1994.

Stevenson, Richard W. *The Rise and Fall of Détente: Relaxations of Tension in U.S.-Soviet Relations, 1953–84*. Urbana, IL: The University of Illinois Press, 1985.

Stone, David. *Wars of the Cold War, Campaigns and Conflicts, 1945–1990*. London: Brassey's, 2004.

Talbott, Strobe. *The Russians and Reagan*. New York: Vintage, 1984.

Tyroler, Charles II, ed. *Alerting America: The Papers of the Committee on the Present Danger*. Washington, DC: Pergamon-Brassey's, 1984. (Attacks Carter's arms control policies.)

Waller, Douglas C. *Congress and the Nuclear Freeze: An Inside Look at the Politics of a Mass Movement*. Amherst, MA: University of Massachusetts Press, 1987.

Wallison, Peter J. *Ronald Reagan: The Power of His Conviction and the Success of His Presidency*. Boulder, CO: Westview Press, 2003.

Weihmiller, Gordon R. *U.S.-Soviet Summits: An Account of East-West Diplomacy at the Top, 1955–1985*. Lanham, MD: University Press of America, 1986.

Wohlforth, William Curti. *The Elusive Balance: Power and Perceptions during the Cold War*. Ithaca, NY: Cornell University Press, 1993.

END OF THE COLD WAR

Beschloss, Michael R., and Strobe Talbott. *At the Highest Level: The Inside Story of the End of the Cold War*. Boston, MA: Little, Brown and Company, 1993.

Carrere d'Encausse, Helene. *The End of the Soviet Empire: The Triumph of the Nations*. New York: Basic Books, 1993.

English, Robert D. *Russia and the Idea of the West: Gorbachev, Intellectuals and the End of the Cold War*. New York: Columbia University Press, 2000.

Hogan, Michael J., ed. *The End of the Cold War*. New York: Cambridge University Press, 1992. (See especially Richard J. Barnet, "A Balance Sheet: Lippman, Kennan and the Cold War," and Denise Artaud, "The End of the Cold War: A Skeptical View.")

Hough, Jerry F. *Russia and the West: Gorbachev and the Politics of Reform*. New York: Simon & Schuster, 1987.

Kaiser, Robert G. *Why Gorbachev Happened: His Triumphs and His Failure*. New York: Simon & Schuster, 1991.

LeBow, Richard Ned, and Janice Gross Stein. *We All Lost the Cold War*. Princeton, NJ: Princeton University Press, 1994.

Lebow, Richard Ned, and Thomas W. Risse-Kappen, eds. *International Relations Theory and the End of the Cold War*. New York: Columbia University Press, 1995.

Lundberg, Lirsten. *The CIA and the Fall of the Soviet Empire: The Politics of "Getting it Right."* Case Study C-16-94-1251.0. Intelligence and Policy Project, The John F. Kennedy School of Government. Cambridge, MA: Harvard University, 1994.

Matlock, Jack F. *Autopsy of an Empire: The American Ambassador's Account of the Collapse of the Soviet Union*. New York: Random House, 1995.

Rowen, Henry S., and Charles Wolf, Jr., eds. *The Impoverished Superpower: Perestroika and the Soviet Military Burden*. Oakland, CA: Institute for Contemporary Studies Press, 1990.

Schweizer, Peter. *Victory: the Reagan Administration's Secret Strategy that Hastened the Collapse of the Soviet Union*. New York: Atlantic Monthly Press, 1994.

Shelton, Judy. *The Coming Soviet Crash: Gorbachev's Desperate Pursuit of Credit in Western Financial Markets*. New York: Free Press, 1988.

Summy, Ralph, and Michael E. Salla, eds. *Why the Cold War Ended: A Range of Interpretations*. Westport, CT: Greenwood Press, 1995.

Walt, Stephen M. "The Gorbachev Interlude and International Relations Theory." *Diplomatic History* 21(3) (Summer 1997). (Review of Lebow and Risse-Kappen; defends "realist" interpretation.)

Zubok, Vladislav M. "New Evidence of the End of the Cold War." *The Cold War International History Bulletin* 12/13 (Fall/Winter 2001): 5–23. (An excellent overall source on the Cold War's end.)

PERSONALITIES

Baker, James A., III. *The Politics of Diplomacy*. New York: G. P. Putnam's Sons, 1995.

Bush, George, and Brent Scowcroft. *A World Transformed*. New York: Alfred A. Knopf, 1998.

Callahan, David. *Dangerous Capabilities: Paul Nitze and the Cold War*. New York: Harper & Row, 1990.

Canon, Lou. *President Reagan: The Role of a Lifetime*. New York: Simon & Schuster, 1991.

Carter, Jimmy. *Keeping the Faith: Memoirs of a President*. New York: Bantam, 1982.

Deaver, Michael K. *A Different Drummer: My Thirty Years with Ronald Reagan*. New York: HarperCollins, 1987.

Ford, Gerald R. *A Time to Heal: The Autobiography of Gerald R. Ford*. New York: Harper & Row, 1979.

Gates, Robert M. *From the Shadows: The Ultimate Insider's Story of Five Presidents and How They Won the Cold War*. New York: Simon & Schuster, 1996.

Haig, Alexander M., Jr. *Caveat: Realism, Reagan and Foreign Policy*. New York: Macmillan, 1984.

Helms, Richard, and William Hood. *A Look Over My Shoulder: A Life in the Central Intelligence Agency*. New York: Random House, 2003.

McFarlane, Robert C., and Zofia Smardz. *Special Trust*. New York: Cadell & Davies, 1994.

Meese, Edwin, III. *With Reagan: The Inside Story*. Washington, DC: Regnery Gateway, 1992.

Reagan, Ronald. *An American Life: The Autobiography*. New York: Simon & Schuster, 1990.

Rearden, Steven L. *The Evolution of American Strategic Doctrine: Paul H. Nitze and the Soviet Challenge*. Boulder, CO: Westview Press, 1984.

Shultz, George Pratt. *Turmoil and Triumph: My Years as Secretary of State*. New York: Charles Scribner's Sons, 1993.

Talbott, Strobe. *Master of the Game: Paul Nitze and Nuclear Peace*. New York: Alfred A. Knopf, 1988.

Weinberger, Caspar. *Fighting for Peace: Seven Critical Years in the Pentagon*. New York: Warner Books, 1990.

SOVIET

Chernyaev, Anatoly S. *My Six Years with Gorbachev*. University Park, PA: The Penn State University Press, 2000.

Dobrynin, Anatoly. *In Confidence: Moscow's Ambassador to America's Six Cold War Presidents*. New York: Times Books, 1995.

Gorbachev, Mikhail. *Memoirs*. London: Doubleday, 1995.

———. *Reykjavik: Results and Lessons*. Madison, CT: Sphinx Press, 1987.

Palazchenko, Pavel. *My Years with Gorbachev and Shevardnadze: The Memoirs of a Soviet Interpreter*. University Park, PA: The Penn State University Press, 1997.

Sakarov, Andrei. *Moscow and Beyond*. New York: Alfred A. Knopf, 1991.

ARMS CONTROL

Adelman, Kenneth L. *The Great Universal Embrace: Arms Summitry—A Skeptic's Account*. New York: Simon & Schuster, 1989.

Alibek, Ken, and Stephen Handelman. *Biohazard: The Chilling True Story of the Largest Covert Biological Weapons Program in History—Told from the Inside by the Man Who Ran It*. New York: Random House, 1999.

Carnesale, Albert, and Richard H. Haass, eds. *Superpower Arms Control: Setting the Record Straight*. Cambridge, MA: Ballinger, 1987.

Duffy, Gloria. *Compliance and the Future of Arms Control*. Cambridge, MA: Ballinger, 1988.

Foerster, Schuyler. "The Reagan Administration and Arms Control: Redefining the Agenda." In *Defense Policy in the Reagan Administration*, edited by William P. Snyder and James Brown, 5–44. Washington, DC: National Defense University Press, 1988.

Graham, Thomas, Jr. *Disarmament Sketches: Three Decades of Arms Control and International Law*. Seattle, WA: University of Washington Press, 2002.

Kartchner, Kerry M. *Negotiating START: Strategic Arms Reduction Talks and the Quest for Strategic Stability*. New Brunswick, NJ: Transaction Publishers, 1992.

Landais-Stamp, Paul, and Paul Rogers. *Rocking the Boat: New Zealand, the United States and the Nuclear-Free-Zone Controversy in the 1980s*. New York: Berg Publishers, 1989.

Miller, Judith, Stephen Engelberg, and William Broad. *Germs: Biological Weapons and America's Secret War*. New York: Simon & Schuster, 2001.

Mosher, David, and Michael O'Hanlon. *The START Treaty and Beyond*. Washington, DC: Congressional Budget Office, 1991.

Scheer, Robert. *With Enough Shovels: Reagan, Bush and Nuclear War*. New York: 1982.

Shimko, Keith L. *Images and Arms Control: Perceptions of the Soviet Union in the Reagan Administration*. Ann Arbor, MI: The University of Michigan Press, 1991.

Talbott, Strobe. *Deadly Gambits: The Reagan Administration and the Stalemate in Nuclear Arms Control*. New York: Alfred A. Knopf, 1984.

MILITARY FORCES AND STRATEGY

Coleman, David G., and Joseph M. Siracusa. *Real-World Nuclear Deterrence: The Making of International Strategy*. Westport, CT: Praeger, 2006.

Gervasi, Tom. *The Myth of Soviet Military Supremacy*. New York: Harper & Row, 1986.

McGwire, Michael. *Military Objectives in Soviet Foreign Policy*. Washington, DC: Brookings Institution Press, 1987.

Mendel, Richard A. *The Defense Game: An Insider Explores the Astonishing Realities of America's Defense Establishment*. New York: Harper & Row, 1986.

Nolan, Janne E. *Guardians of the Arsenal: The Politics of Nuclear Strategy*. New York: Basic Books, 1989.

Odom, William E. *The Collapse of the Soviet Military*. New Haven, CT: Yale University Press, 1998.

Pratt, Erik K. *Selling Strategic Defense: Interests, Ideologies, and the Arms Race*. Boulder, CO: Lynne Rienner, 1990.

Rowen, Henry S., and Charles Wolf, Jr., eds. *The Impoverished Superpower: Perestroika and the Soviet Military Burden*. Oakland, CA: Institute for Contemporary Studies Press, 1990.

STRATEGIC DEFENSE INITIATIVE

Burns, Richard Dean, and Lester M. Brune. *The Quest for Missile Defenses, 1944–2004*. Claremont, CA: Regina Books, 2004.

Lakoff, Sanford, and Herbert F. York. *A Shield in Space? Technology, Politics, and the Strategic Defense Initiative*. Berkeley, CA: University of California Press, 1989.

Pratt, Erik K. *Selling Strategic Defense: Interests, Ideologies, and the Arms Race*. Boulder, CO: Lynne Rienner, 1990.

Pressler, Larry. *Star Wars: The Strategic Defense Initiative Debates in Congress*. New York: Praeger, 1986.

Waller, Douglas C., *The Strategic Defense Initiative: Progress and Challenge. A Guide to Issues and Reference*. Claremont, CA: Regina Books, 1987.

AFGHANISTAN AND AFRICA

Bradsher, Henry. *Afghan Communism and Soviet Intervention*. New York: Oxford University Press, 1999.

Clough, Michael. *Free at Last? U.S. Policy toward Africa and the End of the Cold War*. New York: Council on Foreign Relations Press, 1992.

———, ed. *Reassessing the Soviet Challenge in Africa*. Berkeley, CA: Institute of International Studies, University of California, 1986.

Coll, Steve. *Ghost Wars: The Secret History of the CIA, Afghanistan, and Bin Laden from the Soviet Invasion to September 10, 2001*. New York: The Penguin Press, 2004.

Crile, George. *Charlie Wilson's War: The Extraordinary Story of the Largest Covert Operation in History*. New York: Atlantic Monthly Press, 2003.

Klinghoffer, Arthur J. *The Angolan War: A Study in Soviet Policy in the Third World.* Boulder, CO: Westview Press, 1980.

Laïdi, Zadi. *The Superpowers and Africa: The Constraints of a Rivalry, 1960–1990.* Trans. by Patricia Baudoin. Chicago, IL: The University of Chicago Press, 1990.

Lefebvre, Jeffrey A. *Arms for the Horn: U.S. Policy in Ethiopia and Somalia, 1953–1991.* Pittsburgh, PA: The University of Pittsburgh Press, 1993.

Marte, Fred. *Political Cycles in International Relations: The Cold War and Africa, 1945–1990.* Amsterdam: VU University Press, 1994.

Windrich, Elaine. *The Cold War Guerrilla: Jonas Savimbi, the U.S. Media and the Angolan War.* New York: Greenwood Press, 1992.

CARIBBEAN, SOUTH AND CENTRAL AMERICA

Adams, Jan S. *A Foreign Policy in Transition: Moscow's Retreat from Central America and the Caribbean, 1985–1992.* Durham, NC: Duke University Press, 1992.

Arnson, Cynthia. *Crossroads: Congress, the Reagan Administration, and Central America.* New York: Pantheon, 1989.

Coleman, Kenneth M., and George C. Herring, Jr., eds. *Understanding the Central American Crisis: Sources of Conflict, U.S. Policy and Options for Peace.* Wilmington, DE: SR Books, 1991.

Landau, Saul. *The Guerrilla Wars of Central America: Nicaragua, El Salvador and Guatemala.* New York: St. Martin's Press, 1993.

LeoGrande, William M. *Our Own Backyard: The United States and Central America, 1977–1992.* Chapel Hill, NC: The University of North Carolina Press, 1998.

Miller, Nicola. *Soviet Relations with Latin America, 1959–1987.* New York: Cambridge University Press, 1989.

Moreno, Dario. *U.S. Policy in Central America: The Endless Debate.* Miami, FL: Florida International University Press, 1990.

Pavlov, Yuri I. *The Soviet-Cuban Alliance, 1959–1991.* New Brunswick, NJ: Transaction Publishers, 1994.

Wiarda, Howard J., and Mark Falcoff, eds., *The Communist Challenge in the Caribbean and Central America.* Washington, DC: American Enterprise Institute for Public Policy Research, 1987.

GRENADA INVASION

Adkin, Mark. *Urgent Fury: The Battle for Grenada.* Lexington, MA: D. C. Heath & Company, 1989.

Beck, Robert J. *The Grenada Invasion.* Boulder, CO: Westview Press, 1993.

Burrowes, Reynold A. *Revolution and Rescue in Grenada: An Account of the U.S.-Caribbean Invasion.* New York: Greenwood Press, 1988.

O'Shaughnessy, Hugh. *Grenada: An Eyewitness Account of the U.S. Invasion and the Caribbean History That Provoked It.* New York: Dodd, Mead and Company, 1984.

EL SALVADOR AND NICARAGUA

Byrne, Hugh. *El Salvador's Civil War*. Boulder, CO: Lynne Rienner, 1996.

Cockbury, Leslie. *Out of Control: The Story of the Reagan Administration's Secret War in Nicaragua*. New York: Atlantic Monthly Press, 1987.

Kagan, Robert. *A Twilight Struggle: American Power and Nicaragua, 1977–1990*. New York: Free Press, 1996.

Konbluh, Peter. *Nicaragua: The Price of Intervention*. Washington, DC: Institute for Policy Studies, 1987.

Walker, Thomas W., ed. *Reagan versus the Sandinistas: The Undeclared War on Nicaragua*. Boulder, CO: Westview, 1987.

EUROPE

Allin, Dana H. *Cold War Illusions: America, Europe and Soviet Power, 1969–1989*. New York: St. Martin's Press, 1995.

Blinken, Antony J. *Ally versus Ally: America, Europe, and the Siberian Pipeline Crisis*. New York: Praeger, 1987.

Breyman, Steve. *Why Movements Matter: The West German Peace Movement and U.S. Arms Control Policy*. Albany, NY: State University of New York Press, 2001.

Costigliola, Frank C. *France and the United States: The Cold Alliance Since World War II*. New York: Twayne Publishers, 1992.

Creswell, Michael. *A Question of Balance: How France and the United States Created Cold War Europe*. Cambridge, MA: Harvard University Press, 2006.

Goldstein, Walter, ed. *Reagan's Leadership and the Atlantic Alliance: Views from Europe and America*. Washington, DC: Pergamon-Brassey, 1986.

Hutchings, Robert S. *American Diplomacy and the End of the Cold War: An Insider's Account of U.S. Policy in Europe, 1989–1992*. Baltimore, MD: Johns Hopkins University Press, 1997.

Kirk, Roger, and Mircea Raceanu. *Romania versus the United States: Diplomacy of the Absurd, 1985–1989*. New York: St. Martin's Press, 1994.

Kovrig, Bennett. *Of Walls and Bridges: The United States and Eastern Europe*. New York: New York University Press, 1991.

Sodaro, Michael J. *Moscow, Germany and the West from Khrushchev to Gorbachev*. Ithaca, NY: Cornell University Press, 1990.

Zelikow, Philip D., and Condoleezza Rice. *Germany Unified and Europe Transformed: A Study in Statecraft*. Cambridge, MA: Harvard University Press, 1995.

MIDDLE EAST

Brune, Lester H. *America and the Iraqi Crisis, 1990–1992*. Claremont, CA: Regina Books, 1993.

Freedman, Lawrence, and Efraim Karsh. *The Gulf Conflict, 1990–1991: Diplomacy and War in the New World Order*. Princeton, NJ: Princeton University Press, 1993.

Freedman, Robert O. *Moscow and the Middle East: Soviet Policy since the Invasion of Afghanistan*. New York: Cambridge University Press, 1991.

Golan, Galia. *Soviet Policies in the Middle East: From World War Two to Gorbachev.* New York: Cambridge University Press, 1990.

Hiro, Dilip. *Desert Shield and Desert Storm: The Second Gulf War.* New York: Routledge, 1992.

———. *The Longest War: The Iran-Iraq Military Conflict.* New York: Routledge, 1991.

Jentleson, Bruce W. *With Friends Like These: Reagan, Bush, and Saddam, 1982–1990.* New York: W. W. Norton, 1994.

Keddie, Nikki R., and Mark J. Gasiorowski, eds. *Neither East nor West: Iran, the Soviet Union, and the United States.* New Haven, CT: Yale University Press, 1990.

Quandt, William B. *Peace Process: American Diplomacy and the Arab-Israeli Conflict since 1967.* Washington, DC: Brookings Institution Press, 2001.

Sick, Gary. *All Fall Down: America's Tragic Encounter with Iran.* New York: Random House, 1985.

Smolansky, Oles M., and Bettie M. Smolansky. *The USSR and Iraq: The Soviet Quest for Influence.* Durham, NC: Duke University Press, 1991.

REFERENCE WORKS

Beisner, Robert L., ed. *American Foreign Relations since 1600: A Guide to Literature.* 2 vols. 2nd ed. Santa Barbara, CA: ABC-Clio, 2003.

Brune, Lester, comp., and Richard Dean Burns, ed. *Chronology of the Cold War, 1917–1992.* New York: Routledge, 2006.

Burns, Richard Dean, ed. *Encyclopedia of Arms Control and Disarmament.* 3 vols. New York: Charles Scribner's Sons, 1993.

DeConde, Alexander, Richard Dean Burns, and Fredrik Logevall, eds. *Encyclopedia of American Foreign Policy.* 3 vols. 2nd. ed. New York: Charles Scribner's Sons, 2002.

Higham, Robin, and Donald J. Mrozek, eds. *A Guide to the Sources of United States Military History.* Supplements I to IV. Hamden, CT: Archon Books, 1975 to 1998.

U.S. Department of State. *[Papers Relating to the] Foreign Relations of the United States.* Washington, DC: GPO, 1861–.

U.S. President. *Public Papers of the Presidents of the United States.* Washington, DC: GPO, 1961–.

INDEX

Note: Bold numbers denote reference to illustrations.

ABOUT THE AUTHORS

NORMAN A. GRAEBNER, Randolph P. Compton Professor of History and Public Affairs, Emeritus, the University of Virginia and recipient of the University's highest honor, the Thomas Jefferson Award, is an internationally acknowledged authority on U.S. international affairs. He is a leading exponent of the realist school in the study of American diplomacy. Widely acclaimed as an outstanding speaker, Dr. Graebner has received many high awards, including honorary degrees from more than a half-dozen other universities. He also was a Harold Vyvyan Harmsworth Professor of American History at Oxford University and a Thomas Jefferson Visiting Scholar at Downing College, Cambridge. Professor Graebner is the author, coauthor, or editor of more than thirty books and some 130 articles, essays, and book chapters. Included among his most influential works are: *Empire on the Pacific: A Study in American Continental Expansion* (1955, 1983); *Ideas and Diplomacy: Readings in the Intellectual Tradition of American Foreign Policy*, with commentary (1964); *Foundations of American Foreign Policy: A Realist Appraisal from Franklin to McKinley* (1985); and *America as a World Power: A Realist Appraisal from Wilson to Reagan* (1984). He published his memoirs in 2002 titled *A Twentieth-Century Odyssey: Memoir of a Life in Academe*.

RICHARD DEAN BURNS is Professor Emeritus and former chair of the History Department at California State University, Los Angeles. He has authored and edited more than a dozen books and two-dozen in-depth articles covering arms control, diplomatic history, international law, and American foreign policy. He most recently coauthored *The Quest for Missile Defense, 1944–2003* (2004). A bibliographer, essayist, and editor, Burns has long been involved in preparing reference books such as the internationally recognized *A Guide to American Foreign Relations Since 1770* (1983) and the critically acclaimed twentieth century presidential bibliography series. Dr. Burns designed and edited a three-volume *Encyclopedia of Arms Control and Disarmament* (1993), which also received two national awards, coedited the three-volume *Encyclopedia of American Foreign Policy*, second edition (2002), and edited a three-volume *Chronological History of United States Foreign Relations* (2002) and a *Cold War Chronology, 1917–1992* (2005).

JOSEPH M. SIRACUSA is Professor of International Diplomacy and Director of Global Studies in the School of Global Studies, Social Science and Planning at the Royal Melbourne Institute of Technology, where he is a specialist in nuclear politics and global security. A native of Chicago and long-time resident of Australia, he is internationally known for his writings on nuclear history, diplomacy, and presidential politics. Professor Siracusa is also a frequent political affairs commentator in the Australian media, including ABC Radio National. He has worked with Merrill Lynch, in Boston, the University of Queensland, and for three years served as senior visiting fellow in the Key Centre for Ethics, Law, Justice and Governance, Griffith University. Among his numerous books are *A History of United States Foreign Policy* (with Julius W. Pratt and Vincent DeSantis); *Depression to Cold War: A History of America from Herbert Hoover to Ronald Reagan* (with David G. Coleman), *Presidential Profiles: The Kennedy Years, Real-World Nuclear Deterrence: The Making of International Strategy* (with David G. Coleman), and *Nuclear Weapons: A Very Short Introduction*.